SCHÄFFER
POESCHEL

Jürgen Weber/Utz Schäffer

Introduction to Controlling

2008
Schäffer-Poeschel Verlag Stuttgart

Bibliografische Information Der Deutschen Nationalbibliothek
Die Deutsche Nationalbibliothek verzeichnet diese Publikation in der Deutschen
Nationalbibliografie; detaillierte bibliografische Daten sind im Internet
über http://dnb.d-nb.de abrufbar.

Gedruckt auf chlorfrei gebleichtem, säurefreiem und alterungsbeständigem Papier

ISBN 978-3-7910-2759-3

www.schaeffer-poeschel.de
info@schaeffer-poeschel.de

Einbandgestaltung: Willy Löffelhardt
Druck und Bindung: Kösel, Krugzell • www.koeselbuch.de
Satz: Dörr + Schiller GmbH, Stuttgart

Printed in Germany
April 2008

Schäffer-Poeschel Verlag Stuttgart
Ein Tochterunternehmen der Verlagsgruppe Handelsblatt

Preface

The English language has gained tremendously in importance at German-language universities, an ongoing development that continues to be driven by the Bologna process as well as the increasing globalization of academia and business practice. Lectures in Bachelor and Masters programs are increasingly being held in English, and students are required to write reports and final theses in English as well. Managers and controllers working for large German companies are confronted with similar challenges, as they find themselves using English as a company-wide language while working with colleagues in an international context.

An obvious response to this development is to rely increasingly on English-language textbooks that have proved their worth in the United States or the United Kingdom. However, as controlling practice in Germany and parts of mainland Europe differs significantly from management accounting in the Anglo-Saxon countries – and there are many indications that suggest such differences do exist – this may not be good enough. Textbooks which focus on the country-specific characteristics of controlling and controllership need to be used alongside the international classics. We therefore decided to provide our readers with access in English to those chapters of the well-established German standard textbook »Introduction to Controlling« which address the specifics of controlling in German-speaking areas in depth. In addition, the English version may turn out to be relevant for managers and accountants with an international education who deal with companies from German-speaking countries.

Chapter 1 provides a first overview of the empirical findings on controllership as well as controlling conceptions and controlling-related theories. Chapters 2 and 3 establish a deeper understanding of controlling as assuring management rationality in a context dominated by coordination based on plans. These three chapters correspond to the first three chapters of the German textbook. Chapters 4 and 5 deal with the design of controller units; they correspond to chapters 14 and 15 of the German textbook.

In conclusion, we would like to thank several persons who participated in the genesis of »Introduction to Controlling«. Firstly, we would like to thank Sebastian Becker for his highly motivated and consistently good-humored commitment to coordinating the many activities involved in realizing this project. Dr John Endres also deserves our profound gratitude for his support in translating the text into English, as well as the incredible patience he demonstrated in innumerable conversations dealing with the nuances of alternative formulations while putting the finishing touches to the text. Finally, we would like to thank Andreas Bahke, Sebastian Becker, Pascal Nevries, and Christian Schürmann for carefully proofreading the text. Naturally, we take responsibility for all remaining errors, but we are confident that we have made a good start into the world of English textbooks with this manuscript.

Jürgen Weber   Utz Schäffer

Vallendar/Germany, February 2008

Contents

1 Controllers, controllership and controlling: Basic principles and categories

Guiding questions:

1 How has controlling developed in practice? What exactly is it that controllers do?

2 How does controlling differ from country to country?

3 How has controlling developed as an academic discipline?

4 Which different types of controlling conceptions are there?

5 What do the different accounting theories teach us?

1.1 Introduction

1.1.1 Terminology

A good textbook begins with an accurate description of what it aims to teach. This introduction to controlling is no different; however, providing such a description is certainly not easy. You will have noticed that the title of this chapter uses three similar expressions: controllers, controllership and controlling. Is there no way to simplify this? Unfortunately not, as there are significant problems with defining the term controlling. »Everybody has their own idea of what controlling means or should mean, and everybody means something different« (Preißler 2007, p. 14). The expressions controlling and controller are especially prone to being confused: When managers say »Our controlling does that«, they usually mean the controllers! We will therefore use the following working definition to start with:

- A *controller* is a person who carries out a certain set of tasks for a manager (e.g. making cost information available, monitoring results, and many other things).
- *Controllership* means the entire set of tasks that controllers are responsible for and/or carry out.

  Controllership as the sum of a controller's tasks

- Finally, *controlling* is a special management function that is carried out by different persons – including, but not limited to, controllers.

  Controlling as the function underlying the tasks of controllers

Controllers and controllership can be seen as belonging primarily to an institutional, »actor-based« perspective, whereas controlling tends to be part of a functional perspective. Such a co-existence of two perspectives is not at all unusual in management studies (e.g. analyzing companies from the perspective of production theory versus the institutional economics perspective). This does not necessarily make the topic easier to understand; but both perspectives are needed to answer different questions.

1.1.2 Basic approach

As mentioned earlier, controlling and controllership are not among the most clearly defined terms in management studies. A great diversity of terms and concepts characterizes both theory and practice. Empirical studies show that both the tasks of controllers and opinions regarding what controlling entails are very diverse.

The research on controlling recognizes and accepts this diversity, as shown by another frequently-used quotation: »In practice, people with the title of controller have functions that are, at one extreme, little more than bookkeeping and, at the other extreme, de facto general management« (Anthony 1965, p. 28). But controlling research has not really helped to clarify matters; instead, it is also characterized by many extremely diverse opinions and concepts, especially regarding controlling as a function. At first (and second) glance, a convincing integration into the theoretical edifice of business administration has not yet taken place. Overall, the situation for the three potential groups of readers of this book is therefore not very satisfying:

> ▸ *Academics* are bothered by two things: Firstly, the existing approaches explain neither the significant success controlling and controllers' tasks have had in practice nor their diversity. Secondly, they do not provide any prognoses regarding their future development. These two aspects – the ability to explain observations and make predictions for the future – are, however, core functions of research.
> ▸ *Students* want to know the key findings and specifics of an area of study. Knowing these makes it easier to separate what is important from what is not – making life a lot easier, especially during exam times. However, specific aspects cannot be clearly identified by simply collecting facts from practice, but also require being fitted into the existing theoretical edifice of business administration.
> ▸ *Controllers in practice* are interested in knowing – amongst other things – how they should design the controlling function in their organization and whether the tasks they are currently performing will remain relevant in the future, or whether some of them will disappear while new ones will appear. Some of them may feel a certain distaste at the word »theory« (»ivory tower«), but theories can provide valuable ideas and – when linked to design-oriented controlling conceptions – give orientation for daily activities.

In the first chapter, we will try to bring some order to the variety of expressions and concepts, and we will therefore identify three separate elements (cf. also Scherm/ Pietsch 2004b, pp. 6–7): (1) the »pure« description of controlling practice and of controlling as an academic discipline (sections 1.2 and 1.3), (2) controlling conceptions (section 1.4) and (3) theories relevant to controlling (section 1.5).

Theories are here defined as systems of statements that describe and explain phenomena observed in practice and that can be used to make predictions about future developments. The goal of business administration to design and thereby contribute to changes in practice is only indirectly reflected by such a theoretical perspective. In addition, predictions from research should strictly speaking only be derived from laws that apply without limitations in time or space (so-called nomological statements). Such statements are, however, generally not available for questions of business administration; instead, stochastic statements predominate. The

---

The words »controlling« and »controllership« have a multifaceted nature.

There are several reasons why these vague expressions should be specified more clearly.

Three levels are identified for this purpose:
(1) The empirical perspective
(2) The conceptual level
(3) The underlying theories

result is that there is often a wide gap between theory on the one hand and design recommendations for practice on the other hand.

Therefore, controlling research needs systems of statements that are not only aimed at describing and explaining observations, but that also focus on providing design guidelines for practice. »Such practice-oriented, normative systems of statements can be termed ›conceptions‹. These play the role of an intermediary between theory and practice by making eclectic use of theoretical statements with the aim of deriving design recommendations, combining them with normative postulates and relating them to practice. ... They create ... a framework that has to be concretized in corporate practice by taking into account the specific conditions of each individual case« (Scherm/Pietsch 2004b, p. 8).

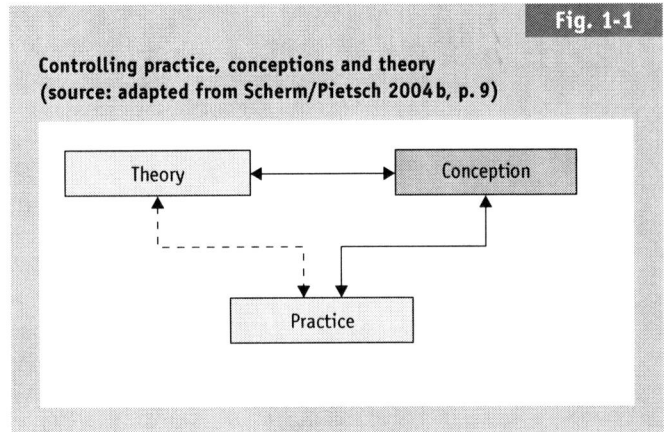

Fig. 1-1

Controlling practice, conceptions and theory
(source: adapted from Scherm/Pietsch 2004b, p. 9)

Controlling is primarily a phenomenon found in practice, and academics in German-language controlling research have traditionally placed a greater emphasis on the design rather than the explanation task of research. It is therefore not surprising that the academic debate on the topic of controlling in Germany has resulted in several conceptions (see section 1.4.2), and it is only in recent years that the research objectives of description and explanation have begun to gain importance. Nevertheless, we briefly want to present the key accounting theories related to controlling in section 1.5. They open up interesting perspectives on the field and may stimulate readers of this introductory textbook to reflect in an unconventional way on the subject matter. First, though, we will sketch the practice and theory of controlling in the light of empirical research and present key controlling conceptions.

1.2 The practice of controlling: first impressions

1.2.1 A brief description of how controller positions emerged in the USA

The first controllers worked in the public sector in England and in the USA. As early as the 15th century, the job title »countroller« was used for the role of keeping records about incoming and outgoing funds and goods at the royal court in England. In a similar function, a »comptroller« was responsible for monitoring the balance between the national budget and expenditure in the USA since 1778.

Controllers first emerged in the public sector in the USA.

Further historical roots of controlling in the public sector can be found in the positions of the »controller of the currency« (as head of the federal banking super-

1.2 **Controllers, controllership and controlling: Basic principles and categories**
The practice of controlling: first impressions

4

vision, from 1863) and the »comptroller general« at the head of the supreme auditing agency (from 1921) in the USA. These origins in the areas of accounting and supervision correspond to two responsibilities of controllers whose key importance has not changed to the present day, as will later be shown in detail.

In private sector institutions, controllers (called »comptrollers«) appeared for the first time in Atchison, Topeka & Santa Fe Railway System (1880), a transport company. Comptrollers essentially carried out financial duties: »The duties of the Comptroller are largely financial and relate to the bonds, stocks, and securities owned by the company« (from Santa Fe's articles of association, as cited by Jackson 1949, p. 8). Controller positions only became widespread much later, however, from the 1920s onwards. An empirical survey carried out by Jackson in 1948 amongst 143 U.S. enterprises showed an »average age« of about 20 years for controller positions (cf. Jackson 1949, p. 7). This was a consequence of the changed economic circumstances in the USA in the 1920s:

> The number of large corporations grew. These found themselves confronted with increasing problems of internal communication and coordination.

The first controller position in a company dates back to 1880.

From the source

Excerpts from the article »The Comptroller: His Functions and Organization« by J. Hugh Jackson on the emergence of comptrollers (1949):

»This expansion of American industry, and the unprecedented growth in the size and complexity of individual business units, increased correspondingly the demand for better management practices, which in turn required more adequate and scientific accounting and more exact financial control. The result has been the development during the last half-century of the functional field commonly known as ›comptrollership‹, and the addition of business concerns of an executive designated as the ›comptroller‹.

The modern offices of president, secretary, and treasurer have long been recognized as indispensable to proper corporate organization, and, as a result, custom and business practice, as well as statutory provision, have caused these officers to be included in the managements of American corporations. ... The history of the comptroller in business corporations, however, is quite different. This office is a development in corporate practice of more recent years, and, while the importance of the comptroller's position in industry is unquestioned, it has not reached the universal usage and more uniform treatment accorded to the offices of secretary and treasurer. So far as the writer has been able to determine, based upon studies of corporate reports and of inquiries made of several hundred corporations, the earliest American comptrollership in a business corporation dates back only to

1880, and the average ›age‹ of the 143 comptrollerships already referred to in this study is a matter of only some twenty-two years. ...

The comptrollership may be considered, therefore, as a logical outgrowth of the offices of secretary and treasurer when it became necessary, because of the large volume of accounting work involved, or advantageous for other reasons, to separate the accounting functions from the secretarial and financial functions of the corporate business. ...

In summary, the underlying causes for the changes in organization leading to the present stage of comptrollership development are to be found chiefly in two basic requirements of business: (a) the increasing necessity for a greater degree of concentration and specialization in the conduct of the accounting, auditing, and tax functions; and (b) the need not only for preserving one of the important ›checks and balances‹ of the corporate mechanism – whereunder the process of accounting and internal auditing may better serve as an independent check upon the receipt, disbursement, and custody of corporate funds – but also in further strengthening the controls over expenditures, costs, and profits so essential to the successful conduct of business today. Both requirements have increased immeasurably in importance during the past half century through the increase in the size and complexities of our modern industrial units« (Jackson 1949, pp. 5–14).

▸ As production plants became more productive because of technological inno-vation, the share of fixed costs increased and thereby limited entrepreneurial flexibility.

▸ Innovative management tools – as yet rarely used in practice and not widely known – became available at the same time as the need for them increased as a result of economic turbulence.

Controller positions are a response to increasing competitive pressure and the growth in company size.

In this context, the typical set of tasks of controllers also changed: whereas their responsibility as chief accountants, auditors or treasurers previously consisted mainly in tracking transactions that had already taken place, they now also had to introduce planning procedures based on accounting language, and coordinate and analyze budget-related data. By switching its focus to the user-customized collec-tion and processing of information by controllers, accounting evolved from being a pure recording and monitoring tool to being an instrument for dealing with the future. This helps explain why its importance increased and how it led to the insti-tutional upgrading of the role of controllers.

These changes also resulted in the foundation of the »Controller's Institute of America« in 1931. This institution, which was later renamed the »Financial Execu-tives Institute«, subsequently managed to create a widespread consensus about controllers' duties and responsibilities. In an often-cited catalog of tasks, controller-ship is represented as a subset of tasks within financial management, counterbal-anced by the tasks of treasurers. This catalog of tasks is shown in *Figure 1-2*. The tasks listed are neither arbitrarily thrown together, nor do they depict wishful thinking on the part of the controllers who were members of the institute. Instead, they are mutually dependent or can be derived logically from one another, as shown in the following.

At the core of controllers' tasks lies their *responsibility for planning*. As was briefly outlined above, the need to create plans for a company's future activities was a key input leading to the emergence of controller positions. Corporations became too big for a single person – the entrepreneur – to manage. Allocating management responsibilities to various managers in a sensible way meant it was necessary to have precise descriptions of their respective competencies and objectives. But creating such a description could not be done without prior planning. The increasing uncer-tainty inherent in the company's environment required explicit planning: simply extrapolating historical data was no longer helpful in dynamic times. Planning and the plans resulting from the process were seen to be the appropriate tool for ensuring that companies remained manageable. The newly created controller posi-tions thereby became responsible for developing a concept for results-oriented plan-ning, creating the required sub-planning processes and providing support for the planning process.

Results-oriented plan-ning is at the focus of attention.

Goals defined in plans are ineffective if compliance is not monitored. In the absence of monitoring, there is no opportunity to learn from deviations, nor is there sufficient motivation to make people really want to achieve their objectives (at least, this is the case for most people). Building up planning systems and formu-lating consistent, coordinated plans therefore requires creating systems and procedures for *monitoring* purposes. In addition to contrasting planned-vs.-actual values (»reporting«), it also includes analyzing the reasons for variances (»interpre-

Anything that is planned also needs to be moni-tored.

1.2 **Controllers, controllership and controlling: Basic principles and categories**
The practice of controlling: first impressions

6

Fig. 1-2

Controllership vs. treasurership according to the Financial Executives Institute 1962, p. 289

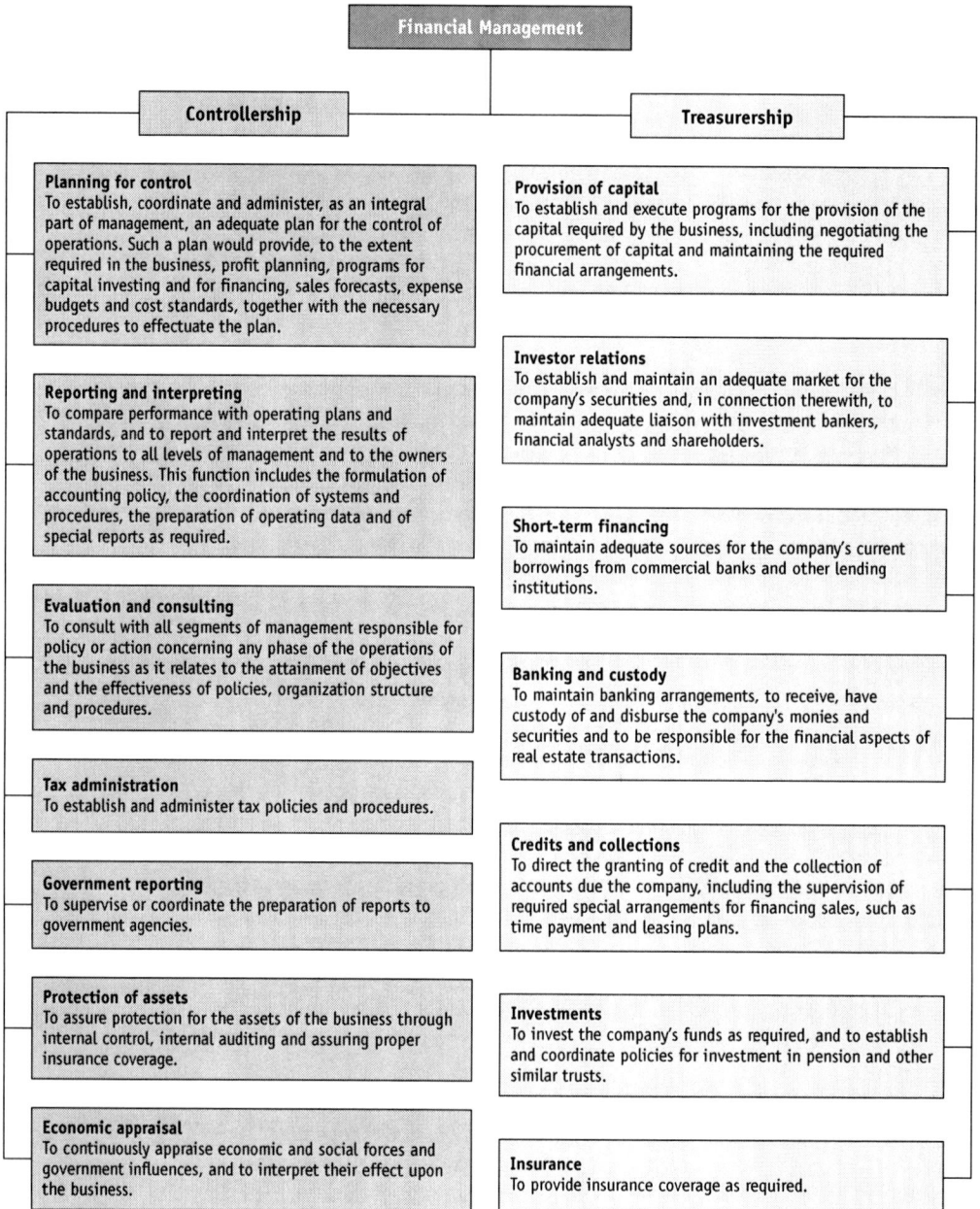

Financial Management

Controllership

Planning for control
To establish, coordinate and administer, as an integral part of management, an adequate plan for the control of operations. Such a plan would provide, to the extent required in the business, profit planning, programs for capital investing and for financing, sales forecasts, expense budgets and cost standards, together with the necessary procedures to effectuate the plan.

Reporting and interpreting
To compare performance with operating plans and standards, and to report and interpret the results of operations to all levels of management and to the owners of the business. This function includes the formulation of accounting policy, the coordination of systems and procedures, the preparation of operating data and of special reports as required.

Evaluation and consulting
To consult with all segments of management responsible for policy or action concerning any phase of the operations of the business as it relates to the attainment of objectives and the effectiveness of policies, organization structure and procedures.

Tax administration
To establish and administer tax policies and procedures.

Government reporting
To supervise or coordinate the preparation of reports to government agencies.

Protection of assets
To assure protection for the assets of the business through internal control, internal auditing and assuring proper insurance coverage.

Economic appraisal
To continuously appraise economic and social forces and government influences, and to interpret their effect upon the business.

Treasurership

Provision of capital
To establish and execute programs for the provision of the capital required by the business, including negotiating the procurement of capital and maintaining the required financial arrangements.

Investor relations
To establish and maintain an adequate market for the company's securities and, in connection therewith, to maintain adequate liaison with investment bankers, financial analysts and shareholders.

Short-term financing
To maintain adequate sources for the company's current borrowings from commercial banks and other lending institutions.

Banking and custody
To maintain banking arrangements, to receive, have custody of and disburse the company's monies and securities and to be responsible for the financial aspects of real estate transactions.

Credits and collections
To direct the granting of credit and the collection of accounts due the company, including the supervision of required special arrangements for financing sales, such as time payment and leasing plans.

Investments
To invest the company's funds as required, and to establish and coordinate policies for investment in pension and other similar trusts.

Insurance
To provide insurance coverage as required.

ting«). Monitoring depends on the availability of precise, objective actual data to contrast with planned figures. Under these conditions, it makes sense also to give controllers responsibility for ensuring the availability of information, which can at the same time be used as the basis for planning.

Information is needed for planning and monitoring.

The third area of responsibility of controllers seamlessly connects to planning and reporting/interpreting. Whoever is intimately involved in creating plans and analyzing deviations (monitoring) will have enough knowledge about the company and the subject matter to provide *valuation and consulting services to management.*

The other four controller tasks listed in the FEI catalog do not fit this line of argumentation, but are related to two specific aspects of the U.S. context:

▸ U.S. companies do not maintain separate financial and operational accounting systems. Stand-alone cost accounting systems, which have been standard in Germany since the 1920s in large companies, are a rarity. On the one hand, controllers in the USA therefore carry out tasks that are usually part of external accounting in Germany (e.g. »tax administration«, »government reporting«). On the other hand, as central information sources, they also capture the interface between a company and the economy in which it operates.

▸ The capital market acted more »directly« in the USA than in Germany. The intermediary position between capital providers and management that German banks typically held is not as pronounced in the U.S. As a consequence, controllers were also given the function of securing assets, almost as an extended arm of the shareholders. Such considerations were alien to German thinking. However, the recently increasing popularity of value-based management is resulting in significantly more advanced approaches in this direction.

At its beginnings and during the early stages of evolution, controllership appeared as a diverse, but consistent and precise concept.

1.2.2 The evolution of controllership in Germany

In Germany, the expression »controller« remained unknown for a long time. Even early contributions to the debate dating from the 1950s and resulting from trips by German academics to the USA did nothing to change this (see the excerpts from Auffermann 1952). The dominant attitudes were rejection and a lack of understanding (see the quotation from Goossens 1959). Even at the end of the 1960s, controllers were usually only found in German subsidiaries of U.S. companies. Then, suddenly, things appeared to change: According to an often-cited study by McKinsey (basis: 30 typical German enterprises with sales greater than 1 billion DM), 90 percent (!) of the companies had controller positions by 1974 (Henzler 1974, p. 63), even if these were not always thus named. The general validity of this finding – which at first glance appears excessively high – was confirmed in the following years by other empirical surveys (for an overview, cf. Richter 1987, pp. 23–29).

Controllers have become more common in German companies too – but the process took over 20 years.

The development becomes clearer in an analysis of job advertisements in the Frankfurter Allgemeine Zeitung, a major German newspaper, for the period 1949 to 1994 (for more detail cf. Weber/Kosmider 1991, pp. 17–35, and Weber/Schäffer 1998, pp. 227–233). In order to depict the way the expression might have changed,

1.2 Controllers, controllership and controlling: Basic principles and categories
The practice of controlling: first impressions

8

job advertisements for positions similar to that of a controller were also included in the analysis. In accordance with the functions and roles typically covered by controllers, these included all advertisements mentioning the areas of business administration, accounting, and planning. Concerning the quantitative development of the job advertisements, the survey provided three key findings:

▸ The first advertisement for a controller dates back to 1954.
▸ As was assumed in the relevant literature, the controller positions were initially mainly offered by local subsidiaries of U. S. parent companies.
▸ The number of controller positions developed exponentially; but only in the 1980s did it exceed the number of positions similar to that of a controller.

From the source

Foreword from a report by a study commission on the role of controllers in the USA:

»This report by the English study commission that traveled to the USA in 1950 to investigate the causes for the greater productivity of American industrial accounting as well as its methods has caused a stir not only in England, but also in Germany on the basis of the publication and discussion of excerpts. ...

One could focus on many interesting and important issues raised in the report, such as the description of the sense of responsibility for costs, performance-based pay, reporting systems or cost control and cost analysis. However, this is not the place to go into such detail. The report should speak for itself. Nonetheless, it should be pointed out how important the institution of the ›controller‹ in the USA appeared to the English study commission. The controller's tasks are hard to describe: As a result of their special [!] accounting knowledge, ›controllers‹ or ›controller‹ departments analyze business data to monitor the performance of individual departments and generate and disseminate business metrics to top management, department heads and supervisors, thereby enabling the business side of the company to be run properly. The greater productivity of U. S. companies is often explained as resulting from the key position held by ›controllers‹ in the organization's management. In many cases, both the head of bookkeeping and the head of the entire cost accounting department report to him.

In Germany, only a few large companies have oriented themselves towards the same concept by creating a central business management department that compiles and prepares the figures that the executive

management needs to make decisions. I am convinced that a significant improvement in performance could be achieved if we introduced an institution such as that of the ›controller‹ into our companies« (Auffermann 1952, p. 6).

Excerpts from a paper by Goossens dating from 1959: »The ›controller‹ – head of the company without overall responsibility«:

»So the controller is a man who designs his own plans, coordinates them – and even monitors them! Not only that, he also controls ... the entire organization and auditing, production monitoring, cost accounting, bookkeeping, balance sheets and taxes. In this way, the controller essentially becomes the head of the company, but without appearing externally as the head or taking the overall responsibility associated with that position. Even on its own, vesting the combination of planning, production monitoring and reporting in one person amounts to an inordinate concentration of power in a large company. But if *organization* and *auditing* are added, then all other office bearers – including the chairman of the board and the supervisory board – become insignificant, marginal figures. ...

One should always and everywhere learn from others – and not only from the USA. But the ›controller‹ does not really fit into the legal structure of German corporate management. Adopting him in Germany would hardly signify progress, but rather sliding back to the conditions which German organizational research believed had been overcome a long time ago – at least in its theoretical findings and on the basis of practical experience« (Goossens 1959, pp. 75–76).

Fig. 1-3

Changes in controller's task descriptions as reflected in a longitudinal analysis of job advertisements (source: Weber/Schäffer 1998, p. 229)

Task area / Time period	1949–1959	1960–1964	1965–1969	1970–1974	1975–1979	1980–1984	1985–1989	1990–1994
Reporting	–	14.3	6.5	4.7	8.4	8.5	11.4	13.2
Short-term/annual/operational planning	–	–	6.5	6.2	9.6	12.0	9.2	11.6
Strategic planning	–	–	–	1.6	4.0	7.1	3.6	3.6
Advice and consulting on business issues	25.0	4.8	4.8	2.3	3.2	3.7	4.8	4.7
Capital budgeting/cost-effectiveness analyses	–	4.8	3.2	2.3	4.0	2.9	4.4	6.5
Budgeting and budgetary monitoring	–	4.8	12.9	9.3	11.9	8.8	10.1	7.9
Planned-vs.-actual comparisons/variance analyses/cost monitoring	–	9.5	8.1	7.0	11.1	6.8	12.4	10.7
Financial planning, monitoring liquidity, financing issues	–	4.8	8.1	9.3	6.8	6.3	4.2	3.4
Collaboration on company policies and goals	–	–	–	–	2.0	1.5	1.7	0.8
Management and control tasks	–	–	1.6	0.8	2.8	2.2	1.6	3.1
IT organization	–	4.8	8.1	3.8	7.2	8.0	5.5	3.3
Project coordination/special analyses	–	–	–	4.7	3.2	3.4	3.4	5.1
Drawing up balance sheets/group balance sheets	–	14.3	3.2	6.9	2.4	2.7	2.7	4.2
Bookkeeping	–	9.5	4.8	7.8	3.2	3.4	2.1	2.5
Cost accounting/costings	50.0	18.9	14.5	11.6	5.5	9.5	7.7	6.4
Taxation	25.0	9.5	4.8	5.4	3.6	2.0	1.2	0.8
Other	–	–	12.9	16.3	11.1	11.2	14.0	12.1

Figures represent percentage share of all tasks during a given period

From a task-related perspective, controller job advertisements are characterized essentially by the simultaneous listing of budgeting and budgetary monitoring, planned-vs.-actual comparisons, variance analyses and cost monitoring. This combination of aspects differentiates them in a statistically significant way from positions similar to those of a controller (cf. Weber/Bültel 1992, pp. 535–546). The analysis further shows a clear change of tasks over time (e.g. towards integrating controllers more strongly into strategic management issues, see *Figure 1-3* for details), although there was no change in the fundamental bundle of tasks.

Controller positions are characterized above all by the specific combination of tasks they encompass.

1.2 Controllers, controllership and controlling: Basic principles and categories
The practice of controlling: first impressions

10

The genesis and ongoing development of controlling in practice can also be traced by interviewing contemporary witnesses. In the following, we show some quotes by prominent individuals who tracked the development of controlling in Germany over many years (as quoted by Binder 2006, pp. 96–105 and 128–130):

Rudolf Mann: »The need was simply there. And more people felt that controlling was needed now. There was something in the air. ... Essentially, what people were looking for was a consistent system of control rather than just raw figures«.

Rainer Bramsemann: »The integrative approach, and therefore the necessity of having rigorously to think things through from beginning to end, from analyzing sales and profits to analyzing the origin of funds and their usage. This was not being provided by the traditional partial planning and budgeting systems. The value added by marketing was also limited to market and customer-based integration«.

Hans-Ulrich Küpper: »From my perspective, what is right about this development is that accounting is removed from a pure role of generating figures. I see an independent function and task in having instruments and systems for managing such complex systems«.

Albrecht Deyhle: »Well, we got the word or the expression controller from the USA. The word controlling is not as wide-spread in the USA, as far as I know. When talking about the ensemble, they usually talk about controllership. We set it into motion ourselves. It was probably I who did it. I did it as a twin sister for marketing. Marketing from the customer perspective and controlling from the results perspective«.

Andreas Schmidt: »U.S. companies were successful with this, they had better information, financial, and accounting systems and thereby set the benchmark. The German corporate groups were characterized most strongly by cost accounting. Controlling was an approach aimed at creating a more comprehensive reporting system«.

Péter Horváth: »My explanation of the diffusion is that, in certain industries, transparency and efficiency were not really at the focus of attention in Germany in the 1960s, 1970s and 1980s. Companies were earning so much money that this question was simply not very interesting – when looking at banking, insurance or trading. Only when these topics became more important as a result of pressure to use resources more efficiently and effectively did one naturally start thinking more about controlling«.

Ekkehard Kappler: »The practical development was determined mostly by Albrecht Deyhle. He promoted this area of study in practice through his tireless efforts. ... With the Controller Academy in Gauting, he achieved almost complete coverage of practice; he was also astute in building the Controllerverein as an analog of the Marketing Club's organization form. But diffusion took a long time«.

Dietger Hahn: »I believe that in 10 to 20 years we will still find controlling departments. The expression has established itself in the German-speaking regions. ... This area of activity will continue to exist for quite some time yet, at least that is how we see it in Germany today. ... But we are just a very small country on the planet. ... Whether the Chinese and Japanese will be prepared some day to talk about controlling, this is a question I want to leave to the future. ... Someday we will have to ask ourselves why the Americans nowadays get by almost without using the expression«.

1.2.3 Empirical findings on the current state of controllership

Companies formulate workplace requirements for controllers in job advertisements. In order to find out what it is that controllers really do, case studies or large-scale questionnaire-based empirical studies can be used. Many such studies have been carried out in recent years. We would like to show some selected findings in the following to provide further insight into the »real world of controllers«.

Empirical studies have confirmed the large variety of tasks as well as the core tasks of controllers.

One of the first studies on the state of controllership in Germany, concluded in 1988, was conducted by von Landsberg and Mayer. Amongst other things, controllers were asked which importance they placed on specific tasks and how much effort they invested in them. The resulting »hit list of tasks« shown in *Figure 1-4* was derived from the 260 answers received in total. It confirms the findings of the analysis of job advertisements: controllers are inextricably linked to the ongoing operational planning of companies (budgeting, investment planning). They design and manage the

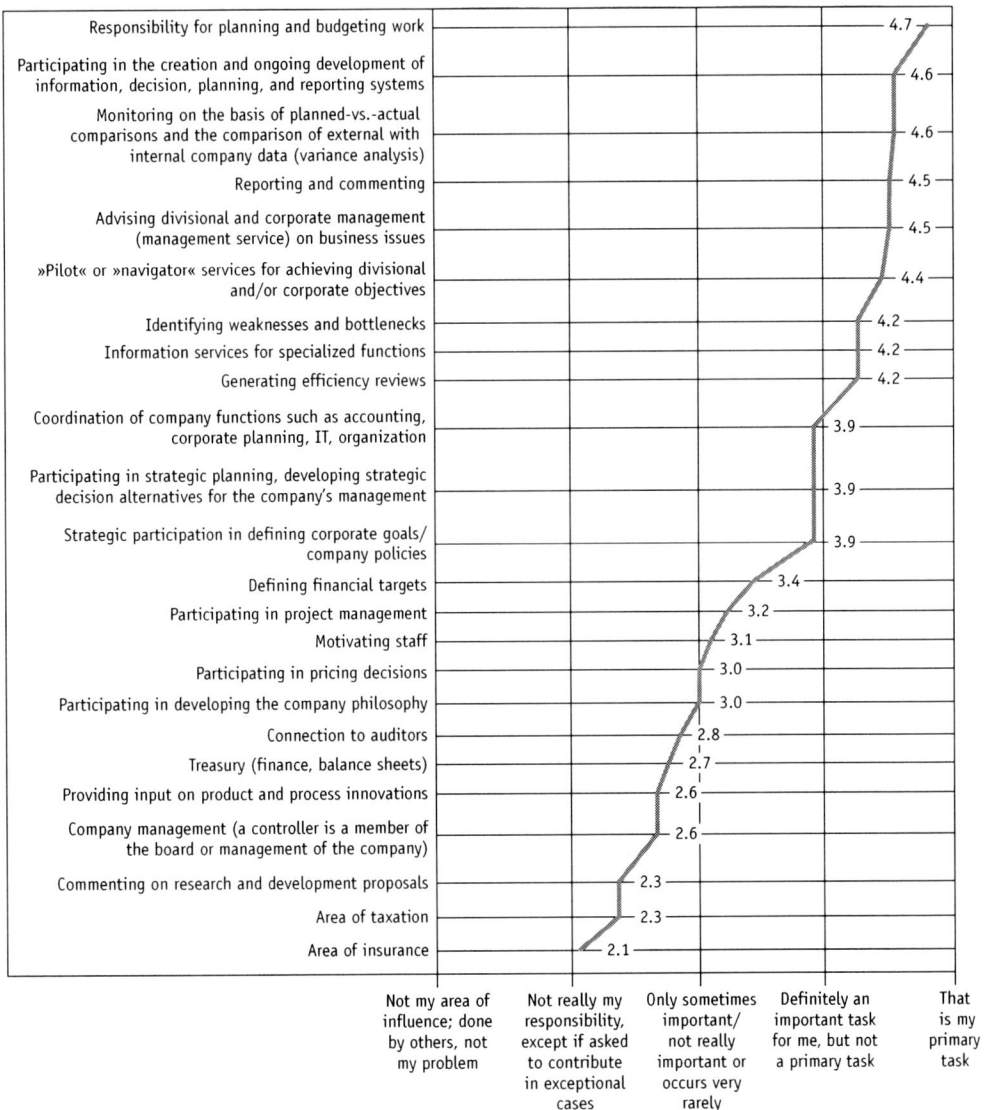

Fig. 1-4

Controller tasks according to von Landsberg/Mayer 1988, p. 71

Task	Value
Responsibility for planning and budgeting work	4.7
Participating in the creation and ongoing development of information, decision, planning, and reporting systems	4.6
Monitoring on the basis of planned-vs.-actual comparisons and the comparison of external with internal company data (variance analysis)	4.6
Reporting and commenting	4.5
Advising divisional and corporate management (management service) on business issues	4.5
»Pilot« or »navigator« services for achieving divisional and/or corporate objectives	4.4
Identifying weaknesses and bottlenecks	4.2
Information services for specialized functions	4.2
Generating efficiency reviews	4.2
Coordination of company functions such as accounting, corporate planning, IT, organization	3.9
Participating in strategic planning, developing strategic decision alternatives for the company's management	3.9
Strategic participation in defining corporate goals/ company policies	3.9
Defining financial targets	3.4
Participating in project management	3.2
Motivating staff	3.1
Participating in pricing decisions	3.0
Participating in developing the company philosophy	3.0
Connection to auditors	2.8
Treasury (finance, balance sheets)	2.7
Providing input on product and process innovations	2.6
Company management (a controller is a member of the board or management of the company)	2.6
Commenting on research and development proposals	2.3
Area of taxation	2.3
Area of insurance	2.1

Not my area of influence; done by others, not my problem	Not really my responsibility, except if asked to contribute in exceptional cases	Only sometimes important/ not really important or occurs very rarely	Definitely an important task for me, but not a primary task	That is my primary task

1.2　Controllers, controllership and controlling: Basic principles and categories
The practice of controlling: first impressions

12

Ranking by importance of controlling tasks in Austrian companies according to Niedermayr's study 1994, p. 215

Rank	Controlling tasks	Values
1.	Budgetary monitoring + planned-vs.-actual comparisons	5.3
2.	Responsible for cost accounting	5.0
3.	Responsible for reporting	5.0
4.	In charge of budgeting	5.0
5.	Variance analyses	4.9
6.	Budget coordination	4.9
7.	Budget consolidation	4.7
8.	System development	4.6
9.	System monitoring	4.5
10.	Interpretation of reports	4.5
11.	Internal business consulting	4.3
12.	Evaluating investments	4.1
13.	Participating in strategic planning	4.1
14.	Central business information service	3.9
15.	Initiating corrective measures	3.7
16.	Balance sheets	3.7
17.	Financing and finance	3.7
18.	Strategic planned-vs.-actual comparisons	3.5
19.	Coordination of early warning systems	3.3
20.	Initiating preventive measures	3.3
21.	Strategic variance analysis	3.1
22.	Information technology	3.1
23.	Information service for strategic planning	3.1
24.	Organisation and administration	3.1
25.	Taxation	3.0
26.	Internal auditing	2.5

planning process and are involved in defining goals. They report on whether the objectives have been achieved, are responsible for ongoing monitoring of the planned values and feed back the results to management. In addition, they provide management support in the form of comprehensive information services and are responsible for building and maintaining the required systems. They act as coaches, consultants and counterparts to managers on all issues related to business administration. In a »typically German« fashion, other financial functions are carried out by other departments: Controllers do not see themselves as being responsible for balance sheets, taxes, finances and insurance – at least, this was the case in 1988. Nevertheless, in the global view the impression that emerges is that of a broad spectrum of tasks with a solid core, but rather unclear boundaries.

This impression is not limited to Germany, as shown by the Austrian study carried out by Niedermayr in 1994. The almost 300 answers received were used to generate the list of controller activities shown in *Figure 1-5*, sorted as above by the importance accorded to each task. The result once again shows the dominance of planning/budgeting, monitoring and information supply, which are confirmed as »classical« controller tasks in their daily operations.

Once you leave the German-language area, however, greater differences emerge. According to a study by Stoffel (1995), the following key differences were found for U.S. controllers at the end of the 20th century (see also *Figure 1-6*):

In the international comparison, there are clear differences between the tasks of controllers.

▸ They are responsible for a major part of budgeting activities, but they share the overall area of budgeting with other staff or support units.

▸ Their position in operational planning relating to time, quantities and qualities – a preceding step to budgeting – was also found to be significantly weaker.

▸ In the area of information supply and reporting, U.S. controllers focus strongly on the information needs of parties external to the company. This leads to additional fields of activity for which controllers in Germany are responsible only in exceptions to date, such as liquidity management, corporate taxation, debtor accounting and company insurance.

Fig. 1-6

Controller tasks: an international comparison (source: Stoffel 1995, p. 157)

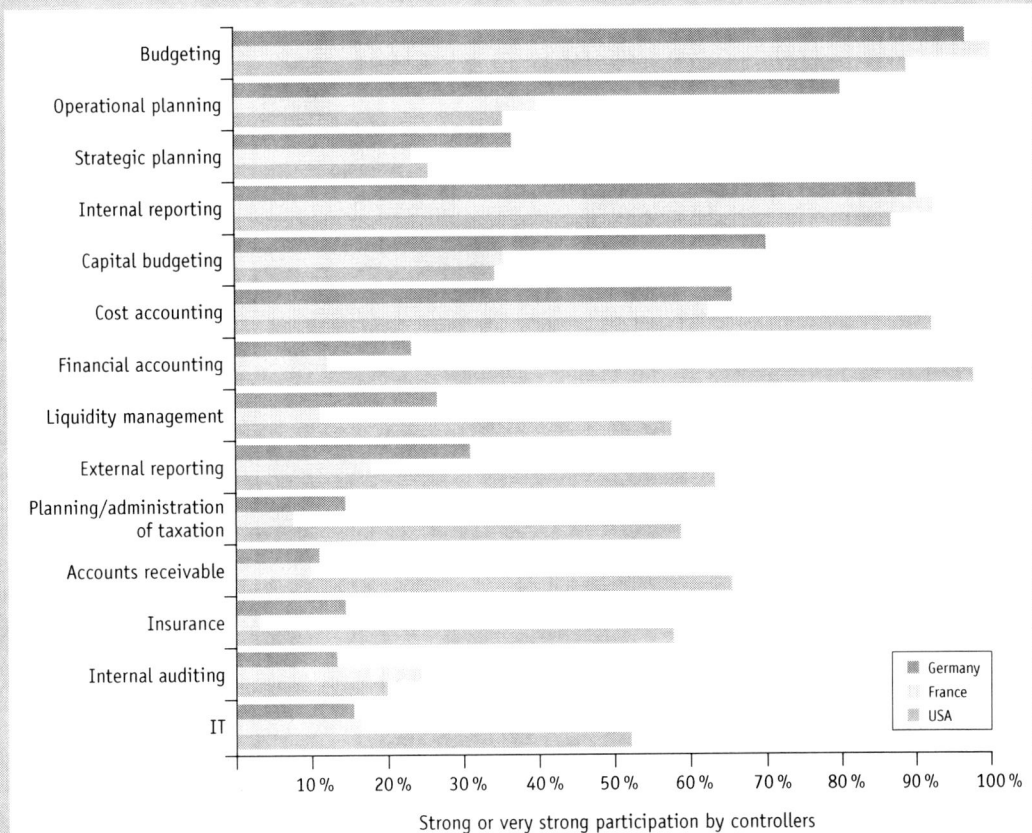

	Germany	France	USA
Budgeting			
Operational planning			
Strategic planning			
Internal reporting			
Capital budgeting			
Cost accounting			
Financial accounting			
Liquidity management			
External reporting			
Planning/administration of taxation			
Accounts receivable			
Insurance			
Internal auditing			
IT			

Strong or very strong participation by controllers

As a rule, U. S. controllers have a strong *financial focus*, as evidenced by the fact that they are generally part of the finance department. But here, too, changes can be observed: Whereas an early survey by Simon et al. (1954) found controllers to be pure accounting men who enhanced their numerical data to create an information tool, later studies (Skousen/Zimmer 1970; Henning/Moseley 1970; Siegel/Kulesza 1996) found a much wider set of tasks that Siegel/Kulesza succinctly characterized as follows: »From numbers-crunching preparer of financial statements to high-level decision-support specialist« (Siegel/Kulesza 1996, p. 26).

Controllers became more common in French companies only in the 1970s, thereby mirroring the development observed in Germany. Like their German colleagues, French controllers are consistently not responsible for the additional accounting and finance-related tasks which occupy most of controllers' attention in the USA. In their basic orientation, the following two types can be identified. The first-mentioned is clearly dominant in business practice:

The differences between tasks in the USA, Germany and France in detail

1.2

Controllers, controllership and controlling: Basic principles and categories
The practice of controlling: first impressions

14

▸ In those cases where controllers in France report to the finance department, their planning- and monitoring-related tasks deal exclusively with budgeting. This is supplemented by internal reporting, and, as a basis, internal accounting as additional areas of responsibility.

▸ In contrast, when controllers report directly to management, they participate in the planning process itself. However, they participate to a lesser degree than in Germany.

The bundling of planning, monitoring and information supply tasks in controller positions may therefore – as shown by this short comparison – differ significantly from country to country. The large accounting share in the USA results in a focus dominated by financial figures. In France, controllers usually also report to the finance department, but are only at the third management level (at most) and therefore have little influence. Where planning, monitoring and information supply tasks tend to be seen as being of equal importance, as is the case in Germany, a significant part of controllers' tasks consists in influencing and accompanying the planning processes themselves. Correspondingly, controllers are ranked at a higher level in the company's organizational structure. As a result, controllership becomes a phenomenon that is determined greatly by context and culture.

Controllership is very much context-dependent and culture-specific.

A study by Ahrens that gained a lot of international attention focused not on comparing the areas of responsibility, but rather on researching the practices and the self-view of management accountants or controllers in British and German breweries respectively. On the basis of participant observation, interviews and document analysis, he identified some clear differences: Whereas controllers in the German breweries participating in the study perceive their company through notions of plans and planning and accordingly view accounting as being an abstract and operationally detached form of expertise, management accountants in Britain and their cooperative operational managers seek early involvement in emergent operational proposals and claim a substantial – as opposed to just a formal – influence for the day-to-day ordering of organizational action. Correspondingly, companies appear primarily as technical units in the case of German breweries, within which controlling is responsible for ensuring that technical processes are profitable. In British breweries, on the other hand, accountants have a dominant position. A »good manager« is one who is able to manage his or her area of responsibility successfully within the budget framework prescribed by accounting or profit expec-

Fig. 1-7

Distribution of controllers' tasks in the companies participating in the WHU benchmarking controlling working group (source: Weber/Weißenberger/Aust 1998)

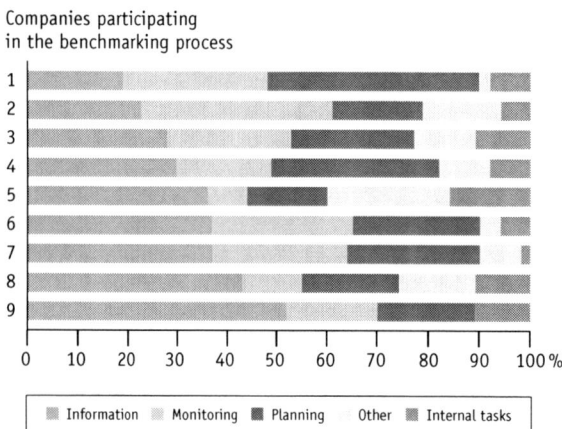

Companies participating in the benchmarking process

■ Information ■ Monitoring ■ Planning Other ■ Internal tasks

tations. The company appears to be more economically focused in this case (cf. Ahrens 1999).

There also appear to be differences between Germany and Great Britain.

Naturally, the findings made in the breweries studied by Ahrens cannot be generalized by extrapolating them to all German or British companies; still, it is apparent that controllers' activities are embedded in a cultural context. This context may not necessarily show itself via questionnaires and the reading of manuals, but should under no circumstances be ignored in a comparative analysis.

Differences in perceived controllership relate not just to the spectrum of tasks and controllers' practices, but also become visible in the share of time used on the different tasks. This is clarified by the results of a benchmarking working group in which several large companies participated in order to compare their controller units (cf. Weber/Weißenberger/Aust 1998). *Figure 1-7* shows the different areas of responsibility, clustered in five groups. The first three (planning, monitoring, and information) are sufficiently clear at this stage of the discussion. The »internal tasks« cluster includes elements such as planning one's own resources, meetings between controllers, internal training, and management tasks in the controller unit. To summarize, companies choose very different configurations of controller tasks to match their individual needs – even though the fundamental view is the same. This »real variability« (Amshoff 1993, p. 71) requires explanation!

**Summary
(see guiding questions 1 and 2)**

▶ The first controller positions in private-sector companies were established in the USA at the end of the 19th century. They only arrived in Europe almost three quarters of a century later.

▶ The core tasks of controllers were – and continue to be – designing the planning process, monitoring whether or not goals are achieved, supplying management with relevant information, and providing business support to managers.

▶ In spite of all the similarities, controllers' tasks differ from country to country and from company to company in an economic region. This is what makes controllership such a multi-faceted subject.

1.3 Development of controlling as an academic discipline

In parallel to its impressive development in practice, controlling has become a recognized discipline in academia as well – in spite of some reservations (cf. Küpper/ Wagenhofer 2002, p. X; Ahn 1999, p. 110). According to a study by Binder/Schäffer, there were no fewer than 72 chairs explicitly carrying the label »controlling« at the 92 business administration faculties of the German-language universities and business schools in 2004 (cf. Binder/Schäffer 2005a, p. 101). Furthermore, some aspects of controlling as a subject are often covered by other chairs that do not explicitly use the expression controlling as part of their name.

Controlling has become a recognized discipline.

A closer analysis of the chairs' labels shows that only 15 percent of the 72 chairs are »pure« controlling chairs. The remaining 85 percent of chairs are linked to other subjects. The diversity of combinations clearly shows that controlling can be linked to very different aspects – and thereby represents a classical cross-sectional function. Combinations with accounting (36 percent) and auditing (13 percent) head

Visit www.whu.edu/ controlling for a listing of German-language controlling chairs.

1.3 Controllers, controllership and controlling: Basic principles and categories
Development of controlling as an academic discipline

16

From the source

The emergence and ongoing development of controlling as an academic discipline can also be traced by interviewing those who helped shape the field. In the following, we have collected some quotations from prominent individuals who tracked the development of controlling as an academic discipline in Germany over many years (as quoted by Binder, 2006, pp. 143–150, 164–169 and 196):

Jürgen Weber: »It's not that we first found something and then looked for a name. Instead, we took something for which there already was a label in business practice, but in the beginning we did not quite know what it was. ... Fundamentally, my view of controlling is that the whole thing was initiated and driven by practice. This was the key driver. In the area of research, we really just looked at the phenomenon afterwards and tried to understand and explain it«.

Hans-Ulrich Küpper: »I do see a clear contrast to marketing here. In the case of marketing, there was already a crew behind it: the sales people. In the case of the standard textbook by Nieschlag/Dichtl/Hörschgen – as a student, I bought the first volume when it was titled ›Lehre von der Absatzwirtschaft‹ (›Sales‹) – the word ›Marketing‹ was added at the beginning of the title for the 3rd edition in 1970. This shows that the academic group was already there, and the chairs already existed as well. From my point of view, that is a different starting position«.

Klaus Brockhoff: »My general concept of how focus points emerge in scientific progress – including business administration studies – is basically the ›needs-driven perspective‹. Somewhere, there is a need. People then focus their attention on somehow satisfying this need. ... The necessary condition is that there have to be people who have drive and who develop a solution. The most important sufficient condition for such a phenomenal development such as that undergone by controlling is that there has to be a clearly recognizable need for such a thing, otherwise it [the process] aborts much earlier«.

André Zünd: »The academic community did not deal with controlling very much, or even at all. It simply did not fit into the scientific concept, into the university landscape, the disciplines. This may have played a role. Controlling is actually something multidisciplinary. It is not just plain one-sided accounting, it hardly fits into the German understanding of the faculties, disciplines and the classic categorization of business administration (Kosiol and others) very well. Controlling simply does not fit. It is not only accounting, it is also accounting. It is not only human resources management, it is also human resources management. This interdisciplinary idea of controlling worked against the academic understanding of business administration«.

Péter Horváth: »One can see a classical development in the adaptation process. At first, there was – as always – a certain resistance. This was characterized by the fact that the degree of innovation of new ideas was denied or that the purpose of the ideas was questioned. And this was the case in practice as well as academia. A typical question: What is there that is new about it, what is there that could be viewed as a new idea contributed by controlling? ... So this is how questions came up regarding the delimitation in relation to other disciplines, the existence of an autonomous research question and of specific instruments that can be used here. ... There are many colleagues who even now say: Controlling is nothing new. It is either a camouflaged kind of general business administration (Betriebswirtschaftslehre) or, on the other hand, it may simply be a bloated form of accounting«.

Jürgen Weber: »There was no controlling community. ... There was no reason for it, since it seemed to be only a hindrance. The scene appears to live on the highly diffuse character of the discipline, which allows everyone to hide oneself. Everyone can say: ›I have my own definition of Controlling and I know what is really happening‹. Nobody can be questioned, not even rudimentarily. There is no organized process of discussion within the community, because there is no community«.

Péter Horváth: »In my view, research developed ever more strongly towards a certain independence and autonomization of the controlling issue. In the 1970s and 1980s, practice was at the focus of attention. Now we have a new generation of researchers who no longer deal with practical issues so much as with formal, analytical models, mainly influenced by institutional economics. A relatively strong divergence between practice and theory can be observed«.

the list. According to Hirsch, »the combination of the sub-disciplines ›controlling‹ and ›accounting‹ in a chair's name is an indication of the great closeness of these two disciplines« (Hirsch 2003, p. 255). Nevertheless, 36 percent of chairs are characterized by other combinations.

The institutional development of German-language controlling at universities and business schools began in 1973, when Péter Horváth was offered the newly created chair of controlling at the Darmstadt technical university. After that, progress was slow until the end of the 1980s: In 1989, just 17 of today's 72 controlling chairs existed. Then things started speeding up (see *Figure 1-8*). In just a few years, 14 controlling chairs were established in former East Germany, while the number grew by 41 in the former West German Bundesländer.

The first chair for controlling was created in 1973.

This rapid institutionalization of controlling chairs can be traced back mainly to changes in business practice. The analysis of job advertisements by Weber/Kosmider and Weber/Schäffer for the years 1949–1994, which was described earlier, showed a significant increase in the number of controller positions as well as similar jobs. The expansion of university capacity in the field of controlling also led to a clear increase in publications relevant to controlling in the academic journals of the German-speaking regions: Whereas the share of articles on controlling hovered between 4 and 6 percent in the 1970s and 1980s (see *Figure 1-9*), that figure doubled to an average of about 12 percent at the beginning of the 1990s.

In addition to universities and business schools, universities of applied science *(Fachhochschulen)* played an important role in the development of the specialization. As early as 1971, Elmar Mayer launched the AWW Köln *(Arbeitsgemeinschaft Wirtschaftswissenschaft und Wirtschaftspraxis im Controlling und Rechnungswesen)*, a

Fig. 1-8

Growth of the number of German-language controlling chairs (source: Binder/Schäffer 2005a, p. 102)

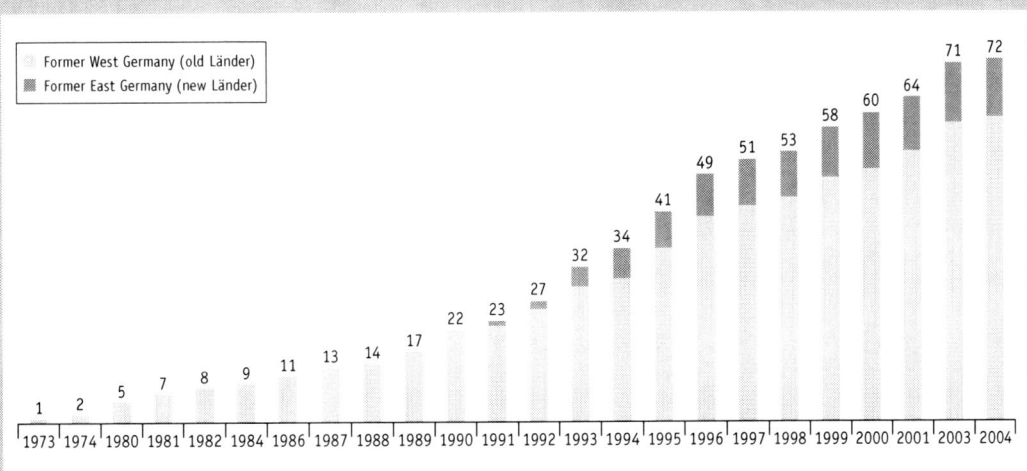

Former West Germany (old Länder)
Former East Germany (new Länder)

1973: 1
1974: 2
1980: 5
1981: 7
1982: 8
1984: 9
1986: 11
1987: 13
1988: 14
1989: 17
1990: 22
1991: 23
1992: 27
1993: 32
1994: 34
1995: 41
1996: 49
1997: 51
1998: 53
1999: 58
2000: 60
2001: 64
2003: 71
2004: 72

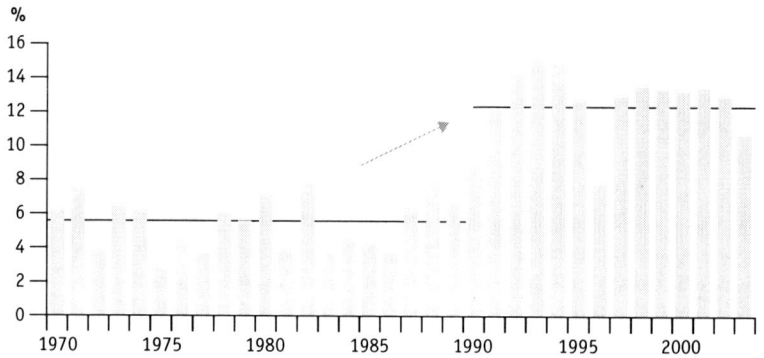

Fig. 1-9

Growth of controlling-related contributions to German-language scientific journals
(source: Binder/Schäffer 2005b, p. 608)

working group on the role of business administration theory and practice in controlling and accounting, at the business department of the Cologne University of Applied Science. In 1974, Mayer accepted the chair of business administration, controlling and accounting at the same institution. By the end of 1989, 34 out of 40 accounting chairs at universities of applied science already carried the extended designation »accounting and controlling« (cf. Mayer 1990).

Summary
(see guiding question 3)

▸ Controlling has become a recognized discipline not only in practice, but also in research.

▸ The development of controlling as an academic discipline was driven to a large degree by practice. As a result of the increasing integration of the German research in controlling into the international scientific community, this tight linkage could become looser in the future.

1.4 Controlling conceptions

A vast number of sources dealing with controlling can be found in the literature, but there are not many that try to build a bridge between what controllers do and what controlling means. In the following, we will begin by introducing a conception of controlling, developed in practice, that does build such a bridge. It originated with the Internationaler Controller Verein (ICV, *International Controller Association*). Afterwards, we will present the current controlling conceptions in the academic discussion and the relevant theoretical building blocks used in accounting research.

1.4.1 The ICV's practice-based conception of controlling

The *Internationaler Controller Verein* is the dominant association of controllers in the German-speaking countries. It was founded and strongly influenced by Albrecht Deyhle, the best-known trainer of German-speaking controllers. His understanding of controlling played a key role in the development of controlling in German companies, not least because of the very large number of controllers he coached. The *International Group of Controlling* (IGC), which is closely linked to the ICV, formulated a position paper *(»Leitbild Controller«)* that begins with a short introductory statement (Internationaler Controller Verein eV, www.controllerverein.de, as of 2002):

> »Controllers design and accompany the management process of defining goals, planning and controlling and thus have a joint responsibility with management to reach their objectives.

This means that:
- ▸ Controllers ensure the transparency of business results, finance, processes and strategy and thus contribute to higher economic effectiveness.
- ▸ Controllers co-ordinate secondary goals and the related plans in a holistic way and organise a reporting-system which is future-oriented and covers the enterprise as a whole.
- ▸ Controllers moderate and design the controlling process of defining goals, planning and management control so that every decision maker can act in accordance with agreed objectives.
- ▸ Controllers provide necessary company management data and information.
- ▸ Controllers develop and maintain controlling systems«.

Next, the relationships between controllers and controlling are depicted as intersecting sets, as illustrated in *Figure 1-10*. Further explanations are provided to aid understanding (as of 2006):

> »Controlling means steering or regulating, i.e. leading to the practical achievement of the agreed objectives. A controller ensures that everyone has the possibility of controlling themselves within the framework of the elaborated goals and plans. The figure with intersecting circles illustrates the division of tasks and roles between a manager and a controller in a team. Managers carry out the task and controllers provide for the transparency of the economic result. Thus it is clear that

This overview of controlling conceptions begins with the work of Albrecht Deyhle, who rendered outstanding services to controlling.

Internationaler Controller Verein e. V. http://www.controllerverein.de

International Group of Controlling (IGC) http://www.igc-controlling.org

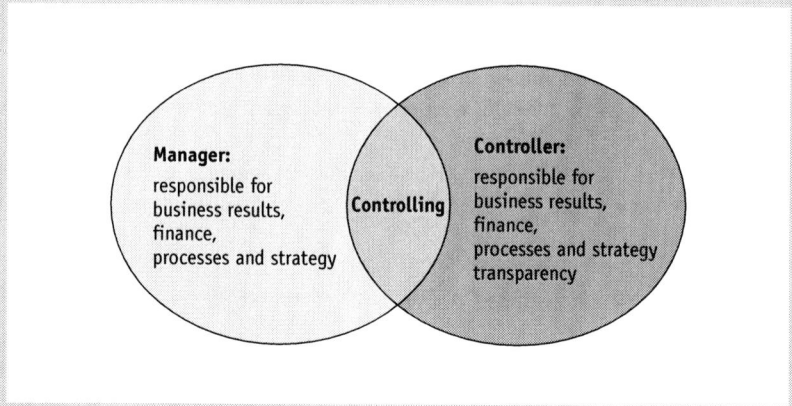

Fig. 1-10

Managers and controllers as a team (ICV, as of 2006)

Manager:
responsible for business results, finance, processes and strategy

Controlling

Controller:
responsible for business results, finance, processes and strategy transparency

it is not only controllers who perform the controlling. Controlling as a process and mental attitude is represented by the intersecting part of the circles. It constitutes the result of the cooperation of a manager and a controller in a team (controlling as applied business management).«

Summarizing the key ideas of the Controller Verein's statement shows that

The key ideas of the ICV conception: an overview

▸ controlling is viewed as a core management function that results from the tight-knit cooperation between managers and controllers,
▸ controlling is defined as directing, steering or regulating, and
▸ a management context characterized by systematic planning is presupposed.

These basic elements can also be found – more or less clearly – in the controlling conceptions developed by university professors. In this context, we will be outlining the key findings of a survey amongst ICV members in various sections of this textbook (the »ICV study«, Weber et al. 2006).

1.4.2 Controlling conceptions in the German-language literature

There are many different controlling conceptions in the relevant German-language literature and there is no such thing as a unified understanding of controlling, much less of »Generally Accepted Controlling Principles« (Küpper/Weber/Zünd 1990, p. 282). Often, the »original« contribution of a conception is essentially just a more or less successful reformulation of existing definitions and concepts. The majority of conceptions can also be accused of being largely normative; it remains unclear why controlling is defined in a certain way and not in another.

Unfortunately, there are no »Generally Accepted Controlling Principles«.

Under these circumstances, it is understandable that the number of attempts to create some kind of order in the »tangle of concepts and definitions« has skyrocketed. For a long time there were hardly any doctoral theses dealing with controlling that did not dedicate many pages to this purpose (for an example of a successful approach to categorization, cf. Zenz 1999). But even these attempts at creating order are still far removed from being homogenous or even similar. The structure shown in the following therefore cannot claim to be representative. It should also be noted that individual approaches usually do not belong to just one of the four definition types shown, i.e. there are usually overlaps. The categorization refers to the basic focus of the conception cited in each case.

It is not only the interpretations of controlling which vary considerably, but also the attempts at categorizing them.

1.4.2.1 Controlling as an information supply function
Early controlling conceptions usually focused on information supply as the essence of controlling. Such an understanding is shown in the following two statements, for instance:

- Controlling as »management support through information« (Hoffmann 1972, p. 85) or
- Controlling as »obtaining, preparing and coordinating information to be used by management in directing business to achieve certain goals« (Heigl 1989, p. 3).

Early controlling conceptions usually focused on information supply as the essence of controlling.

The point of reference is usually accounting, although in very different forms. Some authors equate controlling with an American type of accounting, thereby including areas such as statistics, budgeting, taxes and internal auditing in the ambit of controlling (e.g. Harbert 1982, pp. 68–69). Other authors see the idea of controlling realized not so much in a functional expansion of accounting as in a material change to it. Their point of reference is a very technocratic understanding of accounting. This becomes particularly clear in Bannow's statement, who »[sees] the responsibility of a head of accounting as lying essentially in capturing and recording the information (figures) underlying the business processes of a company in accordance with accepted accounting principles to enable the accounts to be drawn up at a later stage so that management can be granted discharge at the end of defined periods (financial year)« (Bannow 1983, p. 22). Apart from mixing an institutional and a functional perspective, such statements negate the control function that has been inherent in accounting since its origins (cf. e.g. Schneider 1992b, pp. 19–20) as well as the evolution of cost accounting into a management tool. From a theoretical perspective, it makes little sense to relabel the established concept of decision oriented accounting »controlling«.

This criticism applies in a similar way to approaches that try to derive the essence of accounting as controlling from an intensive analysis of information use, i.e. the recipients of the financial data. The image of »customer-unfriendly« accounting that underlies such a definition is relevant in practice. In theory, however, the question of how the »proper« financial information should be shown to different information recipients in the company has already been assigned to an area of research: it is the different types of behavioral research that deal with this issue (cf. Schweitzer/ Küpper 2003, pp. 584–710 for an overview).

The attempt to define controlling as a »central unit of company information systems« (Müller 1974, p. 683) is also problematic. According to this and similar conceptions, controlling is associated with a set of tasks ranging from determining information requirements in cooperation with those who need them, to information acquisition, to preparing information in a manner that addresses the problems and

Extracts from Müller (1974): »Coordination between information needs and information supply as the central responsibility of controlling«:

»The corporate function of controlling – which had been somewhat forgotten for a relatively long time – is currently arousing increasing interest in both business administration teaching and the academic debate. This renaissance of the controlling conception did not just emerge out of the blue. It should be seen in a close relationship with increasing attempts to free corporate accounting from its current limits and to convert it into a highly effective tool for managing planning and decision making tasks in companies. ...

Earlier attempts to create awareness in Germany of the controlling conception developed in the USA were characterized by highly divergent understandings of the functional aspects of this area as well as the tasks of controllers. This reflected the variety of forms in which controlling appears in practice in the USA, where many variants of the position of controller are known, ranging from head accountant to a member of the executive top management. In contrast, the most recent discussion on controlling shows a certain agreement in the attempts to use controlling to close an ever more obvious gap in the functional structure of companies, which is caused by the increasing – and often excessive – measures dedicated to processing information. Correspondingly, there is a general tendency to interpret and conceive of controlling as a central organ of a company's information management. ...

The closer analysis of controllers' tasks shows ... a potential function which has not received any attention in theory or practice, even though it should be considered as the vertex of a systematic information-related activity. This becomes clear when one sorts the different areas of responsibility ... by the task categories of obtaining information and using information for the purposes of planning, decision making or monitoring. Even though the delimitation of the individual task areas ... does not always allow their unambiguous allocation to one of the two categories, it nevertheless becomes quite clear that the tasks of controlling are not limited to obtaining information, but rather also hold an important share of information usage, especially in planning and monitoring.

This special, overarching construction of the controlling area enables it to assume an important task: coordinating information supply within the company with the information needs that have to be satisfied to solve subsequent tasks. The central function of controlling should not lie in the area of routine tasks of accounting and budgeting. The coordination task is much more important: It should consist in constantly, efficiently, and innovatively matching the information requirements of a company's planners and decision makers to the activities of company information supply and processing« (Müller 1974, pp. 683 and 686–687).

Viewing controlling as being equivalent to information supply covers only a (small) part of controllership.

recipients, to explaining the information. Sometimes controlling is limited to an »essentially information-related dimension« in the hopes that the »appearance of omnipotence« (Link 1982, p. 261) can thereby be effectively counteracted. However, there are good reasons for doubting that this is a sensible way of addressing the question of demarcation. The approach essentially offers nothing more than relabelling a field of research (information systems and management) that has been studied for a long time. This is not really convincing, particularly if one considers that the responsibilities of controllers go far beyond pure information tasks in practice.

1.4.2.2 Controlling as results-oriented control

The second type of early controlling conceptions emphasizes controlling as a sub-area of corporate management tasked with results-oriented control or with consistently aligning the company with its goals. Mann (1973, p. 11), for instance, explicitly speaks of controlling as »profit control«.

In this generalized form, however, the approach is not helpful: It is not just controlling, but also the entire management of a for-profit company that directs all its energies primarily towards making a profit. It also remains unclear whether the exclusive reference to the profit goal purposefully excludes other company goals or stands for an abbreviated representation. Such a limitation oriented towards the profit goal makes little sense: Consider that it would mean that non-profit organizations (such as state hospitals, for instance) would by definition not be able to use controlling. It is hard to see a sufficient reason for this. However, if one extends »profit-oriented« to »results-oriented«, the added value of the explanation is, in practical terms, equal to zero: Results orientation as a basic element of corporate management is something with which students become sufficiently acquainted as early as the first semester!

A possible meaningful interpretation of this controlling conception does not address profit orientation itself, but rather the way in which it is realized. This becomes clear from Hahn's (1987, p. 6) definition: »The way in which controlling works as a management philosophy includes ... results-oriented planning, and supervision by means of target agreements ... and analyses of goal achievement ... using the figures provided by accounting and finance«. This conception is based on a view of management that describes it in terms of a control cycle, as shown below.

> Controlling as results-oriented control is based on a control-cycle perspective.

The starting point lies in defining the objectives which the company and its units want to achieve, and which they are supposed to achieve. These are generated

From the source

Extracts from the book »Praxis des Controlling« (*The Practice of Controlling*) by Rudolf Mann:

»The task of controlling consists in assuming responsibility for profits as defined as the company's objective by top management. If seen in this way, it extends far beyond the solely information-related responsibility of accounting. Its focus lies on a monitoring and control function that constantly adapts itself to new situations.

Control means using regulating tools to stabilize agreed-upon goals when there are deviations. The use of corrective measures takes place either between colleagues at the same level of hierarchy, i.e. between a controller and the affected department head (decentralized conflict resolution) or as centralized conflict resolution by including the company's top management.

The difference compared to conventional finance and accounting lies in the following areas:
▸ Finance and accounting produce (standard) reports as required either internally or by external agencies.
...

▸ In contrast, controlling uses the findings obtained by finance and accounting to create checks and analyses of deviations. The analyses depend on the situation and are directed at the respective focus areas. The responsibility of controlling lies in
▸ the timely recognition of developments that endanger goal achievement and
▸ the use of tools to correct such developments, if necessary with the help of the company's top management.

With this task definition, the author consciously distances himself from other conceptions, which free the treasurer from all routine tasks of finance and accounting and give them to the controller. ...

Effective controlling has three task areas: planning, information and monitoring, control.

The focus lies on monitoring and control. (›To control‹ is here understood in its overall semantic meaning, i.e. not just as ›monitoring‹, but also as ›steering, directing, managing‹.) The basis of these tasks is a working planning and information system. This has to be built and constantly improved« (Mann 1973, pp. 20–22).

in a planning process and are provided to the respective managers at various levels in the company in the form of plans. The managers try to achieve their objectives through their daily management activities. The extent to which they succeed in their efforts is recorded, for instance, through cost accounting as a means of measuring outputs. The values thus identified then form the basis for comparing planned with actual values. If any deviations are found, the information can be fed into two directions: The newly gained knowledge can be used in a *feedback loop* to modify execution in such a way that the goals are achieved after all. For instance, cost overruns in February should thereby be compensated by the end of the year at the latest. In the case of a *feed-forward loop*, the deviation data is used to question the validity or achievability of the plans. In the airline industry, for instance, it made no sense to try to achieve the annual targets after what happened on September 11th, 2001.

Viewing controlling as a control-cycle as just described converts it into a synonym for »managing by plans«, which at the same time creates strong links to the roots of controllership: Controller positions were introduced when entrepreneurs had to change their management behavior for reasons of size and dynamics, when plans started substituting (or at least accompanying) personal instruction. Management that focuses heavily on individuals, as is typically the case in medium-sized companies, or bureaucratic, rule-based management structures, as found in the public sector, marked other »management philosophies«. Controlling would thereby have to be defined as a specific form or philosophy of management. A large part of the management literature already deals with »plan-based« management, however. Furthermore, planning would be completely absorbed by controlling in this perspective.

A further, potentially sustainable delimitation is provided by Krüger's (1979, p. 161) definition: »Controlling is a system of coordinated measures, principles, goals, methods and techniques used for system-internal, results-related control and monitoring«. Siegwart (1986, p. 109) similarly equates controlling with »profit-oriented control and monitoring«. Such definitions prove to be useful when a further management function is identified in addition to control/steering and monitoring/supervision, namely goal-setting or decision making. Such a differentiation is by no means uncommon in the literature; it is, as a matter of fact, widely known. However, the innovative contribution of such a controlling definition would only consist in the shared perspective on existing management elements, especially monitoring (of results) and parts of planning (e.g. the relationship between planning levels).

Controlling as a systematic linking-up of results-oriented planning and monitoring

1.4.2.3 Controlling as a coordination function

The controlling conceptions in this, the third group, see the central task of controlling as lying in the coordination between different sub-systems of management.

This perspective, in which controlling is linked exclusively to a coordination function, was to a large degree formed by Horváth and Küpper. The original contribution was published in 1978 (cf. Horváth 1978, pp. 194–208). Horváth chooses a *systems-based approach* and bases his argument on differentiating a company's management system into a planning and monitoring system on the one hand and an information (supply) system on the other hand. This differentiation generates a

Horváth introduced a systems-based perspective on controlling.

Extracts from the contribution »Controlling – Entwicklung und Stand einer Konzeption zur Lösung der Adaptions- und Koordinationsprobleme der Führung« (Controlling – development and status of a conception for solving the adaptation and coordination problems of management) by Péter Horváth:

»Today, controlling is a supporting management sub-system that coordinates planning, monitoring and information supply ...

There is an important reason why we are using the language of the systems approach for our definition; we believe that the systems approach, if it includes the dimension of information, is the approach most likely able to describe the controlling function and to come up with problem solutions in this area:

▸ The systems approach elevates the linkages and coordination between different task sets within an organization to a central problem.
▸ Based on the systems approach, information and information processing can be described as a fundamental dimension of an organization.

Coordination as the main function of controlling has two aspects:

▸ On the one hand, it means delimiting, forming and coordinating planning and monitoring systems as well as information supply systems (*system differentiation*).
▸ On the other hand, coordination has to take place on an ongoing basis within the existing systems structure of planning and monitoring, and the supply of information has to be ensured (*system coupling*).

At this point, it has to be emphasized that the content of the planning and monitoring process does not form part of the controlling function, but rather lies with those who carry the responsibility for implementation. In order to provision the planning and monitoring system with information, it is necessary that information sub-systems be formed within the controlling system, which supply the information needs with the suitable degree of accuracy, condensation, and timeliness. The most important information systems are:

▸ The system of environmental analysis used to obtain information about the environment.
▸ The system of internal accounting, which provides information on past and future states and movements of assets and liabilities, both in a quantitative and a monetary dimension.
▸ The system of tax information, which captures the taxation consequences of the company's business activities.

The system of information supply is inconceivable without an instrumental basis. This is nowadays mainly represented by the system of automated data processing, which we also consider to be part of the controlling system. ...

As the company's system of objectives is characterized by conflicts and vagueness in reality and because system differentiation and coupling do not always work properly, there is a need for ongoing comparisons between actual and planned values in these areas. This is the function of internal auditing, which we view as part of the controlling system, as a kind of monitoring of coordination« (Horváth 1978, pp. 202–204).

---

need for coordination which is covered by controlling. It thereby becomes the third management sub-system. Horváth sees the task of coordination as not being limited to relationships between systems (e.g. matching planning and monitoring information), but also includes coordination within the planning and monitoring system as well as within the information supply system as part of the responsibility of the controlling function (e.g. coordinating strategic with operational planning).

Schmidt built on Horváth's approach and extended it. His enhancements focused not on coordination itself, but rather on the objects of coordination: »The coordination function of controlling relates to the management system and to the phases of the management process. Its activities aim primarily at the company-wide internal coordination and integrative linking of the information, goal, planning and monitoring and organization systems« (Schmidt 1986, pp. 56–57). This structural

Horváth identified three management sub-systems, which are coordinated by controlling.

Fig. 1-11

**Controlling as part of a company's management system
(source: Küpper 1987, p. 99)**

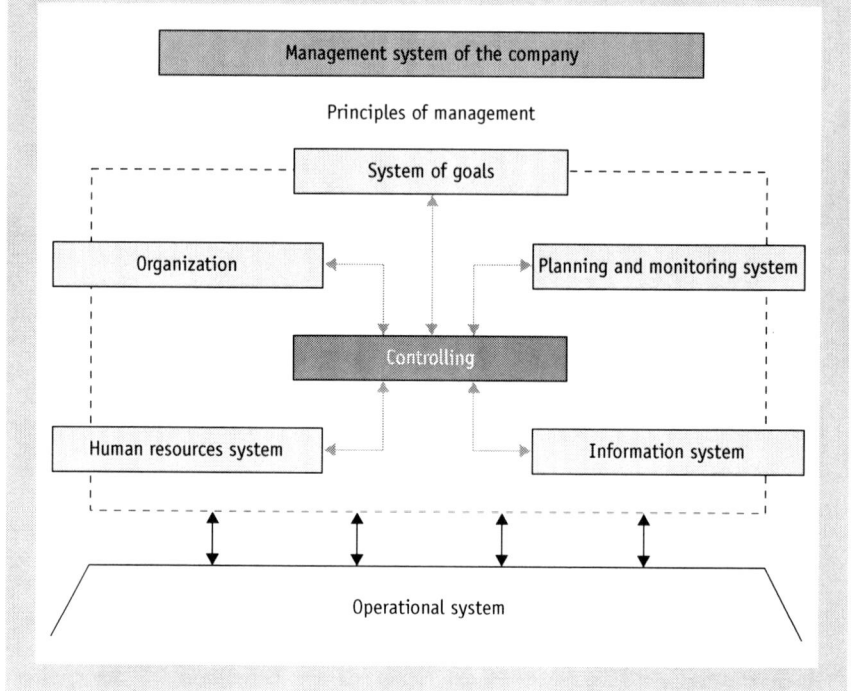

Küpper introduced two additional management sub-systems requiring coordination.

approach was adopted – with slight modifications – by Küpper (1987), from whom the illustrative *Figure 1-11* was taken. The benefit of the greater differentiation is that it uncovers additional coordination problems waiting to be solved: »Planning and monitoring systems, which are supposed to ensure a high degree of coordination, can be achieved primarily through appropriate organizational structures. However, this creates a need to coordinate planning and monitoring with the organization. Furthermore, the type of behavioral influencing is important for achieving coordinated action in the company. If controlling is to result in coordinated action, it also has to work to create appropriate incentive systems. In this way, however, its link to a further management system, human resources management, becomes apparent« (Küpper 1987, p. 96).

By taking on such a coordination task, controlling aims to achieve exactly the same with regard to management as management does with regard to execution: Controlling deals with efficiency (achieving an objective with the least inputs) and effectiveness (using inputs to achieve objectives that provide the highest utility). Coordination deficits within the management system lower both. For instance, if a new remuneration system is introduced without first ensuring that the required information is available in the necessary quality, demotivation, performance drops and management opportunism result. The coordination task reaches its limits when it becomes too expensive to carry out or when the knowledge needed to execute it adequately is lacking.

If controlling is defined in this way, it enters into any form of management of a (productive) institution. The existence of the function (coordination) is at its core influenced neither by the concrete objective nor by specific leadership styles or models. Consequently, controlling has to exist in »classical«, bureaucratically organized public administrations as much as in medium-sized companies managed personally by the head of the company. Under such a broad perspective, the range of tasks related to coordination in the management system is very wide on the one hand. However, coordinating management in »normal« large companies – with the concomitant importance of systematic, results-oriented planning and monitoring – is subject to requirements completely distinct from those in a bureaucracy or a typical medium-sized company. On the other hand, the concept of controlling then only matches the way it is understood in practice to a very limited degree: In classical bureaucracies, one finds neither controlling as a concept nor persons whose job title is controller. It was therefore proposed (cf. Weber 1992, p. 176) that the coordination task of controlling should be limited to management systems where the planning system is of exceptional importance, in other words, where operations are mainly coordinated through plans. In this case, the coordination tasks of controlling are concentrated on the planning system. The monitoring system, human resources management system, organizational and information systems are respectively and primarily coordinated towards the planning system; the need to coordinate direct interdependencies between the other management subsystems becomes less pronounced.

The coordination-based perspective on controlling is – independently of the definition variant used in each case – not undisputed in the current debate. The criticism starts with the systems-based perspective, which is considered to provide descriptive rather than explanatory value. A further criticism addresses the fact that there are usually no clear statements about where the exact boundaries of the sub-systems lie and how these are formed (or should be formed) (cf. Weber/ Schäffer 2000a). In this way, both Küpper and Horváth define sub-systems in different ways in different sources (cf. e.g. Küpper 2005, p. 30 compared to *Figure 1-11*, which was quoted earlier). In the practical reality of companies, there are furthermore already problems with separating management from operational systems (e.g. in modern group concepts in production). The lacking theoretical attention dedicated to defining system boundaries denies an answer to the question of the completeness as well as the meaningfulness of the differentiation. Furthermore, the coordination-based controlling approach is also not immune to overlaps with traditional sub-disciplines of business administration. Instead, if taken to its logical conclusion, it leads to a counterintuitive separation from management, allocating to controlling the entire task of management design (»meta-management«) (cf. Weber 1997; Zenz 1999, pp. 93–94). Finally, the coordination-based approach – especially in its interpretation by Küpper – is far removed from the focus of controllers' activities (cf. Weber et al. 2006, pp. 32–38) and thereby from the empirical roots of controlling (for further details on the criticism, cf. Schneider 1992a; Schäffer 1996; Kappler/Scheytt 1999; Wall 2000; Becker 2003).

There are some objections against the coordination-based approach to controlling as well.

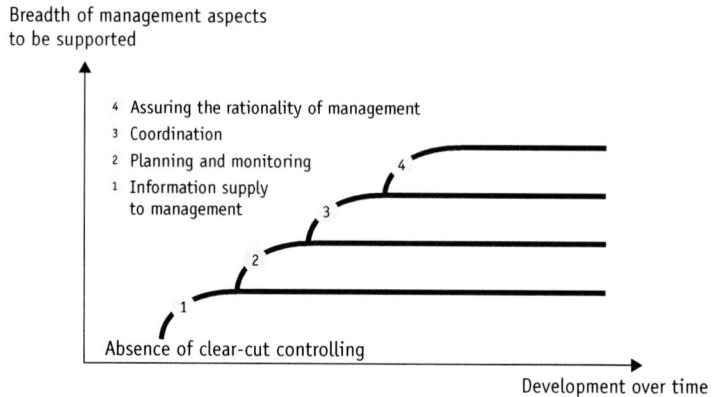

Fig. 1-12

Understanding of controlling in German-language literature
(source: Weber et al. 2006, p. 30)

1.4.2.4 Controlling as assuring the rationality of management

On the basis of a critical discourse around the coordination approach (cf. Weber/ Schäffer 2000a), a new approach has been developed according to which controlling deals with assuring the rationality of management (cf. Weber/Schäffer 1999; Schäffer/Weber 2004).

A specific management perspective forms the basis of this view. Management is performed by economic actors (especially managers) who strive to achieve individual goals and who are endowed with cognitive abilities. These are subject to individual limitations. Deficits of rationality may result from a manager's limited abilities (»skill«) and motivation (»will«). Starting from these deficits inherent in the actors, assuring rationality means acting to increase the likelihood that the execution of the management actions corresponds to the anticipated means-end relationship in spite of the deficits. To this aim, the function deals with how to recognize rationality deficits and how to reduce or eliminate them. This understanding of controlling also corresponds to a large degree with the »classical« definition of

Summary
(see guiding questions 4):

▶ In spite of many attempts to find a satisfactory definition, there is to date no solid terminological foundation for controlling in business administration (however, this is also the case for many other terms in business administration – such as planning, information or organization).

▶ Information-based, results-based and coordination-based approaches to developing a controlling conception can be distinguished. The three approaches exist largely in isolation from one another and reveal problems upon closer scrutiny. These relate either to the lacking originality of the approaches or the stringency with which they are theoretically deduced.

▶ As a result of a critical discourse around the coordination approach, which has dominated for an extended period of time in textbooks, a new approach has been developed which views controlling as assuring rationality. It deals with recognizing, preventing and eliminating deficits in management rationality.

management control by Anthony. According to that definition, »management control [is] the process by which managers assure that resources are obtained and used effectively and efficiently in the accomplishment of the organization's objectives« (Anthony 1965, p. 17).

Viewing controlling as assuring rationality is currently the most recent perspective on controlling.

In the second chapter, we will derive the rationality-assuring approach on which this textbook is based from the tasks of controllers and introduce it in greater depth.

1.5 Selected controlling-related accounting theories

There is no similar debate about the essence of controlling or about *the* correct understanding of the subject in the English-language literature (cf. Meyer/Schäffer/ Gmür 2008 for an overview of recent research in accounting). However, there is a whole series of distinct accounting theories, the various perspectives of which can also be used to review controlling. In the following, we will be introducing these theories in brief and will highlight some of their implications for controlling, the reason being that we want to create an awareness amongst readers for the diversity of possible perspectives on the subject.

First, however, we will take a closer look at the relationship between accounting and controlling. It should be noted that English-language accounting research deals both with internal accounting (management accounting and costing) and external accounting (financial accounting). Management accounting and controlling, which is particularly widespread in German-speaking regions, are generally considered to be equivalent in most respects (cf. Wagenhofer 2006). Correspondingly, the standard textbooks on management accounting deal with similar issues and essentially the same tools as controlling textbooks. The most important difference is that controlling (or controllers) are given more tasks related to shaping systems and actively providing advice (cf. Becker 2003).

1.5.1 Accounting theory based on institutional economics

The »mainstream« of accounting theory is based in essence on institutional economics, especially on principal-agent theory. According to this theory, controlling is seen as a tool for solving agency problems, i.e. for designing and monitoring the mutually agreed-upon contractual relationship between a principal and an agent (cf. Lambert 2007, pp. 247–250). The underlying assumptions are:

Assumptions of the principal-agent theory

▸ that conflicts exist between the principal's goals and interests and those of the agent,
▸ that the agent behaves opportunistically (»self-interest seeking with guile«, cf. Williamson 1985, p. 47) and
▸ that the agent has private information to which the principal cannot gain access at no cost (information asymmetry).

1.5 **Controllers, controllership and controlling: Basic principles and categories**
Selected controlling-related accounting theories

30

Information asymmetry
as a cause of problems of
delegation

This private information, which results in an advantage for the agent, is in the first instance a consequence of an intended specialization that gives the agent degrees of freedom, as is the case, for instance, in a profit center organization. At the same time, however, the agent has the possibility of pursuing his own goals to the detriment of the principal under the cover of the asymmetric distribution of information. The resulting reduction of the principal's expected utility is described as agency costs. The goal is to minimize such costs by optimizing the design of contractual agreements. Agency costs are a central object of investigation, but their exact value cannot be measured empirically. Instead, they have to be derived on the basis of a model-theoretical »trick«, namely as the difference between an ideal situation without information asymmetry (»first-best« situation) and a state where information is indeed distributed asymmetrically (»second-best« situation).

Differentiating between
positive and normative
PA theory

Principal-agent theory is subdivided into two key theoretical branches. The *positive branch* mainly works empirically and conceptually, concentrating on analyzing complex institutions of corporate practice, such as the cooperation between the executive board and the supervisory board. The fundamental contributions in this area are considered to be the analysis by Jensen/Meckling (1976) and the book by Watts/Zimmermann (1986). Owing to the empirical focus, the analysis concentrates on institutions for which data is readily available, for instance via annual reports or market statistics. The *normative branch*, on the other hand, mainly investigates the formal, analytical derivation of optimal incentive systems, taking into account risk aspects. In this area, Holmström's (1979) investigation is considered to be one of the fundamental contributions. Owing to the formal approach used, it is – in contrast to the positive branch – often necessary to work with restrictive assumptions, which in turn means that the results are usually not directly applicable in practice. Nevertheless, some proponents of the coordination-based controlling view see the normative principal-agent theory as being a key instrument for deriving theoretical statements about controlling (cf. especially Küpper 2005, pp. 76–78).

Different forms of
information asymmetry
lead to different PA
models: hidden action
and hidden information.

Based on the type of asymmetric information distribution, two model types can be distinguished: *Hidden action models* focus on the agent's behavior, which is often represented as work effort (without having to be limited to it). Hidden action occurs after an agreement has been reached and arises because the agent's actions are unobservable by the principal and hence cannot be contracted upon. This situation is also described as moral hazard. The proposed solution is to agree on results-based remuneration. Agency costs resulting from sub-optimal risk sharing between the principal and the agent can best be reduced in long-term relationships. This is also described as the trust-building effect of long-term contracts: Although the principal does not explicitly observe the agent's behavior, he can rest assured that the agent will not exploit the asymmetrical information to achieve his own, deviating goals.

In the case of *hidden information models*, the agent already has an information advantage at the time the agreement is concluded, e.g. concerning his ability to execute a certain task or about exogenous influences. The agent can exploit this information advantage to the detriment of the principal when formulating the agreement. The consequence, adverse selection, can, however, be avoided at least in part by the principal. By cleverly designing several different contracts, the principal can tempt the agent to select the contract most beneficial to him, thereby revealing his private information (self-selection).

Fig. 1-13

Information asymmetry in principle-agent theory (source: Weißenberger 1997, p. 148)

Type	Hidden action		Hidden information	
	Hidden effort	Hidden knowledge	Hidden characteristics	Hidden information in the strict sense
Cause	Difficulties in observing agent's manual activities	Difficulties in observing agent's mental activities	Difficulties in discriminating relevant characteristics	Lacking knowledge of exogenous disturbances
Point in time	After agreement concluded		When concluding agreement	
Consequence	Moral hazard		Adverse selection	
Focus of analysis	Trade-off between optimal risk sharing and motivation		Mechanisms for revealing agent's information advantage	

1.5.2 Behavioral approaches: behavioral accounting and controlling

In the English-language literature, a substantial body of behavioral accounting research has emerged since the 1950s and 1960s. Instead of restrictive model assumptions such as those underlying principal-agent theory, this research aims to achieve the most realistic understanding possible of the actors involved.

The term »behavioral accounting« was introduced by Bruns/DeCoster in 1969. They understand it to mean »thinking concerned with behavioral elements and the integration of knowledge from the behavioral sciences into accounting« (Bruns/ DeCoster 1969, p. V). The meaningfulness of such a perspective can also be justified for controlling:

▸ Controlling systems are integral components of corporate management and should influence the behavior of actors in companies. To do this, reliable knowledge about behavioral effects is required.

▸ Controlling theories rely on explicit and/or implicit assumptions about behavior, which need to be checked and – if necessary – substantiated through empirical findings.

The first main focus of behavioral accounting research analyzes *human information processing* in the accounting and auditing context. The analysis concentrates on processes of information selection before and during decision making in the audit process, types of judgments and the cognitive style of the actors (cf. Libby/Lewis 1977, 1982). It was found that »accountants and other experts may not be as proficient at certain aspects of decision making as was thought. Inaccuracies appear to result from both inconsistencies in application of decision rules and misweighting of evidence. The probabilistic judgment literature has suggested that misweighting of evidence results from use of simplified decision rules often called heuristics. ...

Behavioral accounting deals primarily with the human processing of accounting information and the effects of accounting tools on individuals.

Controllers, controllership and controlling: Basic principles and categories
Selected controlling-related accounting theories

32

Problem representations based on intuitive causal models or frames seem to drive many decision making strategies« (Libby/Lewis 1982, p. 273).

The second main focus analyzes the *effect of controlling systems* – especially of budgets – on the actors within the company. As an example, we would like to briefly introduce Argyris's (1952) »classical« study on the behavioral effects of budgets. The American Accounting Association commissioned Argyris to analyze the behavioral effects of budgets on lower- and middle-level managers in four industrial companies. The research showed that:

▸ Budgets create considerable pressure on superiors and workers. This leads in some cases to resistance on the part of the workers, but it is the superiors in particular who are subject to considerable personal and emotional stress.

▸ There is a conflict between the »budget people« and the »factory people«. The success of the former rests on the failure of the latter insofar as one of their most important tasks is to uncover budget overruns on the part of the line managers.

▸ The ways in which people express their interest in budgets and the ways in which they describe and use them are directly related to the pattern of leadership they use in their daily industrial life.

▸ Budgets promote departmental egoism. When pressure is exerted via budgets, the budgets become the yardstick for reward and punishment. Consequently, line managers orient themselves exclusively towards the success of their immediate areas of influence, and not on overall corporate success. This can lead to considerable conflict among departments.

In the German-language controlling literature, behavioral findings were employed only at a comparatively late stage and by few authors in any substantial way (cf. Küpper 2005; Weber 2005 and Hirsch 2006).

1.5.3 Alternative accounting theories

A large part of the alternative theories has emerged from an explicit distancing from institutional economics and – in part – from the behavioral approaches which it criticizes. The different streams have in common that they embody a stance which questions objectivity, »accurate representation« and normative approaches in the first place and therefore seek alternative descriptions for what accountants do and the role accounting plays. The following streams are distinguished:

The various types of alternative accounting theories analyze concrete effects of accounting on the behavior of managers.

▸ Interpretive accounting theory: controlling as result and means of social construction

▸ Institutional theory: controlling as a means for legitimizing companies and organizational units,

▸ Radical accounting theory: controlling as a means for establishing and maintaining power and authority, and

▸ Postmodern accounting theory: controlling as a discourse of imposing discipline

Interpretive accounting theory is based on interpretive sociological approaches, especially symbolic interactionism and ethnomethodology. The focus lies on viewing *reality as socially constructed*. Individuals do not act based on an objective reality that exists independently of human beings and has a determinate nature, but rather on the basis of subjective meanings and interpretations. These emerge from the continuous social interactions with other actors and are reproduced and modified on an ongoing basis. Controlling systems are, in this sense, both the outcomes of social constructions and their means.

The interpretive and institutional accounting theories both view reality as socially constructed.

This is illustrated in a study by Dent (1991) on the transformation of a railways company from a technical engineering to an economically oriented organization: The existing cost accounting of the company captured costs for the purpose of analysis, but was uncoupled from budget responsibility and day-to-day activities. Economic and accounting concerns were incidental to technical-rational engineering and production concerns. This gradually changed with the appointment of »business managers« in the company: »Planning and budgeting activities began to assume a new significance. Formerly, they were introverted acts of cost containment. Now they came to symbolize the search for profit-maximizing opportunities« (Dent 1991, p. 720). At the same time, the use and interpretation of cost accounting was a vehicle for changing the prevalent self-image in the railways company: »The continuing attacks on the competence of public sector managers had worn morale down. To be business-like was ›good‹, it gave them pride, and made the railways modern. Increasingly people came to share the normative symbolism of the ›bottom line‹« (Dent 1991, p. 720). In the trajectory of events, the importance of cost accounting changed. At the same time, it helped change the way in which actors interpreted their company. Similar processes of change could be observed in Germany, for instance when state-owned enterprises such as telecommunications and postal services were privatized.

Institutional theory has been influenced mostly by the institutionalism of organization theory and sociology. Here, controlling is primarily considered to be an instrument for *legitimizing* a company or an organizational unit in its environment. Institutional theory also starts from the assumption of a socially constructed reality and attributes great importance to cognitive and symbolic aspects of controlling systems. In addition, institutionalism also emphasizes external determinants of companies. Companies rely not only on information and materials as inputs from their environment, but also on sufficient legitimacy as a prerequisite for mobilizing resources. In order to be accepted by their environment as being legitimate, companies have to correspond to the shared and rationalized views and »taken for granted« rules in their society or culture about what companies are and how they work. They do this by creating formal structures and practices that match institutionalized expectations (cf. Meyer/Rowan 1977, pp. 343–346). Consequently, companies of a certain size have to carry out efficiency calculations, they need to have controlling systems, follow value-based control concepts and have other, similar characteristics – independent of whether these would really be necessary in a world without legitimation needs.

Using controlling tools also serves to legitimize the company within its environment.

An interesting example of this approach is found in Ansari/Euske (1987). The object of their case study is »uniform cost accounting«, which the U.S. Department of Defense introduced in 1975 to monitor and control maintenance expenditures in military repair facilities. However, most of the depots investigated continued to have other accounting systems in use, most line managers were unfamiliar with the system and the Department of Defense neglected to analyze the data it received

Controllers, controllership and controlling: Basic principles and categories
1.5 Selected controlling-related accounting theories

34

from the system during the first three years. Ansari/Euske therefore interpreted the system as an »important means to demonstrate rationality ... Both accounting systems and accountants are symbols of rationality for external groups. They therefore play an important role in reifying the abstract qualities of efficiency, productivity and accountability that are valued by an organization's external constituencies« (Ansari/Euske 1987, p. 563).

Radical accounting theory is based on neomarxist conceptions and on work done in the tradition of labor process theory (cf. Baxter/Chua 2003 and Roslender/Dillard 2003). It analyzes accounting and controlling with a focus on their roles as instruments of (class) dominance and concludes that they are not neutral tools of documentation, but rather *tools of domination* that serve the interests of the owners of capital. »Management accounting is ... seen ... as a way of controlling workers and legitimating systems of control« (Loft 1991, p. 18). From this viewpoint, controlling limits opportunities for resistance because it provides a legitimate language within a company with expressions such as added value, efficiency and cost awareness, thereby influencing the attitudes and the behavior of management and workers in accordance with shareholders' wishes. At the same time, the instrumentally rational thinking of controlling serves to shape actions and imposes discipline through incentive systems and »the requirements of the situation«. Workplaces in company units that are not sufficiently profitable or too expensive in the international comparison unfortunately have to be cut – even if the company as a whole is generating record profits (cf. Armstrong 1985).

Finally, *postmodern accounting theory* orients itself predominantly towards the contributions by Foucault (cf., for instance, Foucault 2004 and Miller/O'Leary 1987). Accounting and controlling are here seen as components of a historical discourse of *imposing discipline*. The way disciplining works can be described using three principles (cf. Hopper/Macintosh 1998):

▸ According to the *principle of enclosure,* people are gathered in closed rooms, military barracks, factories, prisons, hospitals etc. on the basis of functions or purposes and brought into a homogenous social order through the construction of hierarchies where tight control can be exercised. In a case study at ITT, Hopper/Macintosh observed how the principle of creating decentralized profit centers and cost accounting under the new CEO Geneen was realized in the 1960s and 1970s.

▸ Such a created order is the precondition for disciplining the actors, which is described through the *principle of efficient body*. According to Hopper/Macintosh, this principle is implemented on the basis of a rigid reporting system at ITT: »The financial control system and the monthly meetings provided the means for training ITT managers in the correct manoeuvres. The signals from Geneen and the financial control systems automatically triggered the required proper behaviour. ITT managers performed as docile, efficient bodies« (Hopper/Macintosh 1998, p. 135).

▸ The *principle of disciplined bodies* is concretized in three techniques of disciplining: hierarchical surveillance for a disciplinary gaze, normalizing sanctions and examination. At ITT, the principle is realized, according to Hopper/Macintosh, through direct and primary reporting to headquarters and a rigid monthly review and analysis of monthly reports on the basis of controlling information.

Postmodern accounting theory with its radical statements deviates most strongly from the dominant perspectives on accounting and controlling.

Hopper/Macintosh interpret this as »examinatory practice, featuring an alphanumeric-inquisitional process of reading, examining and re-writing each manager as text« (Hopper/Macintosh 1998, p. 143).

Summary
(see guiding question 5)

▶ The »mainstream« of accounting theory is based in essence on institutional economics. In controlling research, it is above all principal-agent theory and the concept of the *homo oeconomicus* that are used.

▶ Behavioral approaches distance themselves from the restrictive assumptions of the homo oeconomicus and try to integrate findings from the behavioral sciences to a larger extent into the analysis of controlling.

▶ Alternative accounting theories also position themselves through explicit distancing from the institutional economics approaches. The different schools of thought provide interesting perspectives on the object of this textbook: controlling as a result and means of social construction, controlling as a means to legitimize or secure dominance or controlling as a discourse of imposing discipline.

1.6 Summary

The introductory motto at the beginning of this chapter could have been: »Controlling is a multifaceted thing«. We have purposefully decided not to reduce the complexity underlying controlling artificially, but to provide a broad overview from context- and culture-dependent controller practice to different controlling conceptions and controlling-relevant theories of accounting research. This made it possible to provide a (mostly) neutral impression of the different facets and perspectives on the subject.

However, we did not want to leave it at that level of heterogeneity and complexity – even less so in an introductory textbook. Instead, we will go into greater detail in describing our own perspective, which was briefly introduced in section 1.4.2.4. It can be described as a behaviorally oriented approach that can largely be matched to the practical development of controllership.

Taking a clear position makes it easier for the reader to evaluate the descriptions and to place them into context. In business administration, there is no single theory or conception that explains everything. Economic reality is much too varied for this to be possible. Theories and conceptions are like glasses that one uses for specific purposes and which are less suitable for other purposes. The question is not whether a theory is right or wrong, but whether it is useful or not useful. We believe that our pair of glasses is especially suitable for designing and shaping controllership in companies – and that it therefore makes sense to use this perspective as a basis for this introductory textbook.

Recommended reading ...

... The practice of controlling: first impressions
Amshoff 1993, pp. 243–368
Horváth 2006, pp. 18–75
Stoffel 1995, pp. 123–246
Weber et al. 2006
Weber 2007
Weber/Schäffer 1998, pp. 227–233

... Development of controlling as an academic discipline
Binder/Schäffer 2005b
Messner/Becker/Schäffer/Binder 2008
Schäffer/Binder/Gmuer 2006
Wagenhofer 2006

... Controlling conceptions
Becker 2003, pp. 7–47
Eschenbach/Niedermayr 1996, pp. 65–94
Friedl 2003, pp. 148–178
Horváth 2006, pp. 77–146
Küpper 2005, pp. 28–44
Weber/Schäffer 1999
Weber/Schäffer 2000a
Zenz 1999, pp. 7–119

... Selected controlling-related accounting theories
Ahrens et al. 2007
Baxter/Chua 2003
Becker 2003, pp. 82–192
Chua 1986
Hirsch 2006
Lambert 2001
Napier 2006
Scherm/Pietsch 2004a

2 Controlling: assuring management rationality

Guiding questions:

1 Which tasks are controllers responsible for when assuring rationality?

2 Is controlling what controllers do?

3 Is there any unique aspect that sets controlling apart from other business functions? Which aspect would that be?

4 Which understanding of rationality underlies the conception of controlling used in this book?

Controlling conceptions can (1) be laid down normatively, without detailed justification, (2) be derived from existing accounting theories (*deduction*) or (3) be generated on the basis of empirical evidence (*induction*). Whereas the first approach seems unsatisfactory, the second is generally difficult to apply in business administration. In contrast to the related discipline of economics, research questions in business administration usually have such a high »degree of resolution« that no single theory on its own is generally able to explain a phenomenon. But using several or many theories in parallel may create an impression of eclecticism or even arbitrariness. Therefore, we have elected to use an *inductive approach* in the following. The benefits of this approach are, on the one hand, that it is based on real-life observations, which is very helpful for an introductory textbook: It is easier to picture a cost center manager talking to a controller than to visualize secondary coordination between a planning and a monitoring system – we will soon show what this means. On the other hand, the inductive method is also chosen because it can be used to obtain statements that can be verified (or falsified) empirically, which helps avoid justified criticism directed at the non-falsifiability of a purely conceptual approach.

We will use an inductive approach to the term controlling.

2.1 Deriving the controlling function from controllers' tasks

2.1.1 Starting point of the analysis

At this point in the discussion, you have already received a comprehensive (but hopefully not confusing) overview of the activities of controllers and different perspectives on what controlling is and is meant to be. The diversity of aspects can be summarized in the following three points, with each point differentiated according to an institutional (controllers or controllership) vs. a functional perspective (controlling):

(1) Relationship to planning and monitoring

Institutional perspective: Controllers' tasks are closely linked to planning and monitoring, i. e. to generating plans and to checking that they are complied with. This is where the origin of controllers' activities lies: Historically, the need for systematic planning and monitoring led to the emergence of the first controller jobs. The same relationship can be seen today in growing medium-sized companies or in public-sector organizations that switch to being managed by objectives (»New Public Management«).

Functional perspective: There is a controlling conception in theory that is – as was shown in chapter 1 – based on precisely this relationship with planning and monitoring (controlling as results-oriented control). In the coordination-based perspective on controlling, too, the planning and monitoring system is of crucial importance, and the view according to which controlling is considered equivalent to assuring management rationality is – as will be shown – explicitly linked to a context where coordination based onplans dominates. The tight link to planning and monitoring is also demonstrated quite clearly by the large number of pages dedicated to these functions in controlling textbooks.

(2) Relationship to information

Institutional perspective: Controllers assume responsibility for creating business transparency for managers. The information they generate is the »language« of planning and monitoring. Neither can be carried out without meaningful and relevant information. Information supply is therefore a key controller task, upon which other tasks are built. The considerable amount of time that controllers spend collecting and preparing management-relevant data in practice is an indication of this fundamental importance.

Functional perspective: Again, there is a controlling conception in theory that bases its definition of controlling on this precise aspect, although it is one of the earliest approaches. Information supply also plays a key role in the control-based and coordination-based approaches and is treated in corresponding depth in both cases.

(3) Closeness to management

Institutional perspective: Tight relationships exist between the activities of managers and controllers. There is a widely-held view that controllers should not carry out management tasks themselves. Nevertheless, they support managers in many different ways. The spectrum ranges from simple information services (»Please provide me with the contribution margins of the two most important product groups during the past four months«) to a complex counterpart function. In the instance of the counterpart function, the interaction between managers and controllers is especially important.

Functional perspective: The discussion about the controlling function is characterized by attempts to achieve a »clean« separation from management. However, this causes significantly greater problems from the functional perspective than from the institutional point of view. In the case of controlling as an information supply function, the separation is easy because information is considered a means to the ends of management – rather than management itself. There are much greater problems of separation for the coordination-based view. On the one hand, coordination forms an original sub-area of management, especially within the task of organizing. On the other hand, it is also difficult not to identify the coordination of management subsystems as being management itself. Finally, conceiving of controlling as results-oriented control makes it identical to a specific type of management.

At this stage, the problem of insufficient terminological and conceptual clarity – which was mentioned at the beginning of chapter 1 – has become very much apparent. Understanding what controlling is clearly depends on which author is giving his or her view – at least as long as the aspects of planning, monitoring and information supply are included. In the same way, it is up to the author's discretion to decide how close the relationships between controlling as a function and controllers as an institution should be.

What is to be done? One can either accept the diversity, the multifaceted nature of controlling and the real-life variability of controllership, as a given fact without a defined cause, or one has to search for an explanation that creates sufficient terminological and conceptual order.

Choosing the latter approach – which is clearly more beneficial for the three target groups of this book (students, academics, and practitioners) – requires further analyses. When reviewing the aspects discussed before – the relationship to planning, to information, and the closeness to management – the greatest knowledge gap obviously exists in the third area: the closeness of controllers and controlling to management and leadership. Here, the contours are, as has been shown, the most blurred, especially regarding the interaction between controllers and managers. In order to understand this interaction better, it is necessary to deal in greater detail with managers on the one hand and controllers on the other hand. More specifically, we need to find out which characteristics are relevant to our questions and can typically be ascribed to managers and controllers. That will be the subject of the following section.

2.1.2 Typical characteristics of managers and controllers

2.1.2.1 Overview: elements of an economic modeling of human beings

Viewing the role of assuring rationality as the core of controlling means that there has to be a possibility that rationality deficits exist. However, no provision is made for such deficits in classical economic theory, where the way in which companies work is seen in terms of a production function. Human labor is a production factor just like plants and machinery or raw materials. The actors' tasks (»their place in the production function«) can be determined with sufficient certainty, just as it is possible to find suitable actors who are capable of carrying them out. Their suitability relates both to their *abilities* (capacity) and to their *motivation* (acting in accordance with the requirements of their task = the objectives of the company). Other, individual characteristics of the actors are of no interest in an environment that is sufficiently predictable in terms of tasks as well as requirements and their fulfillment.

In classical economic modeling there are no rationality deficits …

This classical perspective is thereby based on the assumption that tasks and the requirements imposed on those responsible for carrying them out can be completely determined. This assumption is, however, seldom fulfilled in today's practice. Often, the required knowledge is severely constrained. Such constraints may result either from the impossibility of observing all the factors determining the task in a concrete case or from the fact that outcomes can only be determined to a limited degree in advance. Constraints in the way tasks and requirements are defined create degrees of freedom for those responsible for carrying them out. The degrees of freedom can be used to deviate from the specified task parameters.

... but in reality people operate under cognitive constraints and may behave opportunistically ...

Whenever individuals have degrees of freedom in carrying out tasks, their individuality needs to be taken into account. Accordingly, there has been a long history of attempts to model human beings. The work by Simon and Kahneman/Tversky in particular has become widely known (cf. Simon 1957; Kahneman/Tversky 1973). Their approaches and other, similar ones highlight the cognitive constraints of human beings on a broad front. They relate to

▶ the *perception* of a problem (e.g. the inability of a developer to recognize that launching a new product quickly is more important than achieving a higher degree of technical perfection),

... and the world is set up in a way that means these characteristics have to be taken into account.

▶ the *prediction* of future developments (e.g. extrapolating strong sales growth over an extended period of time, even though one's own success will attract competitors) or

▶ the *evaluation* of alternative decisions (e.g. the inability of people to merge a great number of different evaluation criteria »coherently« into an overall assessment).

Such cognitive constraints on the part of managers play a key role in the spectrum of controllers' tasks; we will deal with this issue in more detail shortly.

In addition to discussing the abilities of managers and controllers, the way they apply their abilities to concrete actions also needs to be taken into account. This aspect does not receive much attention in »classical« business administration. For instance, organizational research considers the management problem to be essentially solved when tasks have been appropriately allocated to persons. The underlying assumption is that people act in accordance with their abilities, at least if they are requested to do so in the form of organizational instructions.

It was the field of human resource studies that first noted that this view lands somewhat short of the mark. Amongst other things, and taking into account findings from psychology, this area of research deals with the motivation of employees. For instance, it aims to establish whether letting employees participate in defining goals leads to a higher acceptance of the goals and thereby to a higher degree of goal achievement or not. We will be dealing with this kind of topic in greater detail in chapter 3. The observation that people do not automatically act in accordance with their employers' goals, but that they rather follow their own goals and sometimes do so using dishonest methods such as deceit or fraud (»opportunistic behavior«), finally led to the development of principal-agent theory, which was outlined in chapter 1 and which has become one of the standard theories in business administration.

Accordingly, human beings have individual characteristics (»abilities« and »motivation«) that should be taken into account for economic analyses. Motivation is determined by individual goals, whereas abilities provide the means for achieving the goals. These two impulses form the foundation for the dynamics of the modeling approach presented here: The motivation of actors, which tends to be expansive in nature, and their abilities, which act as a constraint, drive the dynamic evolution of human action – as long as neither of the impulses dominates the other for an extended period of time. Both mental properties, which were introduced as being independent at the outset, are connected through so-called »internal models«, patterns which shape action. These consist of a »self-image«, which contains assumptions about the actor's own characteristics and their ancillary conditions, and a »world-image«, which consists of hypotheses about reference parameters and the consequences of different actions. It could be said that they form the glasses through which we perceive ourselves and the world. Internal models determine behavioral patterns through assumptions, expectations and attitudes as well as the general rules linked to them. First, let us have a look at how managers and controllers typically differ from one another in terms of their abilities and motivation.

Individual characteristics relate to the abilities and motivation of individuals.

Internal models as a part of the order that shapes actions

2.1.2.2 Modeling managers and controllers

In our search for typical differences between the characteristics of controllers and those of managers, we begin by referring to Deyhle, whom we introduced in chapter 1 in connection with the ICV's understanding of controlling. The following statements by Deyhle are often quoted in the literature on controlling: »Numbers, the relationships between elements of business and economic logic form ... a profession of their own. ... How should a ›non-accountant‹ such as a manager be able to deal with this area of technical expertise? Answer: ›Together with his controller‹. A person called controller ... is tasked with being a business companion, advisor, pilot and an economic conscience. Also because a manager needs a large portion of euphoria – and should perhaps not analyze some things too thoroughly so as not to lose his drive. Such analyses should be entrusted to the controller« (Deyhle 1984, pp. 37–38).

Differences between the characteristics of managers and controllers

In relation to *professional or technical abilities*, this quote creates the impression that controllers are characterized by an explicit specialization in business science that »their« managers might lack. This impression is accurate in many German companies, where managers predominantly come from a technical or natural science background and do not have an additional qualification in business studies such as an MBA – which many of their colleagues in English-speaking countries do have. The impression will, however, not be correct if the manager used to be a controller at an earlier stage in her career and obtained her management position on the basis of her qualifications in business studies. Based on their personal attitudes, controllers and managers are attributed very distinct profiles in the literature. This is exemplified by the following paired expressions.

▸ Controllers are considered to be analytical, matter-of-fact, providing clear reasons, whereas managers are seen as intuitive, emotional, with a tendency to be superficial.
▸ Controllers tend to be reserved, fastidious and self-focused, whereas managers are more aggressive, generous and customer-oriented.

▶ Controllers are viewed as being rigid, schematical and administrative, managers as being flexible, diverse and engaged.
▶ Finally, the risk-averse and holding-back nature of controllers is contrasted with the risk-taking and driving orientation of managers.

An empirical survey carried out at WHU essentially confirmed these assumptions (cf. Weber/Schäffer/Bauer 2000, pp. 20–21). However, controllers appeared to be only insignificantly more risk-averse and rigid than their managers.

The fact that managers and controllers display different characteristics is supported by empirical evidence.

Considerable differences are also assumed to exist between the *motivation and preferences* of controllers and those of managers. With managers, the issue is whether or not they are dedicating their entire effort to achieving the company's goals. The corresponding criticism ranges from accusations of self-enrichment (stock option programs, the Mannesmann legal process or exorbitant salary demands such as those by Dick Grasso, CEO of NYSE), which are particularly frequent nowadays, to »effort aversion« as one of the standard assumptions of principal-agent theory and to the striving for prestige and power combined with delusions of grandeur (»the more resources, the better«). There is no corresponding criticism of controllers. Here, positive statements tend to dominate, in which reference is made to intrinsic

From the source

The idea of productive cooperation between drivers and constrainers is not new, as the following excerpts from a contribution by Sandig, dated 1933, show:

»There is a need for at least one individual in the company to provide drive and thereby be the driver. In most cases, this will be the head of the organization. He is the one who ensures there is ›always something happening‹, i.e. business activity. He ensures that the business moves forward and that it does not fall asleep ... The company's driver is the person responsible for promoting the idea of profits and turning it into reality. ...

Another person in a leading position – someone who has substantial say in company policy – has to become responsible for applying the brake, for holding back. The person who is given this task should be the person with the greatest ability for correctly assessing dangers. ...

Being the person responsible for braking is probably the position with the highest responsibility in a company. A precondition for the man who occupies this post is that he must have the will to the ongoing existence, to the progress, to the successful life of the company. His task is always to keep an eye on the big picture, the fate of the entire organization. The

person responsible for the brakes has to try to anticipate events and the possible influence of individual occurrences on the organization as a whole. ....

Observing economic life shows that dividing up the driving effect and the braking effect in a company and assigning the resulting tasks to two complementary persons intensifies work in the company to an extraordinary degree. It thereby orients itself towards the efficiency of company policy. If the driver exercises his role while being able to confide in someone pulling the brake at any decisive moment, he will be able to accelerate his management speed as a result of the sheer pleasure of sprinting ahead. The joy derived from the company's operations is heightened. The person responsible for applying the brakes, on the other hand, really enjoys his work when there is something for him to slow down from time to time. In this way, the cooperation of the two individuals boosts each one's effectiveness, and there is a mutual incentive for them to give their all for the company's goals.

The result of such driving and braking is controlled entrepreneurial will. Company policy under this interaction of drivers and constrainers would truly be governed by the maxim: Durch Unternehmen erhalten! *(To conserve through entrepreneurial action!)*« (Sandig 1933, pp. 352–360).

motivation and the typical »referee's ethics« (neutrality and independence as well as incorruptibility). Doubts in controllers' good faith are as rare as accusations of their putting insufficient effort into their work (for instance not being responsive enough to managers' wishes or lacking a service mentality). The only question that might unveil a hint of potential opportunism problems of controllers is »Who monitors the controller?«.

To conclude, we can state that strongly diverging characteristics are assumed – and empirically observed – for controllers and managers. Next, we will analyze the effect of such differences on the types of controllers' tasks.

2.1.3 Controllers' tasks derived from the characteristics of managers and controllers

2.1.3.1 Controller tasks as a result of delegation by managers

Managers are responsible for managing the company. Part of their competencies is to decide to whom they should delegate some of their tasks. Managers strive to delegate tasks if at least one of the following three conditions is met:

▸ Their capacity is insufficient or cannot be expanded to enable them to carry out the task by themselves.

▸ Other persons can complete the task faster or to a higher level of quality.

▸ There are other persons available who can complete the task at a lower cost while achieving the same result.

Determinants of the decision to delegate

Whether or not these conditions are fulfilled depends, on the one hand, on the specific context: Whereas a manager who is working during the summer lull (if there still is such a thing) may have time to prepare decisions himself, this could be completely impossible during the Christmas rush. On the other hand, one can also make standard assumptions regarding the different characteristics of managers and other persons who could potentially do the work. For instance, controllers know more about cost accounting than most managers, but earn significantly lower salaries – we will be dealing with these aspects in greater detail. In the latter case, when making his decision to delegate, the manager can therefore justify assigning tasks in general on the basis of capability and cost. In the former case, he may also have to delegate on a case-by-case basis in response to specific situations or modify the general assignation of tasks in particular instances. Leaving aside problems of measurement and assessment for the moment, the decision is made based on a comparison of costs and benefits or opportunity costs.

Applying such an analysis will be difficult for the manager when he does not have a complete understanding of the task he wishes to delegate: For instance, if he is not quite sure of how cost accounting works and what sort of a contribution one can expect from it, he will be unable to make a correct decision about who should be given the task of running the cost accounting function – or whether he even needs cost accounting at all. »*Problems of ability*« on the part of managers can therefore lead to delegation mistakes. If these are expected to be substantial, it makes sense to relieve individual managers of this responsibility and to have a different unit (higher up in the hierarchy) make the delegation decision. The freedom of individual

Decisions to delegate tasks are made at various levels of hierarchy.

managers to make decisions is thereby constrained and they have to accept a »given« range of resources.

Situations of this kind can be found in the practice of companies in vast numbers. For instance, there are cases where local managers cannot decide »on their own« to hire staff or to launch investments of any amount. They lack the overall view that is required for such decisions. A »classical« example relating to controllers is a board decision that obliges all business units to establish their own, decentralized controlling department, which has to cooperate with controlling at headquarters in certain areas.

Such constraints on managers' competency to delegate are even more necessary whenever there is a risk that they may behave opportunistically or when they have already been observed doing so. For instance, they might exceed their competencies, submit incorrect plans or report false information. Such motivational problems can explicitly not be solved at the level of the manager, but require that higher positions in the hierarchy take the necessary measures. Correspondingly, persons who have been »instated from above« serve not only the local manager, but also report to headquarters or a higher hierarchical level.

This applies to a significant degree to the organization of controllers too. For instance, local controllers are obliged to inform controllers at headquarters about obvious misconduct by their local managers so that countermeasures can be taken through the normal channels. The problem is obvious: Cooperation based on trust and loyalty ends where managers violate the rules that apply to them; the only problem is that it is not always clear when this is the case, and managers usually have a different opinion on where the limits are. Controllers are well aware of this dilemma (»betraying my manager«, »spying for headquarters«).

2.1.3.2 Differentiation of delegation-based controller task types
The considerations described above, used in conjunction with the description of differences between the characteristics of managers and those of controllers, make it possible to create a new order within the diversity and heterogeneity of controller tasks. Three different types can be identified (see *Figure 2-1* and cf. Weber/Schäffer/ Prenzler 2001 for more detail):

Unburdening tasks
This category encompasses all tasks delegated from managers to controllers to ensure they are carried out better, faster or with less effort. Managers are able to assess these tasks comprehensively and delegate them based on their own economic judgment (or could do so). A large part of controller tasks can be found in this group: for instance, responsibility for reporting, ongoing variance analysis or for planning processes. By carrying out such unburdening tasks, controllers exercise a pure »supplier function«. They are »of direct use« to the managers and thereby increase the efficiency of management overall.

Managers are directly able to see the benefits of unburdening tasks performed by controllers.

Supplementary tasks
Such a direct usefulness does not exist for supplementary tasks. In contrast to the unburdening tasks, managers are here unable to assess in their entirety the tasks they could potentially delegate in respect of their extent, contents or results. Two possible behavior patterns may result:

Fig. 2-1

Controller tasks as determined by the manager's characteristics

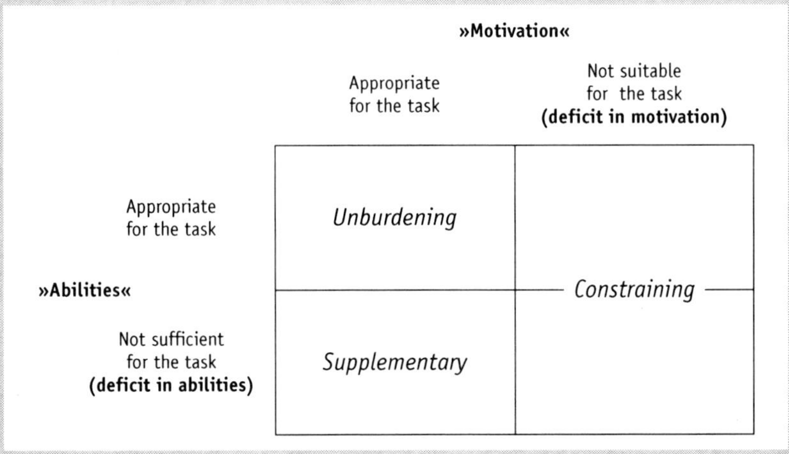

»Motivation«

	Appropriate for the task	Not suitable for the task **(deficit in motivation)**
Appropriate for the task	*Unburdening*	
»Abilities«		— *Constraining* —
Not sufficient for the task (deficit in abilities)	*Supplementary*	

▶ In the first case, managers can at least assess the importance and type of the task and can then make a decision on whether or not to delegate on this basis. One example for such a task is checking existing plans (»monitoring of the creation of plans«). It makes sense for managers to entrust an independent person who has a separate perspective on their ideas with such tasks in order to filter out wrong assumptions and assessments and to avoid simple calculation errors. But managers cannot determine in detail whether or not the benefits of delegating the task exceed the costs or not. In marketing language, such supplementary tasks are credence goods. Customers who consume them expect suppliers to have a strong reputation for quality.

> In the case of supplementary tasks, the benefits are not always apparent at a glance.

▶ In the second case, a higher authority »forces« the manager to accept a supplementary contribution. In other words, higher-level management does not confide in the local manager's insight; his potentially flawed ability to assess situations correctly is healed by the »clear view from headquarters«. As an example, consider a group-wide regulation issued by the executive board according to which capital budgeting plans for all investments exceeding a certain amount have to be countersigned by a controller. Controllers do not necessarily have to »sell« »involuntary« supplementary tasks to »their« managers; but they are always a potential source of atmospheric disturbances between controllers and managers (»Which boss are you really reporting to?«) and may accordingly influence the way in which unburdening tasks are carried out.

Constraining tasks

Constraining tasks can be characterized as a special case of manager supplementation. They result when managers display problems of motivation, in other words, if they do not want to adhere to the guidelines set out for them by a higher authority. Controllers become »custodians of economic morals« in such cases. At first glance,

Constraining tasks are the most problematic in the task portfolio of a controller.

there does not have to be a significant difference compared to the way a supplementary task is carried out; in both cases, for instance, the assumptions and assessments of a plan have to be questioned critically. In the case of opportunistic managers, however, controllers have to expect cunningly concealed distortions as well as a completely different type of conflict when the problem of motivation becomes apparent.

The transitions between the three task types are blurred as their distinct identities depend on the abilities and motivation of the manager. A supplementary task in the context of monitoring the creation of plans would, for instance, be an unburdening task if the manager could also execute it himself. What used to be a supplementary task turns into a constraining task when a manager unexpectedly starts behaving opportunistically. Typical unburdening tasks can also have a constraining focus, for instance when a manager purposefully wants incorrect figures to be presented or when a controller prevents opportunism on the part of the manager by purposefully preparing decisions in a certain way.

For assigning controller tasks to the three task groups, a certain allocation tendency can be identified, as mentioned above. This is also the reason for typical task combinations: When controllers provide explicitly results-related information as an unburdening task, there is a close proximity to the use of this information in similarly explicit decision supporting calculations as well as in »number-driven« variance analyses. Furthermore, the preparation and monitoring of plans indicates an unburdening of management, also in terms of the progression of the planning process. When controllers prove their worth in such unburdening tasks, there is immediate plausibility in also giving them responsibility for related supplementary tasks, such as monitoring the creation of plans. This in turn makes them potentially suitable candidates for assuming the constraining function if necessary.

On the other hand, every categorization also depends on the individual case. This explains why there is often a considerable impact on the controllers' area (such as changes in the organizational position) when an important leader is replaced. It also underscores why introducing cost accounting to a medium-sized company that is run with a strong focus on the organization's leader is a completely different problem compared to the case where a large enterprise acquires a medium-sized company, replacing key managers at the same time as it assumes responsibility for managing the company.

What unburdening, supplementary or constraining tasks entail depends on the individual circumstances.

To summarize: In general, controllers' tasks are activities that support managers in their function as leaders. Such support can take very distinct forms: In the case of supplementary and constraining tasks, the goal is to prevent management mistakes or minimize their impact. Controllers do for management what quality managers do for production. They assure high-quality management by reducing or preventing involuntary or purposeful deviations from the targeted level of managers' performance. The vague expression »targeted level of managers' performance« can be specified as the achievement of sufficiently effective and efficient performance on the part of the company. The aim is to maximize goal achievement using given means (effectiveness) or to achieve a given goal with minimal means (efficiency). This relationship between means and ends is described as rationality in the economic literature. We therefore will be using the expression »assuring rationality« for the task types described above:

▸ In the context of supplementary tasks, controllers can (reactively) check – using different technical and methodological knowledge or a different perspective – whether or not managers are using the right means to achieve the common ends, or (proactively) encourage and enforce the use of suitable means.

▸ In the context of constraining tasks, they can help ensure that potentially opportunistic managers strive for the common goal by (reactively) questioning the outcomes of actions or by (proactively) ensuring that the desired states are modified or that management perceives sanctions to be sufficiently likely.

Controllers (also) deal with management rationality.

Unburdening tasks are tasks which a manager could do himself in principle, but which she delegates to a controller in order to assure an efficient use of internal resources. Unburdening managers thereby focuses not on managers' mistakes, but on their limited capacity: As management support in the strict sense, it contributes indirectly to assuring rationality, in other words, controllers create the necessary conditions for rational action on the part of management by assuring that there is an efficient provisioning of input data and an efficient management cycle.

2.1.3.3 Assuring rationality as a task for controllers

Three key findings of our discussion can be summarized at this stage: (1) It has become even clearer why controllers carry out the tasks described in chapter 1 in parallel. The reason lies in the tight links between the tasks. From the perspective of the persons responsible for carrying out the tasks, the links result from identical or similar requirements placed on controllers' abilities and behavior. From the viewpoint of those receiving the services, controllers earn the right to contradict managers by offering support services that unburden them. (2) The concrete »manager's situation«, i.e. his abilities, attitudes and goals, influence the way in which the tasks are carried out. For instance, providing information can be an unburdening, supplementary or constraining task – depending on the situation. The interaction with the manager has to be adapted accordingly. (3) The concept of assuring rationality forms a goal of controller support functions that »cuts across« the traditional tasks related to information supply, planning and monitoring.

The nature of planning, monitoring and information supply tasks is sufficiently well known. »Modern« cost accountants too, have always performed such tasks in combination. But the function of assuring rationality clearly is a new, specific function of controllers. Whether or not this first impression is accurate can be assessed by asking who else could provide this service. There are three possible answers to this question:

▸ The task is delegated on a case-by-case basis, depending on the situation. For instance, in every decision-making round, a different manager could assume the role of assuring rationality. Such a solution may well work in an appropriate organizational culture; however, it should not be expected to work as a general rule.

Who else could contribute to assuring rationality?

▸ It is also conceivable to designate a »commissioner for assuring rationality«, just as there are quality inspectors, environmental commissioners and commissioners for gender equality in large German companies. Such a commissioner would dedicate himself exclusively to providing supplementary and constraining support to management. However, such a position can quickly become a thorn in the side of a manager (»professional whiner«). Furthermore, there is the considerable problem of proving the position's benefits (»dispensable overhead«), which is reinforced by the fact that the benefits accrue at different levels of the organization's hierarchy. Finally, quantum effects take hold: It is hard to imagine that the daily work of a »professional assurer of rationality« can really be completely fulfilled with doing this task if he is close enough to an individual manager.

▸ In assigning the task to a job role that already exists, it has to be ensured that the person (1) knows management intimately, (2) has sufficient mental distance to management, and (3) has sufficient autonomy. This combination of characteristics is difficult to achieve. For instance, a »fresh« graduate who is employed as assistant to a department head may well fulfill the first two criteria. However, she will hardly be able to assert the force of a better argument if her boss is not interested. Controllers stand a much better chance. The unburdening tasks they carry out provide them with deep and undistorted insights into the quality of management activities. The emphasis on calculation, reflection and analysis forms a good contrast to the approach of managers, who also use their intuition (»gut feeling«). The integration into a controller organization that cuts across hierarchy level ensures – as much as possible – autonomy. Finally, unburdening tasks create a substantial »basic load«, which is capable of making full use of controllers' capacity in conjunction with supplementary and constraining tasks.

In order for a person or unit to be able to efficiently and effectively assure rationality, three conditions have to be met.

It thus becomes clear that although controllers do not assure management rationality in every way, assuring rationality forms a much more comprehensive and important part of their tasks compared with other job roles. Hence, there is ample justification for speaking of an original controllers' task. This is also shown by the observation that many of the simplified images attributed to controllers in practice deal with assuring rationality (cf. Weber 1996b): Alongside the most widely known expressions of the »bean counter« and »number cruncher«, controllers are also known as »wet blanket«, »bloodhounds« and – somewhat more flatteringly – as the »economic conscience«. Managers and controllers are clearly aware of the fact that controllers contribute to an especially large degree to assuring rational management. However – and this should already be emphasized at this point – they are generally not able to assure management rationality on their own. Managers, controllers and other management support services are jointly responsible for this task.

Controllers are not tasked with assuring rationality in its entirety, but their purview covers a major part of it.

2.1.4 Controlling as assuring the rationality of management

In the academic discussion, the question of where to »locate« controlling in the overall edifice of business administration has long been the focus of intense and controversial debate. We presented the four most important schools of thought on controlling in chapter 1. The brief introductions highlighted the difficulties involved in categorizing controlling unambiguously. The information supply function has – in the form of accounting and/or information management – already been taken into consideration, as have planning and monitoring. Coordination between information supply, planning and monitoring is also dealt with within the sub-disci-

For us, controlling means assuring management rationality.

plines. Links to other management sub-systems are debated to a far lesser extent; still, there is a great variety of literature, for instance, on the motivational effects of different planning approaches or on the intensity and design of monitoring. It would not be accurate to say that this area is unoccupied. The charge that controlling lacks a specific core starts from these statements.

As indicated at the beginning of the chapter, we will be taking an inductive approach to deriving controlling. Taking another look at controller tasks in practice shows – as mentioned – a dichotomy: On the one hand, controllers provide information, planning and monitoring services. However, each of these tasks could also be provided by other persons: Accounting staff can supply information, planners can do the planning and monitoring could be performed for instance, by a higher-up manager. The fact that the combination of tasks – as has also been shown – is specific to controllership is similarly of no help in the search for the core of controlling: Essentially, it addresses an issue falling into the bailiwick of organization (coordination based on plans), where it is already being discussed extensively. The remaining option – the last hope, so to speak – is the original controller task of assuring rationality, which is enabled by the specific combination of tasks they are responsible for. This is exactly where we strike gold.

Using theory to answer the question of where assuring rationality is located does not provide a convincing answer: There is no specialized function that deals with the issue of how the rationality of individual managers or of the management function as a whole should be assured. One only finds scattered and sparse references (for instance, under the keyword corporate governance). The statement gains validity the more one switches from an abstract, functional view (e.g. planning) to that of individual manager groups (planning department managers) or individual managers (»manager Smith's contribution to planning«), in other words, the more one takes into consideration concrete cognitive constraints, properties and preferences.

Based on this inductive approach, assuring management rationality thereby seems most suitable for being identified as the original content and essence of controlling. Therefore, it is proposed that *controlling be viewed functionally as assuring management rationality* (cf. also Weber/Schäffer 1999 and Schäffer/Weber 2004). This is a task that has not been considered integrally in the edifice of business administration. Providing an »alternative view« on previously discovered solutions and avoiding mistakes and other rationality deficits before they become effective constitutes an independent, discernable problem. Its specific nature lies in answering the question of how to recognize rationality deficits, and how to reduce or eliminate them. Taking these three things together promises similar benefits from specialization as are known from the separate perspectives of other management functions.

The close relationship to practice does, however, also result in a constraint on the task of assuring rationality. Controllers are, as described, not to be found in every type of organization, but only in those that orient their management towards coordination by means of plans. In the context of other management structures – for instance, in person-oriented management in medium-sized companies or in public administration, which is coordinated by laws and regulations – one does not come across any controllers, and one finds a completely different kind of problem of assuring rationality. We therefore limit the meaning of controlling to

If one wishes to maintain a close link to practice, controlling has to be limited to institutions primarily coordinated on the basis of plans.

Summary
(see guiding questions 1, 2 and 3)

▸ Within the spectrum of controllers' tasks, assuring rationality can be identified as a task type that is not exclusively, but indeed mainly carried out by controllers.

▸ Controlling is defined as assuring rationality in a context where coordination based on plans dominates and integrated as a further specialized discipline into the edifice of business administration.

▸ The inductive derivation of controlling ensures a tight linkage between controlling and controllership. In this way, it is not necessary to postulate controlling normatively; instead, it can be derived empirically.

▸ Three fundamental types of controllers' tasks can be identified: unburdening, supplementary and constraining.

assuring rationality in the context of coordination by plans. This ensures – in accordance with the inductive approach – that the link to practice is maintained.

At this point, the major part of the terminological clarification that was the subject of the chapter has been completed: We know which spectrum of tasks controllers carry out, what is original about these tasks, how controlling is related to controllership, and finally, that controlling means assuring rationality in a specific management context. But we have not completed our task entirely yet. We still have to clarify what rationality and assuring rationality mean in detail.

2.2 Rationality and how to assure it

2.2.1 The concept of rationality

Rationality is a key concept, and not just in business administration. Much older disciplines also discuss it (for instance, philosophy and the theory of science). Not surprisingly for anyone who has read this far, rationality is another expression that is defined in very different ways in the literature. However, this lack of uniformity can easily be circumvented by referring back to means-end (or »instrumental«) rationality, which holds a dominant position in economics. In this case, rationality is measured by the yardstick of efficiently using means to achieve given ends. These ends are usually means for achieving higher-order ends, so that means-end rationality aims at the efficiency and effectiveness of actions (cf. Schäffer/Weber 2004, p. 462).

Our understanding is based on means-end rationality.

But this only helps to overcome the first hurdles. Who defines which ends should be pursued, or which are the correct means to a given end?

In the search for an appropriate reference, one could think – an obvious thought – of a good textbook on business administration, simply following the motto: »There is nothing quite as good for practice as a good theory«. In the simplest case, this means acting according to the following pattern: »Companies pursue the ends of maximizing their profits; from all the alternatives available, they choose the one that promises the highest returns«. In practice, however, managers are somewhat sceptical about this idea, and in most cases, they have good reasons: The theory of business administration can – as has been emphasized various times already – only rarely be formulated in such detail that it delivers reliable, »correct« solutions in concrete cases. For instance, does an exclusive focus on profit maximization not neglect justified demands that society makes on companies? Do the underlying models really take into account everything that could be of importance, e.g. the reactions of competitors to one's own actions? Alternatively, one might consider asking an expert, for instance a manager, an auditor or a consultant. But: who is the right expert in each individual case – and what happens when he or she is wrong? Would it be better to ask more experts? Would only a unanimous view be valid? How should one deal with dissenting or minority opinions?

All of these questions cannot be dealt with in depth in an introductory textbook on controlling, even though they are doubtlessly highly relevant for the daily work of controllers (cf., for instance, the overview provided in Weber/Schäffer/Langenbach 2001, pp. 46–76). Two insights are sufficient at this stage: On the one hand, these questions have already generated an extensive and, in parts, highly controversial debate. On the other hand, one finds solutions that can be used in an attempt to answer our questions. In the following, we will take *rationality* to mean *the domi-*

From the source

**Extract from »Economy and Society«
by the sociologist Max Weber (1922):**

»Social action, like all action, may be oriented in four ways. It may be: (1) *instrumentally rational* (zweck-rational), that is, determined by expectations as to the behaviour of objects in the environment and of other human beings; these expectations are used as »conditions« or »means« for the attainment of the actor's own rationally pursued and calculated ends; (2) *value-rational* (wertrational), that is, determined by a conscious belief in the value for its own sake of some ethical, aesthetic, religious, or other form of behaviour, independently of its prospects of success; (3) *affectual* (especially emotional), that is, determined by the actor's specific affects and feeling states; (4) *traditional*, that is, determined by ingrained habituation.

... Action is instrumentally rational (zweckrational) when the end, the means, and the secondary results are all rationally taken into account and weighed. This involves rational consideration of alternative means to the end, of the relations of the end to the secondary consequences, and finally of the relative importance of different possible ends. Determination of action either in affectual or in traditional terms is thus incompatible with this type.

Choice between alternative and conflicting ends and results may well be determined in a value-rational manner. In that case, action is instrumentally rational only in respect to the choice of means. On the other hand, the actor may, instead of deciding between alternative and conflicting ends in terms of a rational orientation to a system of values, simply take them as given subjective wants and arrange them in a scale of consciously assessed relative urgency. He may then orient his action to this scale in such a way that they are satisfied as far as possible in order of urgency, as formulated in the principle of »marginal utility«. Value-rational action may thus have various different relations to the instrumentally rational action. From the latter point of view, however, value-rationality is always irrational. Indeed, the more the value to which action is oriented is elevated to the status of an absolute value, the more »irrational« in this sense the corresponding action is. For, the more unconditionally the actor devotes himself to this value for its own sake, to pure sentiment or beauty, to absolute goodness or devotion to duty, the less is he influenced by considerations of the consequences of his action. The orientation of action wholly to the rational achievement of ends without relation to fundamental values is, to be sure, essentially only a limiting case« (Weber 1978, pp. 24–26).

Extract from the habilitation thesis *(thesis for a postdoctoral lecture qualification in Germany)* of the business economist Erich Gutenberg (1929):

»Essentially, thinking in terms of relationships between means and ends is the basis of everything, not only in economic life, but in human life in general. ›To act irrationally‹ generally means not to act purposefully; it means not to match means correctly to the ends they are meant to achieve. The type of ends is of no importance« (Gutenberg 1929, p. 30).

We conceive of rationality as the dominant view of experts concerning a specific means-end relation.

nant view held by experts regarding a specific means-end relation. For this to be valid, two conditions in particular have to be met:

▸ The experts have to be recognized as experts by other experts. For instance, an experienced manager would confide in another experienced manager's ability to evaluate a management situation accurately, an auditor would accept the competence of an experienced senior accountant or a manager would concede a controller's ability to perform a net present value calculation correctly. Conversely, and as confirmed by recent experience, there is room for considerable scepticism when somebody entering the job market for the first time formulates high-flying business plans for a startup.

▸ When experts hold different views, there has to be the possibility of an open discourse aimed at arriving at a shared assessment. Participants in such a debate have to be willing to argue rationally, to review all counter-arguments without prejudice and to arrive at a consensus acceptable to all – and they need to have sufficient time to do so. Blind spots, stubbornness or misplaced emotionality are just as harmful to rational solutions as wishful thinking, demonstrations of power or excessive time pressure.

Taking rationality to mean the dominant view of experts is widespread in science, too. Nobel prizes are awarded to those who have published extensively (acceptance by referees), who are cited frequently (acceptance by other scientists) and who have won many scientific prizes previously (another indication of acceptance in the community). Although this method is widespread, it is no panacea for errors: In some cases, a view held by an individual may well be more accurate than the experts' group view. In science, this is typically the case when there are fundamental breaks in the dominant view (»paradigm shifts«). In such cases, genius beats the »academic average«. However, it would be very risky to rely on geniuses; at the beginning, they cannot be distinguished from charlatans – of whom there are many more!

The understanding of what is or is not rational depends on the current state of knowledge – meaning that the dominant view can be wrong.

The reference to science highlights another characteristic of the rationality concept: Rationality always has to be defined relatively, based on the current level of knowledge. Dominant theories are constantly being replaced by newer, more suitable ones. What was rational yesterday no longer has to be so tomorrow. Learning constantly extends the limits of knowledge – and therefore, of rationality. Introducing a new planning tool to a company's planning practice can represent such a shift in what is considered »state of the art«.

In practice, it is usually sufficient to avoid the most flagrant violations of rationality.

In practice (but also in theory), it is not always completely clear who really holds the status of being an expert for a specific problem, or with whom such an expert should debate the correct solution when in doubt. Fortunately, solving practical problems does not require fulfilling theoretically ideal conditions. In other words: It is usually sufficient to keep an eye on clear violations of the conditions in order to avoid significant violations of rationality, and the »problem of the experts« can also be resolved satisfactorily in most cases. But before dealing in greater detail with how to assure rationality, we will take a look at different levels of rationality. Knowing them is of considerable importance for designing measures that assure rationality.

2.2.2 Levels of rationality

As shown above, our argumentation is based on rationality as a means-end relation-ship. Given ends should be achieved with the appropriate means, or given means should be applied to the right ends. This viewpoint can be directly transferred to a concept that forms one of the basic patterns in business administration: Factors are combined in a process in order to obtain a result. The question of the correct means can be further subdivided into questions regarding the right input factors and the right process for combining them. If one includes the right result, three levels of rationality can be differentiated (cf. Weber/Schäffer/Langenbach 2001, pp. 50–53):

Differentiating between results-based, process-based and input-based rationality

▸ *results-based rationality*, also known as »substantial rationality«,
▸ *process-based or procedural rationality* and
▸ *input-based rationality.*

The three levels are interdependent: Input-based rationality is a necessary condition for process-based rationality (»correct« processes cannot be achieved with wrong inputs); the same relationship exists between process-based and results-based rationality. There are two reasons why it makes sense to differentiate between the three levels:

The three levels of rationality are inter-dependent.

▸ Rationality is, as has been shown, linked to the knowledge available. Knowledge deficits of individual decision makers can be corrected or ameliorated by referring to a »state of the art« of knowledge. For instance, this is the case when a manager wants to solve a capital budgeting problem, but does not know what net present value means. At this point, a controller can easily help. There is a series of prob-lems, however, for which such a »state of the art« does not exist. For instance, knowledge deficits regarding the intended result are characteristic for processes of innovation. Such situations are also well known in management: The funda-mental strategic positioning of a company in particular is often marked by such considerable uncertainties that only its approximate direction can be determined – but not the exact strategic goal.

As a remaining, less extensive analysis of rationality, the type of process leading to the uncertain result can be analyzed and shaped. With regard to strategic planning, this could mean, for instance, providing enough time for managers to match their different expectations of the future or to avoid excessive formaliz-ation and quantification. If the knowledge deficits are too great even for assuring process-based rationality, the only option remaining is to assure that the right means are used, in other words, to bring together the right experts for strategic positioning and to wait until a solution has been found that is accepted by all. Different levels of knowledge permit rationality to be determined in diverse ways, in other words: Even when the ends are not completely clear, it is nevertheless possible to make statements about the rational use of means.

▸ The different levels of rationality can be checked at different points in time. It is not always necessary to wait for the result to identify rationality shortfalls; such problems should be identified as early as possible in order to minimize negative consequences. This aspect is of central importance for controllers' activities in particular: For instance, if they recognize inconsistencies at the stage where plans are developed, they have sufficient possibilities of ensuring that ensuing problems are not permitted to crop up during implementation.

To summarize: There is a large variety of approaches to defining rationality in literature. For our purposes, we have selected means-end rationality, which dominates in economics. Depending on the extent of the knowledge deficits, the existence of rationality can be related to three levels, namely results-based, process-based and input-based rationality. In other words: Both the means and the end should be analyzed critically.

2.2.3 Assuring rationality

Defining controlling as assuring management rationality presupposes both that rationality can be operationalized and that specific measures aimed at assuring rationality can be identified. Otherwise, there would be no independent problem to investigate. To check whether this condition is fulfilled, we will begin by taking a look at the use of any specific model in the planning process. The reasoning is shown in *Figure 2-2*. As person responsible for assuring rationality, we postulate a controller who usually carries out the tasks described below.

How can rationality be assured in practice? – An example

We start by assuming that there is a group of managers who want to find out whether a certain investment option is profitable. To do so, they use the net present value model. There are already various conceivable (and potentially sensible) possibilities of assuring rationality during this first phase. They relate to the model itself on the one hand, and to the suitability of the managers for applying the model on the other.

A net present value calculation assumes a decision problem characterized, amongst other things, by the possibility of quantifying capital expenditure effects through a series of payments and by a fixed point in time when the capital is spent. These conditions are often only approximately met. For instance, investing in creating a brand image causes concrete cash outflows. Changes in cash inflows, on the other hand, can usually only be estimated in the broadest possible terms. Also, many investments can either be shifted in time or »stretched« out over time. In both cases, the net present value method may be unsuitable: In the case of extensive knowledge deficits, it suggests a greater accuracy than is actually available (»we can calculate anything«). In such a case, it might be better for decision makers to explicitly take cognizance of the uncertainty underlying the decision, and to trust in intuitive solution approaches. In cases where investments can be designed in phases, preference should be given to real options analysis over the net present value method. Assuring rationality therefore means questioning the basic suitability of a model and checking whether or not the assumptions underlying its application are actually fulfilled. One way in which controllers take charge of this problem is by forming groups of decision problems and assigning specific methods to the groups. In this case, managers have no degrees of freedom with regard to the methods they use or have to reach an agreement with controllers if they do want to use other methods (methodical competence of controllers).

Fig. 2-2

Phases of the process of assuring rationality, using a decision-making model as an example

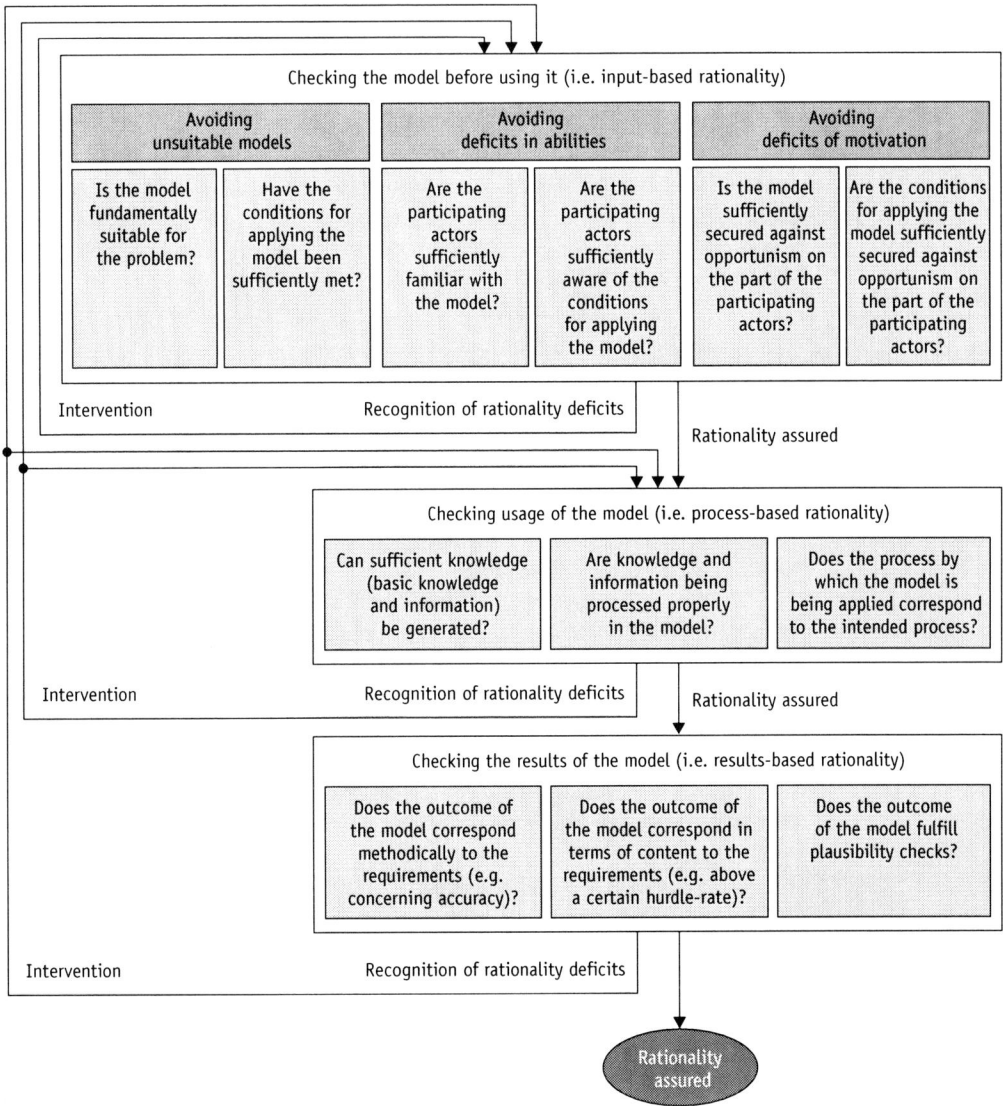

Checking the model before using it (i.e. input-based rationality)

Avoiding unsuitable models		Avoiding deficits in abilities		Avoiding deficits of motivation	
Is the model fundamentally suitable for the problem?	Have the conditions for applying the model been sufficiently met?	Are the participating actors sufficiently familiar with the model?	Are the participating actors sufficiently aware of the conditions for applying the model?	Is the model sufficiently secured against opportunism on the part of the participating actors?	Are the conditions for applying the model sufficiently secured against opportunism on the part of the participating actors?

Intervention — Recognition of rationality deficits

Rationality assured

Checking usage of the model (i.e. process-based rationality)

Can sufficient knowledge (basic knowledge and information) be generated?	Are knowledge and information being processed properly in the model?	Does the process by which the model is being applied correspond to the intended process?

Intervention — Recognition of rationality deficits

Rationality assured

Checking the results of the model (i.e. results-based rationality)

Does the outcome of the model correspond methodically to the requirements (e.g. concerning accuracy)?	Does the outcome of the model correspond in terms of content to the requirements (e.g. above a certain hurdle-rate)?	Does the outcome of the model fulfill plausibility checks?

Intervention — Recognition of rationality deficits

Rationality assured

Using an appropriate model is, however, only a necessary, but not a sufficient condition for rationality. Measures for assuring rationality also have to match the characteristics of those employing the model. In accordance with our basic distinction between abilities and motivation, this means, on the one hand, that managers' knowledge of the functioning and underlying assumptions of the model should be questioned. This aspect is of central importance in practice because – as shown – many managers have knowledge gaps concerning business models and tools (»I've got a controller for that«). On the other hand, it is often helpful to anticipate at which points of using a model there are possibilities of consciously manipulating the result. In this sense, for instance, some companies prohibit the use of cost-benefit analyses because the subjective evaluations introduced into the analysis by those using the tool cannot be checked in sufficient depth to prevent opportunistic behavior. For controllers, this means that they need to be aware as much of the manipulation possibilities of models as of individual managers' tendency to act opportunistically; they then need to take the appropriate measures to address both problems – or recommend using a different model.

> Are managers able to use the model appropriately?

A further criterion worth checking for input-based rationality is the suitability of those responsible for using the model. This relates both to their knowledge of the specifics of the problem and to ensuring a sufficient multiplicity of assessments (diversity of internal models). However, this aspect depends on the concrete decision-making model and is therefore of no relevance for the problem we are currently addressing. Nevertheless, it will play a central role in describing the interaction between managers and controllers.

> Controllers have many opportunities to influence the process by which the model is applied.

If the required conditions for input-based rationality are met, the next phase of assuring rationality focuses on the implementation of the selected model. As shown in *Figure 2-2*, there are three problem areas that should ideally be checked:

▶ Models – such as net present value calculations – require specific knowledge in order to work correctly (for instance, cash in- and outflows and the internal rate of return). This knowledge may be incomplete at the first stages of using the tool, for instance when assessing the capital budgeting proposal; in this case, more information is needed. If there are significant knowledge gaps and if these cannot be adequately filled, the model will generate results that appear to be rational (we have already referred to a comment often made by controllers: »We can calculate anything«). Assuring that there is sufficient knowledge is therefore of critical importance for process-based rationality – and it is in this area that controllers had and continue to have a core responsibility.

▶ Having sufficient knowledge does not necessarily mean that it will be used correctly in the model. We have already made mention of constraints on the ability to make predictions and assess situations. Furthermore, individual opportunism may lead to rationality defects at this stage: For instance, controllers can recount innumerable stories about managers who, from a large pool of information, always select exactly the data that will lead to a result matching their wishes. Being prepared for such behavioral patterns (e.g. by knowing the person in question very well) usually makes it possible to limit them considerably or to prevent them completely.

▶ Finally, rationality deficits may also result from the way in which the model is used. A typical phenomenon in this context is excessive time pressure. Calculations have to be completed and presented by a certain deadline; there is no time for necessary critical revision loops or for sufficient discourse about specific approaches and assessments. Controllers can help assure rationality in such situations by defining certain requirements (e.g. sufficient buffer time). Discourses can also be constrained by the dominance of individuals or implicit pressure »from above«, for instance when a board member wants to have his favorite project presented in the most favorable light. Here too, including controllers in the process can be beneficial because they are usually more independent from line management and therefore – within limits – can demand and ensure objectivity.

A sufficient diversity of internal models, which was mentioned in the section on input-based rationality, is also important for process-based rationality. Various cognitive constraints may result from the interactions between different participants. They are summarized under the heading »groupthink« in the relevant literature (cf. Janis 1982). They include an excessive predilection for risk and a tendency to accept an illusion of unanimity.

Many mistakes can be made when using new models.

This brings us to the final level of rationality: results-based rationality. Assuring rationality in this case relates in the first instance to assessing the model's result on a »technical« basis. For instance, any controller should become suspicious if capital expenditure options covering a period of eight years are calculated to an implausible degree of accuracy of two decimal points. In addition, the result also has to satisfy requirements as regards content. For instance, there are reports of companies where managers were satisfied for years on end with target values that were scattered around the zero line of the P & L results. Not delivering profits is surely – assuming a company with a typical goal-function – not rational. Controllers have to ensure that sufficiently ambitious goals are set, for instance by referring to capital market requirements or – in other contexts – by generating benchmarks. Another typical rationality deficit is the so-called »hockey stick effect«: The measures being reviewed only achieve the required return because they show excellent results for the final years of the investment period. Unfortunately, these hopes are often dashed on the rocks of economic reality. The competitive situation usually becomes harder, not easier. Recognizing the hockey stick effect and using the irrationality usually inherent in it as a standard answer for such plans is an effective way of assuring rationality. Finally, plausibility checks and sensitivity analyses also contribute to assuring rationality.

The model outcome also has to be analyzed critically.

At this stage, the answer to the question posed initially is clear: Measures for assuring rationality can be identified easily and plentifully. Sometimes the criteria being tested are easy to measure (»yes or no«), but sometimes assessing the evidence of rationality requires substantial tests (for instance, determining whether or not managers have sufficient knowledge of the tools being used). Sometimes the checks can be formalized objectively (»Was the most recent market research data taken into consideration when making the decision?«), sometimes a large degree of subjectivity cannot be avoided (for instance, when trying to evaluate the reliability of plan estimates).

Rationality can be assured in many ways. Specializing on this task can be advantageous.

Assuring rationality is not limited to decision making, but similarly addresses the way in which influencing is carried out (e.g. questioning the consistency of individual plans in annual budgeting) and subsequent enactment is monitored (e.g. »Is random sampling sufficient for a specific monitoring problem?«). Assuring rationality is not limited to after-the-fact checks, but also includes anticipating and preventing rationality defects before they occur (for instance, by coaching managers in the use of certain tools or by specifying rules). The field of assuring rationality is ample and the spectrum of measures diverse.

Summary
(see guiding questions 3 and 4)

▸ Rationality is here understood to signify means-end rationality. The point of reference for the existence of rationality is the »prevailing view« of experts.

▸ The extent and type of tasks dedicated to assuring rationality are determined by the extent and type of management rationality deficits.

▸ The spectrum of measures for assuring rationality is extremely broad. This is one reason for the multifaceted nature of controlling.

▸ The task of assuring rationality is shared by controllers, managers and numerous other internal and external agents, positions and institutions.

▸ Rationality deficits should only be reduced to the degree that the resulting benefits outweigh the costs of assuring rationality.

2.3 Next steps

Having introduced our conception of controlling, the further discussion on how to assure rationality – and therefore, on the controlling function – will limit itself to controllers' activities. Anything else would bloat an introductory textbook beyond measure. We have selected this focus to match the interests of the three potential target groups of this book:

We will be concentrating on controllers in the following.

▸ For academics, the focus on controllers provides the opportunity to model concrete tasks and research them empirically. Abstract functions are usually not observable in practice.

▸ After graduating, students may become controllers or deal with them in the context of their jobs. Modeling controllers and their tasks provides benefits beyond satisfying academic interest.

▸ For managers and controllers in business practice, this focus offers the opportunity of establishing direct links to their actual experience and of receiving useful hints that can be used in practice.

What awaits you in the next chapters of the book?

Chapters 4 and 5 deal with how to design, manage and develop a controller unit. Questions of organization (central versus local, functional versus divisional controlling), of incentive design (»How to motivate a controller?«) and of personnel development (»How do controllers build their careers?«) are addressed, as are perspectives on controllership (controllers are currently exposed to stiff competition within companies, to which they need to react).

The conceptual underpinnings of controlling, however, have not yet been described in full detail. A further chapter is needed because a central aspect of the argument developed so far has not been clarified sufficiently: At several points, we mentioned that controllers are only found in practice in environments where coordination takes place through plans – they are not found in other management contexts. The controlling conception promoted by the Internationaler Controller Verein is based on this viewpoint, as are many definitions of controlling, either explicitly or implicitly. But it remains unclear at this stage what »coordination based on plans« means exactly. More than a vague intuition is not available. However, if the management context is so essential for the work of controllers and controlling's task of assuring rationality, we cannot leave it at such a vague understanding. It is therefore the objective of chapter 3 to clarify this point.

A more exact description and analysis of the management context »coordination based on plans« still remains to be provided.

Recommended reading ...

... Deriving the controlling function from controllers' tasks
David 2005
Schäffer/Weber 2004
Weber 2003, pp. 183–192

... Rationality and how to assure it
Ahn/Dyckhoff 2004
Kirsch 1997, pp. 389–531
Langenbach 2001, pp. 23–125
Pietsch/Scherm 2000, pp. 395–412
Schäffer 2001, pp. 112–121
Schäffer 2004
Schäffer/Weber 2004
Weber 2004

3 The context of controlling: coordination based on plans

Guiding questions:

1 How can the management cycle be described in ideal terms?

2 How would the perspective on individual management cycles have to be extended to describe the interaction of several managers?

3 Where would one expect to find controllers in practice – and where not?

4 What is the difference between coordination based on plans and other coordination mechanisms, and which other ones are there?

5 What exactly does coordination based on plans and »management by objectives« mean?

6 Which facets are there to the problem of defining the right goals properly?

As shown in the first two chapters, controlling is closely linked to a context of systematic planning and monitoring. What this means exactly will be explained in the following chapter, for which we have to start with the question of how management works in general.

There are about as many different opinions on what constitutes management as there are on the nature of controlling. As this book is an introduction to controlling and not to management, though, we will not work out the concept of management in detail, but rather define it in such a way that it is compatible with our perspective on controlling.

> Management is another term with many meanings; we need to define it precisely for our purposes.

The chain of argument starts by focusing on a single management process or cycle being carried out by an actor. Afterwards, the perspective will be broadened to include the interaction of several managers. Some statements from organization theory, which focuses on such issues, will be used for this purpose. This will form the basis we need for taking a closer look at goals. It will enable us to discuss types and effects of goals in greater detail, as well as the role controllers play in the process of deciding on, influencing and monitoring goals.

We therefore have to »extend our reach« in terms of the subject matter. But we will only do so to the degree required for understanding management by objectives and for explaining the tasks of controllers.

3.1 The management cycle

3.1.1 Management by an individual manager

The starting point of the discussion is the question of what constitutes the essence of management. In order to answer it, we will first describe *the relationship between two types of actions: management and execution.* The latter can be pictured as occurring along predefined tracks, »quasi-mechanically«. In other words, *execution* is here defined as an action for which there are no (longer any) degrees of freedom (»robot-like behavior«). On this basis, the definition of *management* is obvious: It is an action that defines and thereby constrains degrees of freedom for one or more other actions. On the one hand, such actions can even be other management actions. Such is the case when managers' degrees of freedom are defined and constrained in cascades throughout a company, starting from the executive board's general objective of increasing company value up to assigning specific production volumes to various production sites. On the other hand, degrees of freedom can also be defined and constrained for execution, such as an instruction being issued to factory worker Jones to process 25 units of a specified material in the required way between 2:00 and 4:00 p.m.

A single management action is furthermore assumed – again in an abstract, ideal way – to have been mentally prepared before being carried out by one or several persons. In other words: Degrees of freedom are defined and constrained on the basis of a conscious process of decision making. Predominantly impulsive or instinctive action is generally not modeled in economic theory – and would hardly correspond to actual practice in companies. Emotional impulses and unconscious actions begin to dominate decision making only when »there is no other choice«, when there is no relevant knowledge available to inform purposeful action, in other words, when one needs to improvise (»trial and error«). They are always there latently, however.

Once the management action has been carried out, its effects become apparent after a certain period of time. The effects may show themselves immediately – for instance, when worker Jones has only processed 20 units of material instead of 25 units, as he was supposed to – or with a considerable time lag, as would be the case when implementing a strategic project with a range of several years. In each case, it makes sense to compare the actual outcome with the results that were anticipated during decision making. Perhaps Jones only managed to do 20 units because he was distracted by private problems, but perhaps the 25 units were overly ambitious to start with. Comparing what was intended with what was actually achieved – which we refer to as monitoring – leads to further important insights to which we will return soon.

For »deliberate« decision making to take place, the individual manager has to fulfill certain requirements: She has to be endowed with the necessary cognitive skills to make a decision (»ability«). On the other hand, she has to know what is important for her and what is not (»motivation«). We will take a closer look at these requirements in the following, and will return to them at many points in this book.

The required cognitive abilities that a manager needs for decision making can fundamentally be subdivided into three forms:

▶ *The ability to perceive*
This expresses the capacity of the manager to perceive relevant aspects of the environment and of herself, thus providing information for later processing. In other words, we only see what we are able to see (and want to see). The ability to perceive acts like a filter that permits data to pass through. What is unknown is generally not seen. This ability may vary greatly from person to person. A manager with an engineering background often has no »appreciation« for economic effects, while many controllers are »blind« to vague strategic changes (»weak signals«). Furthermore, psychology tells us of a wide range of ways in which our perception can be distorted.

▶ *The ability to predict*
This ability makes it possible to form expectations that are likely to be fulfilled (a high probability of occurrence). Amongst others, the ability to predict includes having a keen entrepreneurial sense for market developments as well as knowledge of the large number of forecasting techniques. Individuals' ability to predict is also subject to a considerable number of typical constraints. These include a lacking ability to deal with non-linear developments as well as the phenomenon of overconfidence, i.e. an exaggerated belief in one's ability to keep a problem »under control« during implementation. Many controllers can tell stories about such »illusions of control« by their managers.

Cognitive abilities can be subdivided into the ability to perceive, to predict, and to evaluate.

▶ *The ability to evaluate*
This ability describes the capacity of assigning values to different alternatives and comparing them. The spectrum ranges from intuitively weighing up options to complicated decision-making models. In terms of the interaction between managers and controllers in practice, the latter are usually respected for their high level of competence in the area of evaluation specifically. Errors of evaluation are often caused by a lacking knowledge of methods, but also by the frequently observed human characteristic of attempting to find satisfactory – rather than optimal – solutions.

A manager's motivation can be described in the abstract as a utility function. Such a function assigns utility values to different types of conceivable circumstances (for instance, of predictable action sequences in particular); higher utility values are preferred over lower ones. Economically, we typically assume financial objectives at this point (e.g. maximizing income or profits). Managers are required by their contracts to apply all their efforts and ingenuity to achieving the profit goals of »their« companies. However, psychology, under the keyword »theories of motivation«, presents a cornucopia of additional, individual utility components, such as power or self-realization. Controllers have an infinite supply of stories about managers pretending to follow economic goals while in reality being driven by their own career objectives.

To summarize (see *Figure 3-1*): Under normal circumstances, managers act deliberately, not on the basis of pure »trial and error«. Their decision making is based on cognitive abilities (perception, prediction and evaluation) and their individual motivation (utility function). After the action has been carried out, they check whether the actual result corresponds to the planned outcome. Such monitoring is the basis for systematic learning.

Decision making is carried out on the basis of managers' abilities and motivation.

Fig. 3-1

Basic form of the management cycle

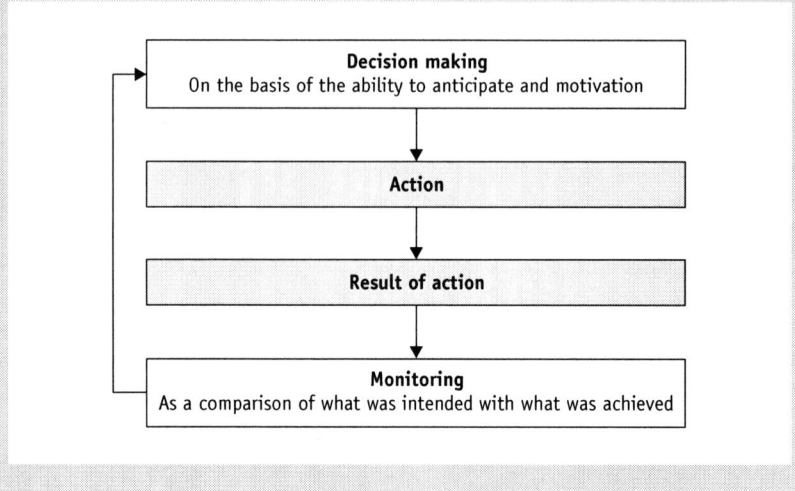

3.1.2 Interaction between managers

3.1.2.1 Basic forms of interaction
Individuals almost always work together to achieve their economic goals. They can –
again from an ideal point of view – work together as equals (»horizontally«) or in
terms of a superior-subordinate relationship (»vertically«). The »classical model« of
a horizontal relationship is the market. This is where supply meets demand on an
equal footing: The buyer does not have to demand anything; the seller is not forced
to supply anything. If a transaction results, it is voluntary and has to benefit both
sides.

As a rule, many people cooperate to achieve a goal.

In companies, however, such a form of cooperation is the exception rather than
the rule. Here, relationships between superiors and subordinates predominate
(»hierarchy«). There are two completely different approaches to designing a hierarchy, which – in keeping with the terminology introduced in the previous section
– are based on different ways of defining degrees of freedom: On the one hand,
hierarchical influence can determine the *process* of subordinates' actions. This
would be the case, for instance, when the head of sales issues instructions to his
staff determining in detail how customers should be addressed. The determination
of degrees of freedom relates to the actions themselves in this case. On the other
hand, there is also the option of only defining the *results* of actions. For example,
management could require employees to achieve certain sales targets – but without
detailing how each sales agent should realize the required sales or contribution
margin targets.

Hierarchically, both the process and the outcome of an action can be specified as an instruction.

Which of the two forms (or which combination of the forms) is chosen depends on
several factors. They include the uniformity of the goods or services rendered (e.g.

for activities that form part of a production process where quality requirements have to be met), the frequency of repetition of actions (standardization makes sense for actions that are repeated often), but especially also the knowledge available concerning the actions: Often, managers are not able to specify each individual action in detail to their subordinates; general knowledge has to interact with detailed knowledge »on site«. In this case, it is only possible to specify the required result.

Deviations from the forms of vertical cooperation in companies only occur in exceptional cases, for instance when companies want to simulate market conditions within the company (»internal markets«). A further important reason results from knowledge deficits: Sometimes there is not even enough knowledge available to define the results of actions. This would be the case, for instance, in parts of a company's research and development department. Here, management and execution have to be closely linked, e.g. by researchers mutually adjusting to one another.

3.1.2.2 Influencing as an additional management task
In the following, let us assume a »normal«, hierarchical management structure. Managers can limit the degrees of freedom of other managers or operational staff. They make a decision about this and later check to see whether the tasks which were meant to be carried out were completed according to the instructions. However, this will not always be the case.

Deviations from what was intended may result from different causes. We will start with reasons inherent in the person being managed. For instance, the person might not dispose of the necessary abilities, or, alternatively, might have wanted to do something else than was expected, in other words, he might have had a different motivation. Problems in the area of abilities might result from excessive demands or unrealistic expectations of the person's abilities (»There is no way Jones could have managed that much work«) or from a situation-based problem of understanding (»Jones did not expect you to actually want all 25 units of material«). Problems of motivation also come in different shapes and sizes. Effort aversion (as one of the standard assumptions of principal-agent theory) is one of the elements that could be mentioned, as are own career goals or a different understanding of business.

However, it is not always the person being managed who is »at fault« for the discrepancy between what was expected and what was achieved. The reasons could also be found on the part of the manager. For instance, the manager may issue ambiguous or vague instructions, or the instructions might have been objectively unrealistic (»overambitious targets«). Finally, the economic environment may also have an impact: The uncertainty inherent in the environment means that not everything will happen exactly as planned by professional management.

To gain a better understanding of management therefore means on the one hand that, in addition to decision making and monitoring the outcome, there is a third type of activity for managers: »*influencing*« (see *Figure 3-2*). In this sense, management also means having to ensure actively that the subordinate will actually enact the decision that was communicated to him or her. This entails activities such as setting special incentives in order to synchronize the objectives or monitoring the execution of the tasks which have been requested. On the other hand, monitoring

Influencing as a distinct management action

Fig. 3-2

Extended form of the management cycle

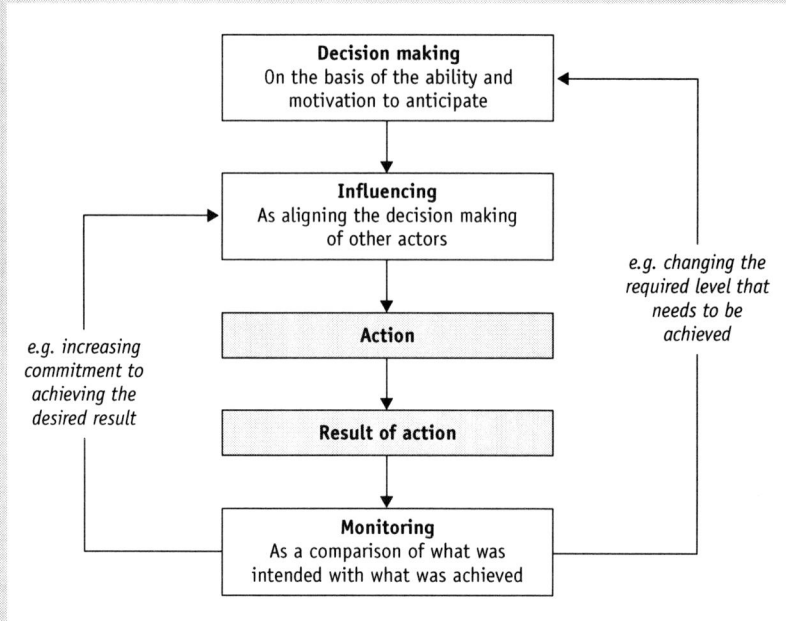

gains a new quality because the reasons for deviations also have to be looked for in the persons tasked with executing instructions. This makes monitoring more challenging because many reasons may be at work simultaneously whilst also interacting with one another: For instance, highly ambitious targets that exceed the subjectively perceived abilities of the actor who is meant to achieve them may lead to frustration, then to stress, and, in the case of continued excessive pressure, to resignation.

Summary
(see guiding questions 1 and 2)

▸ We understand management to mean constraining the degrees of freedom for other actions of management and execution.

▸ Management is a deliberate action carried out by individuals. It is based on cognitive abilities (perception, prediction and evaluation) and the individual's own motivation (utility function).

▸ In the basic model, decision making and monitoring work in combination. The execution of what was anticipated is interposed between decision making and monitoring.

▸ If several persons are involved in management and execution, influencing is added as a further management task.

3.2 Coordination mechanisms as patterns of management

Within business administration research, organization theory in particular has investigated interactions between various individuals. Here, *coordination* plays an important role as the *matching of information and activities between interdependent elements which are organizationally separated as a result of the division of labor.* Under the keyword »coordination mechanisms«, there exists a structural approach that is highly suited to providing an exact definition of coordination based on plans. We will therefore present this structure as a first step.

3.2.1 Coordination mechanisms: an overview

The six coordination mechanisms we would like to present are based on Kieser/ Walgenbach (2003, pp. 108–135) and are differentiated in the first instance by the *institutionalization of the means of coordination.* There are two forms of direct, personal coordination and three mechanisms based on impersonal means, which are therefore labeled »*technocratic*«. At a second level, personal forms of coordination are distinguished according to the direction of the communication flow (vertical vs. horizontal), whereas technocratic coordination specifies different levels of constraints on the coordinated persons' degrees of freedom. The remaining coordination mechanism of organizational culture is based on central norms and values being internalized, thereby shaping action.

Which coordination mechanisms can be identified?

The first type of person-oriented *coordination* is based on *personal instruction.* The coordination task is the duty of an individual manager in this case; he has to carry it out under his own responsibility, without using fixed specifications. The instructions issued can specify either the process of carrying out the task itself (e.g. specifying the use of a specific machine at a specific point in time) or the result that is to be achieved by carrying out the task (e.g. finishing a certain batch by time t) – we already came across this differentiation at the beginning of the chapter. Accordingly, it is either the process or the result of the action that is monitored. Coordination by means of personal instruction is a flexible, easy-to-use coordination mechanism (cf. Kieser/Walgenbach 2003, p. 109). However, a manager's cognitive abilities are not unlimited, which is why the manager may easily be overloaded as the management task becomes more complex, thereby causing a drop in the effectiveness of this coordination mechanism (cf. Kieser/Walgenbach 2003, p. 110). Coordination based on personal instruction may also come up against problems of acceptance by those being managed (who may reject »ad hoc« management activities).

Coordination based on personal instruction

The second basic form of person-oriented coordination views groups instead of individuals as being responsible for coordination. In *coordination based on mutual adjustment*, coordination takes place through group decisions that are binding for the group (cf. Kieser/Walgenbach 2003, p. 111). The coordination can determine either processes whereby something is implemented or the results/outcomes of such processes. The general benefits of coordination by mutual adjustment lie in the

Coordination based on mutual adjustment

greater acceptance of decisions, which increases motivation, and the possibility of reducing the negative effect of individual cognitive constraints by including several persons in the process. Correspondingly, coordination based on mutual adjustment tends to be found in areas of high knowledge deficits (for example, in research) – as mentioned earlier. Conversely, the weakness of the approach lies in the fact that more complex coordination tasks and larger groups make it more difficult to find solutions (cf. Schäffer 1996).

Coordination based on programs

The first of the three forms of technocratic coordination instruments, *coordination based on programs*, can be explained using the term »bureaucracy«. Here, the coordinated actions are determined in advance in respect of both their content and their process. They are then executed »as programmed« when needed (cf. Mintzberg 1996, p. 333). Monitoring focuses on whether or not the rules have been complied with and therefore analyzes the actions that constitute the process. The precondition for being able to use such a form of coordination is a stable environment; only then is it possible – and efficient – to analyze any potential coordination problems in advance and to formulate standards for solving them. Accordingly, coordination based on programs finds its limitations when the management task is too dynamic. Also, it no longer matches the self-image of many managers (»intrapreneurs«) very well.

Coordination based on plans

The second technocratic coordination mechanism is *coordination based on plans*. Plans constrain those tasked with carrying them out by defining binding goals; the achievement of these goals is then monitored. The process by which the goals are achieved is, however, not regulated or monitored – in contrast to coordination based on programs (cf. Kieser/Walgenbach 2003, p. 119). Plans are always tied to a specified time period, which is another difference as compared with program-based coordination; program rules apply permanently or until they are modified. As there are degrees of freedom remaining, coordination based on plans always has to be complemented and completed by other coordination forms. For instance, one often finds department heads or factory bosses in large enterprises who manage their areas just like the founder or managing director of a medium-sized company does. In this sense, plans only provide the framework. Like programs, plans make it necessary to have an analytical understanding of the coordination task, but owing to their limited period of applicability, they have to be adapted much more flexibly to changes in the organization's environment.

Coordination based on internal markets

Finally, the third technocratic form is *coordination based on internal markets*. Here, the coordination task is accomplished by the independent decisions taken by individual managers and the »invisible hand« of the market. Even when supply and demand are balanced efficiently by internal markets within companies, it is not necessary – in contrast to the mechanisms mentioned previously – for the market participants to pursue the same goals with reference to the products or services being traded. Therefore, coordination based on internal markets is very important in many decentralized large companies, where it takes the form of transfer prices.

Coordination based on organizational culture

The remaining mechanism, *coordination based on organizational culture*, starts with a basic assumption: »Members of an organization can coordinate their activities without external specifications to the degree that they have ›internalized‹ the same values and norms and identify with them« (Kieser/Walgenbach 2003, p. 129). The shared convictions then have a coordinating effect. However, it has to be taken into account that organizational culture cannot be »ordered by Monday«, but has to be

Fig. 3-3

Coordination mechanisms (source: Kieser/Walgenbach 2003, pp. 108–135)

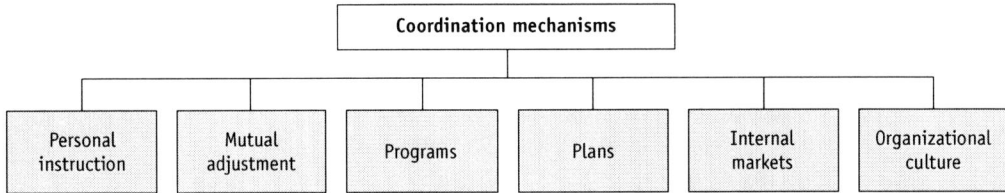

```
                        ┌──────────────────────────┐
                        │ Coordination mechanisms  │
                        └──────────────────────────┘
   ┌──────────┬──────────┬───────────┬──────────┬──────────┬──────────┐
┌────────┐┌────────┐┌─────────┐┌────────┐┌─────────┐┌──────────────┐
│Personal││ Mutual ││         ││        ││Internal ││Organizational│
│instruc-││adjust- ││Programs ││ Plans  ││ markets ││   culture    │
│  tion  ││ ment   ││         ││        ││         ││              │
└────────┘└────────┘└─────────┘└────────┘└─────────┘└──────────────┘
```

cultivated and developed over time. Furthermore, a strong culture may have a negative impact on the flexibility and adaptability of a company. In this way, this coordination mechanism, too, is subject to limitations.

3.2.2 Identifying coordination based on plans as management by objectives

When looking at the different coordination mechanisms described above, it is easy to see that coordination based on plans can be equated to »management by objectives«, which receives a lot of attention in practice: Plans are a formal instrument for formulating and communicating objectives. Management by objectives, just like coordination based on plans, means breaking down the objectives defined for a company by its owner(s) and other stakeholders in such a way across the different levels of hierarchy and organizational units that each local unit contributes to their achievement. Goals successively limit managers' degrees of freedom, from the executive board to the supervisor on site at the production facilities. At the same time, goals allow some leeway that individual managers have to fill with their own knowledge and under their own responsibility. Goals thereby only achieve a »basis« for coordination, which is the smaller the broader the goals are. For instance, only defining financial goals leaves much more freedom for action than simultaneously defining financial and non-financial goals, like when a business unit manager is given market share targets in addition to a required rate of return. Management by objectives is therefore a concept that can be implemented in very different ways. It can be used to contribute local management knowledge and local entrepreneurship, but it can also be used in a way that is very hierarchical and top-down.

Management by objectives can be implemented in distinct ways.

As mentioned in the previous section, coordination based on plans is never the only coordination mechanism used in a company. Instead, management reality is characterized by *the simultaneous co-existence of different coordination mechanisms*:

▸ *Coordination based on programs:*

Mention should be made here of rules resulting from legal regulations. Companies are enmeshed in a (tight) net of process requirements, from environmental protection requirements to accounting rules. In addition, companies also issue

Several coordination mechanisms are always used in conjunction.

various internal rules. For instance, a cost centre manager may not be allowed to commission investments on his own, and unit managers cannot just hire and fire staff as they wish.

▸ *Coordination based on mutual adjustment:*
As mentioned earlier, large knowledge deficits prevent concrete, clear specifications of objectives or processes. A strategic goal can, in this sense, only provide approximate direction, with intense discussions between many managers needed to increase precision.

▸ *Coordination based on personal instruction:*
Here, we see the coordination mechanism that generally strongly complements plans. The available degrees of freedom as defined by the objectives are filled in by the decisions of individual managers and their implementation. The degrees of freedom determine the relationship between the two coordination mechanisms.

▸ *Coordination based on internal markets*:
This coordination mechanism can supplement coordination based on plans whenever knowledge deficits prevent concrete, clear objectives or processes from being specified and when the motivating effect of decentralized entrepreneurship is to be used.

▸ *Coordination based on organizational culture*:
This coordination mechanism also supplements plans. On the one hand, elements of culture – such as mission statements – form an important point of departure for strategic planning, on the other hand, the guiding effect of organizational culture ideally kicks in wherever planning permits or creates decentralized leeway. But this also means that when a company relies to a large extent on

From the source

Extracts from the book »The Practice of Management« by Peter F. Drucker, in which he describes the idea of »management by objectives« for the first time:

»Any business enterprise must build a true team and weld individual efforts into a common effort. Each member of the enterprise contributes something different, but they must all contribute toward a common goal. Their efforts must all pull in the same direction, and their contributions must fit together to produce a whole – without gaps, without friction, without unnecessary duplication of effort. ...

Each manager, from the ›big boss‹ down to the production foreman or the chief clerk, needs clearly spelled-out objectives. These objectives should lay out what performance the man's own managerial unit is supposed to produce. They should lay out what contribution he and his unit are expected to make to help other units obtain their objectives. Finally, they should spell out what contribution the manager can expect from other units toward the attainment of his own objectives. Right from the start, in other words, emphasis should be on teamwork and team results.

These objectives should always derive from the goals of the business enterprise. In one company, I have found it practicable and effective to provide even a foreman with a detailed statement of not only his own objectives but those of the company and of the manufacturing department. Even though the company is so large as to make the distance between the individual foreman's production and the company's total output all but astronomical, the result has been a significant increase in production. Indeed, this must follow if we mean it when we say that the foreman is ›part of management‹. For it is the definition of a manager that in what he does he takes responsibility for the whole – that, in cutting stone – he ›builds the cathedral‹« (Drucker 1954, pp. 121 and 126–127).

organizational culture as a coordination mechanism, it has to limit the level of detail and intensity of coordination based on plans and create sufficient space for action.

With this, the management context – a key determinant of controllers' work and the function of controlling – has been sufficiently analyzed. At this stage in the discussion, it should already have become clear that coordination based on plans or management by objectives cannot be carried out in isolation. Instead, the interaction between individual coordination mechanisms has to be matched to the respective context and the respective situation of the company or business unit.

**Summary
(see guiding questions 3, 4 and 5)**

▸ Organization theory differentiates between various forms of coordination. A common structural approach distinguishes between personal instruction, mutual adjustment, programs, plans, internal markets within companies, and organizational culture as six basic types.

▸ Coordination based on plans and management by objectives characterize the context to which controlling is linked in practice.

▸ Coordination based on plans does not mean that no other coordination mechanisms are used. The degrees of freedom permitted by objectives are typically concretized through personal instruction and mutual adjustment in companies. This relationship determines controllers' work.

3.3 Goals and the process of defining them

Goals play a central role in coordination based on plans. They are (1) an expression of the owners' will (or the will of the capital markets), (2) a means of enforcing this decision on the different levels of the company's hierarchy, (3) an instrument for coordinating the large number of local managers and (4) a basis for organizational learning processes by means of measuring and monitoring the degree of goal achievement. When the wrong goals are set or goals are set in the wrong way, then the competitiveness of the company is very likely to suffer. Goals are therefore the central lever for adjusting the efficiency and effectiveness of management and have to be at the very focus of controllers' attention. We will be reviewing some questions of designing goals in the following, which are of a fundamental nature and therefore find a fitting place in an introductory chapter.

How can the right goals be defined in the right way?

3.3.1 Selecting goals

One of the first lessons learned by students of business administration is that profit maximization is the highest goal of any business activity. However, practice turns out to be somewhat more colorful. Companies strive to achieve a large number of goals simultaneously. On the one hand, as postulated by the stakeholder approach, companies have to serve different target groups (amongst others employees, investors etc.) simultaneously. On the other hand, a purely financial objective is often not sufficient because it cannot be operationalized and concretized sufficiently in

Financial targets on their own are often not enough for management …

response to special management questions. For instance, a financial calculation will usually not be able to tell you whether customer A's order should be processed before customer B's order – or the other way around. The financial effects are too vague. Competitive differentiation – to name another example – may be important for securing a market position, but it is hard to express in terms of »euros and cents«.

Furthermore, profit – as a periodical measure of success – is a lagging indicator in real-life use; it is therefore necessary to direct attention to leading indicators of performance, especially with respect to the strategic positioning of a company. This is underlined by the results of an empirical study in which the effects of logistics on success were analyzed (cf. Dehler 2001). Professional logistics assists in achieving a low logistics cost level on the one hand. On the other hand, it also makes it possible to satisfy customers' delivery requirements faster, more accurately and more flexibly (e.g. 24-hour deliveries, avoiding shortfalls). Upon analyzing the impact on success, it was found – not surprisingly – that lower costs directly improve a company's profitability. However, the by far greater part of the impact on success was derived from increased performance. This influenced the adaptability of the company to market changes, which in turn impacted market success (e.g. the relative market share), which finally affected profitability. Lower costs had no effect on adaptability or market success.

Thus, if managers and/or controllers orient their plans solely towards financial dimensions, there is a great danger that the »really important« levers will be neglected: »What gets measured gets done«. Limiting planning to the financial dimension is nowadays increasingly perceived as not matching the needs of today's extremely dynamic environment. Other goal dimensions have to be taken into consideration in addition to financial objectives, as is the case, for example, in the Balanced Scorecard.

... but there should not be too many goals being used in parallel either.

However, psychological studies show that the number of goals that can be pursued in parallel has a strict upper limit. For instance, a frequently-mentioned figure in the literature is that a »normal person« is not capable of evaluating and comparing more than five to seven goals at the same time (cf. Miller 1956). Insofar, the question for controllers is not only which goals are useful for managing a company, but also how many. Limiting the number is just as necessary as checking critically whether goal dimensions have to be substituted over time in order to avoid neglecting other aspects which were previously not taken into account.

3.3.2 Methods for determining goals

Apart from the question of which goals planning should be based on, one also has to decide on which basis to determine the quantitative level of each goal. Here, (at least) four alternatives can be differentiated in theory.

Historical values

Historical values are often preferred when defining goals (»building on experience«).

The most obvious – and easiest – approach for deriving goals is to check what happened in the past. If one managed not to exceed a certain cost level in the past year, there is good reason to assume that one will be able to do the same in the current year. When one considers the costs of a bookkeeper or the travel budget of a business unit's management staff, the plausibility of such an approach becomes apparent. If goals are generally derived from historical values, a functioning cooperation of all positions in the company should be expected. However, there are also at least two significant objections to be raised:

▸ In turbulent times, the past is a poor predictor of the future. The previous period's profits can quickly turn into losses when the competitive or general business environment changes.

▸ The fact that a target was achieved in the past does not tell you anything about whether it had the right value. It may well be that loafing is simply extrapolated. For instance, the costs of the bookkeeper mentioned above could be completely exaggerated. As a rule, the person or unit defining the goals does not have the knowledge needed to make such an assessment. If anybody at all has it, it would be the person or unit tasked with achieving the goal: From the point of view of managing behavior, such a person or unit would be in a very comfortable position.

Historical values are often problematic in today's turbulent times.

Incentive issues and the fact that historical values quickly become outdated mean that they are suitable as a basis for targets only in exceptional situations in today's competitive environment. If one does decide to use them – for instance, in order to reduce the cost of the target-setting process – then it is the duty of the controller to question the efficiency or effectiveness level very critically in order to address at least a part of the problem of influencing behavior.

Forecast values

The first of the two problems of goals defined on the basis of past values can be significantly reduced by basing the goals on explicit forecasts. This method of derivation can be seen in standard costing. Here, production and cost functions are the basis which permits planning on the grounds of the dependent variable »activity«, which in turn is fed from other planning processes (especially sales planning). If there is a carefully developed basis for forecasting – such as a cost function based on detailed, technical analyses of the achievable level of input factor consumption – the forecast values may be of high quality. When making reference to functional relationships which also formed the basis for the previous year's planning, such an approach also makes it likely that the various partial planning processes again will match.

Both benefits have to be weighed against the costs of making the forecast. Introducing standard costing – in keeping with the example – is expensive. Having constantly to update the underlying forecast functions also causes high additional costs. If this adjustment is not made, the quality of the forecast is reduced. At the same time, forecast values create a false impression of efficiency and effectiveness and can thereby help prevent or handicap necessary improvements. In many companies, controllers should therefore question the quality of their standard costing systems – it will often be worth it.

Finally, from the perspective of incentivization, forecast values are suitable when the person or unit defining the targets knows enough about the forecast function. In the case of standard costing, this often used to be ensured by consultants, who were commissioned by the person or unit to determine the planned cost functions. If

Identifying valid forecast values depends on having a high level of knowledge.

it is only the person receiving the goals who has the necessary forecast knowledge, then rationality deficits are very likely. In this case, the person or unit setting the goals has almost no possibility of arguing against the »professional« forecast basis. In such a case, controllers are also quite powerless.

Basing target values on forecasts is an approach very often chosen in practice. The resulting plans are correspondingly complex and detailed. Controllers can find a wide range of tasks here, as described briefly in chapter 1. Currently, however, the limits of this approach are becoming apparent: The degree of internal changes (e.g. technological transformation) and external changes (e.g. competitive turbulences) has in many cases reached such a pitch that complex forecasting systems are becoming too slow and inflexible, as well as requiring too much effort to be adapted. This provides a bridge to the next two possibilities of defining target values.

Forecast values also suffer from weaknesses and may have side-effects.

Benchmarks

Both of the possibilities presented so far work from an internal perspective: Both extrapolating historical values and deriving targets from forecast functions relate to the internal status quo. External information is only included for the purposes of defining parameters (e.g. factor prices) or variables (e.g. planned sales volumes). Such an approach may have the effect of causing »blindness« to developments in the environment. For instance, in the past companies were often proud of productivity gains of a couple of percentage points per year – even while competitors with substantially larger gains in efficiency started appearing in the course of globalization. Strictly speaking, directing one's attention inwards presupposes that learning from the external environment is not necessary. The lacking willingness to learn systematically from the experiences of others becomes apparent when looking at the instrument of interfirm comparison (»Betriebsvergleich«, cf., for instance, Schnettler 1951). Even though such comparisons were fundamentally suitable for learning from the experiences of others, they usually degenerated in practice to trying to find reasons for the differences that were identified instead of learning from them.

Using external data for comparison means learning from others.

In recent years, a clear change of awareness has occurred in this area. It is based on benchmarking, through which companies are increasingly trying to use the experiences of others in defining their own goals. These may be from the same industry (»best in class«) or from companies that are particularly good at specific functions (e.g. invoicing in a telecommunications company as a model for invoicing in a manufacturing company). All markets are potentially valuable as suppliers of information, capital markets included.

Benchmarks are very common in practice nowadays.

Benchmarks show at which level the competition is operating. Reaching the level of the best competitors improves or creates competitiveness. Benchmarks therefore have a high level of plausibility for setting goals. Also, being able to say that others have achieved this goal level makes it easier to motivate people to strive for the goal. Finally, overcoming the pure inward focus of an organization is a considerable benefit in itself. It creates a new, additional perspective even for areas which usually do not have market exposure.

Benchmarks show »how high one has to aim« in relation to the competition.

Problems result from the limited content-based and time-based comparability of companies; it means that benchmarks first have to be made comparable in both respects. Content-based comparability is given when the benchmarks used (cf. Weber/Linder/Hirsch 2004, p. 69)

- refer to the same object of analysis,
- are available at the same level of aggregation (for instance, related to the relevant market or customer segment),
- are characterized by the same degree of accuracy and
- the context does not exert any one-sided, benchmark- or competitor-specific influences on the reference values (e.g. competitive advantages because of market dominance, lobbying activities by competitors, specific risks based on certain investors' wishes, specific social security systems etc.).

Time-based comparability means that the points or periods in time when the data is gathered have to correspond closely to one another. Ensuring such content- and time-based comparability often causes significant costs. Both the systematic generation of benchmarks and ensuring that the values are comparable are key areas of activity for controllers.

Normatively defined level of goals

The final alternative to be described here consists of defining goal levels normatively. This approach makes sense when the other three alternatives fail: For instance, for »new economy« companies, there was often no role model in the past or in other markets, nor was there any reasonable way to forecast values. Therefore, anyone seeking money from investors had to determine normatively where the company should aim to be in the future. The initial growth spurt of Internet companies clearly showed the perils involved in creating goals »out of thin air«.

On the other hand, goals that are normatively set are justified when their aim is to motivate employees to make a special effort, such as when they are used as visions. One well-known example is Kennedy's goal of having Americans walk on the moon before the Russians. The success of this approach depends on the authority's powers of persuasion as well as the fundamental achievability of the goal. However, visions may easily fail, and visionaries often turn out to be charlatans. For these reasons, controllers should always maintain a critical distance from goals that have been normatively set; it is (very) likely that rationality deficits will occur here.

When can normative goals be recommended?

Upon analyzing management practice, one will usually find a combination of these different approaches. In spite of all caution concerning generalizing statements, it is safe to say that there is currently a trend away from forecast values and towards benchmarks. Companies are thereby reacting to the significant acceleration of business life.

3.3.3 Relationships between goals

Usually, goals cannot be defined independently from one another. There are usually interdependencies between goals at the same level and goals at other levels. Goals may impede (competitive situation) or complement each other. At the level of the company as a whole, one example of such a »classical« conflict is that between profit maximization on the one hand and minimizing environmental impact on the other hand. The achievement of environmental goals is only partially rewarded by the

Companies usually do not limit themselves to just a single way of defining goals.

Goals do not always act together in a complementary fashion – they may also compete against each other.

market (for instance, as a buying preference for products manufactured in a way that protects the environment). One example of complementary goals is improving product quality because this both increases customer satisfaction and reduces the costs of warrantees.

Linkages between goals are discussed in the literature under various keywords (e.g. network effects, synergies, coupled production or interdependencies). In a first step, such linkages between operational goals (and therefore processes) can be traced back to three central groups of causes: interdependencies in procurement, production and sales (cf. Weber 1996a, col. 2144).

The interdependencies between goals can have various causes.

Interdependencies in procurement may emerge when the purchase prices of two products P_A and P_B are linked. For instance, when buying two products from a single supplier or manufacturer, a bigger discount can be obtained (keyword: market power) than if the products are procured from different suppliers (in which case the volume would be smaller for each supplier and therefore economically less significant).

Interdependencies in production, on the other hand, result from process interdependencies or restrictions. Let us take a look at two products, »shortbread« and »coconut macaroons«. A lot of yolk is needed to make shortbread, but no egg-white, whereas egg-white is specifically required to make coconut macaroons. This means that the two are economically linked: The production of shortbread can only be increased if the coconut macaroon production volume is also increased (provided that it is desirable not to waste the excess egg-white). Furthermore, in keeping with the example, there are production interdependencies between the two products with relation to usage of the baking plant. This is constrained by its maximum capacity, so that producing more of one type of cookie is only possible if fewer of the other cookies are produced (assuming no new investments are made to expand capacity).

Interdependencies in sales may exist on the side of consumers or sellers. One very well-known interdependency in sales is the so-called »loss leader«. This is a product – for example, an inkjet printer – which is sold at a loss or at the breakeven price under the assumption that it will enable or boost the sales of a different, extremely profitable product made by the company – such as printer cartridges. If sales-based interdependencies are not taken into consideration when defining profit goals, such a sales strategy cannot be devised or implemented.

The more pronounced such effects become, the less goals can be defined in isolation from one another as this would lead to suboptimal solutions from the perspective of the entire company. In organization theory, this aspect is debated intensely in the context of the benefits and disadvantages of decentralizing decisions. Controllers deal with the issue in many different contexts. These begin in companies at the point where the basic control logic (i.e. integrated group of companies, strategic holding or financial holding) is decided upon and extends from the design of the budgeting system to the setting of transfer prices for products and services exchanged between business units.

3.3.4 Motivational effects of goals

In designing management by objectives, a further important aspect to be considered is how goals affect the behavior of individuals. This aspect is of special importance for influencing. Behavioral researchers have been investigating it for a long time and from many different points of view. But as this is an introduction, we will only refer to a single, though commonly used, approach: goal setting theory by Locke/Latham 1990. This is based on a study carried out by Locke in 1968 and describes how goals should be designed in order to achieve the maximum degree of motivation towards achieving the goal (cf. also Locke/Latham 1984, p. X). As shown by Locke's »classical« studies in 1968, this will to achieve a goal depends on four basic factors: (1) the difficulty of the goal, (2) the acceptance of the goal on the part of the actor, (3) the specificity of the goal, and (4) the commitment to the goal (cf. Locke 1968; Latham/Locke 1991). These four factors will also be used to structure the following paragraphs.

Goal setting theory according to Locke/ Latham

From the source

Excerpts from »Goal Setting – A Motivational Technique That Works« by Gary Latham and Edwin Locke:

»The problem of how to motivate employees has puzzled and frustrated managers for generations. One reason the problem has seemed difficult, if not mysterious, is that motivation ultimately comes from within the individual and therefore cannot be observed directly. Moreover, most managers are not in a position to change an employee's basic personality structure. The best they can do is try to use incentives to direct the energies of their employees toward organizational objectives.

Money is obviously the primary incentive, since without it few if any employees would come to work. But money alone is not always enough to motivate high performance. Other incentives, such as participation in decision making, job enrichment, behavior modification, and organization development, have been tried with varying degrees of success. A large number of research studies have shown, however, that one very straightforward technique – goal setting – is probably not only more effective than alternative methods, but may be the major mechanism by which these other incentives affect motivation. For example, a recent experiment on job enrichment demonstrated that unless employees in enriched jobs set higher, more specific goals than do those with unenriched jobs, job enrichment has absolutely no effect on

productivity. Even money has been found most effective as a motivator when the bonuses offered are made contingent on attaining specific objectives. ...

We believe that goal setting is a simple, straightforward, and highly effective technique for motivating employee performance. ... However, goal setting is no panacea. It will not compensate for underpayment of employees or for poor management. Used incorrectly, goal setting may cause rather than solve problems. If, for example, the goals set are unfair, arbitrary, or unreachable, dissatisfaction and poor performance may result. If difficult goals are set without proper quality controls, quantity may be achieved at the expense of quality. If pressure for immediate results is exerted without regard to how they are attained, short-term improvement may occur at the expense of long-run profits. That is, such pressure often triggers the use of expedient and ultimately costly methods – such as dishonesty, high-pressure tactics, postponing of maintenance expenses, and so on – to attain immediate results. Furthermore, performance goals are more easily set in some areas than in others. It's all too easy, for example, to concentrate on setting readily measured production goals and ignore employee development goals. Like any other management tool, goal setting works only when combined with good managerial judgment« (Latham/Locke 1979, pp. 68 and 80).

3.3.4.1 Motivational effect of goal difficulty

It is a matter of common sense only to accept goals which can realistically be achieved if sufficient effort is expended. Raising the level may have a demotivating effect, just as excessively unambitious goals are not motivating at all. This relationship has been investigated experimentally and empirically in various studies on the optimal level of difficulty in the context of plans. The following schematic statements can be made when differentiating between the aspiration level of the person responsible for carrying out the task (as a self-selected performance goal), the level of performance actually achieved and the level expected (cf. e.g. Höller 1978, pp. 121–123):

▸ During a phase of low expected levels, these are below the person's aspiration level. Based on the person's low motivation, the actual performance will not even meet the level of aspiration. This phase ends when the expected level reaches the aspiration level. This is where aspiration, the expected level and actual performance coincide.

▸ During a phase of high expected levels, the aspiration level increases, but cannot keep up with the pace at which the expected level increases. The same applies for the performance level, which once again falls back behind the aspiration level. The entire phase is characterized by increasing stress on the person, which acts, however, as a positive motivation. The phase ends at the so-called »point of demoralization«, at which the incentive reverses itself completely.

▸ The following phase, during which the expected level continues to increase until it is (much) too high, is characterized by a rapid fall in the aspiration level as well as the performance level achieved.

The motivational effects of goals can easily be reversed to cause demotivation.

Differentiating between aspiration level, performance level and required levels

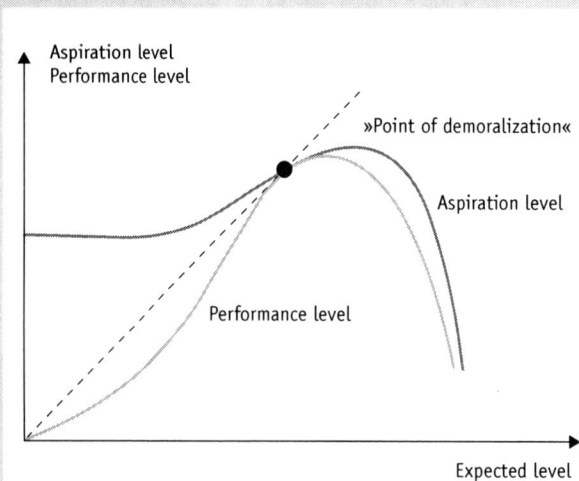

Fig. 3-4

**Motivational effects of the goal level
(source: adapted from Höller 1978, pp. 118–123)**

Aspiration level
Performance level

»Point of demoralization«

Aspiration level

Performance level

Expected level

Several factors influence this relationship. The distinction between success-seekers and failure-avoiders is especially important in this respect (cf. e.g. Wiswede 2007, pp. 65–66). The former prefer activities with a medium level of difficulty, whereas the latter tend to choose very easy or very hard tasks. This phenomenon is explained as follows: Success-oriented people assess their own performance capacity realistically, whereas those who try to avoid failure are moved by their insecurity to prefer very easy tasks, which can definitely be achieved, or very hard tasks, which are almost certainly impossible to achieve, in which case not reaching the goal can easily be explained on the basis of external factors. Based on this observation, one may assume that success-oriented people can be motivated to perform at a higher level by increased

Differentiating between managers who seek success and those who avoid failure

goal levels, as long as the requirements are not excessively hard to achieve. Those avoiding failure, however, are likely not be greatly influenced by variations in the levels of requirements.

3.3.4.2 Motivational effect of goal acceptance

Goal acceptance describes to which degree the subjects accept goals set by their superiors or defined participatively as their own. It is immediately plausible that an employee will dedicate much less effort to achieving a goal that he does not accept (in other words, that he does not view as »his own«). This feeling – which almost everybody has experienced at some stage or another – can be explained through the *locus of control* concept. It describes the perception people have of their ability to shape events and their own environment. They may either believe that they are »masters of their own destiny« in their actions, in other words, that they are able to reach a goal »by their own devices« (internal locus of control); or they may be under the impression that they have no influence on the outcomes of their actions, being subject to influences »from the outside« instead (external locus of control) (cf. Wiswede 2007, pp. 87–88 and 116). If goals are imposed upon someone externally and/or without making use of employees' specific context knowledge, they may come to believe that their ability to achieve the goals will be strongly affected by external influences not taken into consideration when they were defined (external locus of control). If one follows expectancy theory according to Vroom 1964 or one of its current versions, the motivational strength of a goal, the achievement of which appears not to be subject to one's own control, is lower than that of a (comparable) goal where the achievement of the goal can be influenced. In other words, if the goal-setting process allows employees to contribute their own knowl- edge and thereby decrease the perceived »success risk« resulting from external factors, this favors an internal locus of control, which leads to a higher degree of goal acceptance and thereby to more effort being invested. This is also the reason why companies usually rely on goals which are mutually agreed upon or which are defined in participative processes (for a critical discussion on the pros and cons of participation, cf. Macintosh 2003).

> Generally, people are more motivated by goals they set themselves than by goals set by others.

Similarly, just as goals defined in participative processes tend to be more easily accepted (and thereby pursued with greater enthusiasm and commitment), so too do relative goals, oriented towards benchmarks, achieve greater acceptance than abso- lute, normatively defined or internally oriented goals. In contrast to absolute goals, relative goals are characterized by the fact that they remove shared environmental uncertainties from the affected individuals and transfer them to the organization as a whole: Employees are only responsible for their actions. External effects which cannot be influenced (such as market and exchange rate changes) are mitigated by the relative nature of the goals. In consequence, we may conclude for relative goals that they are more likely to contribute to an internal locus of control and will thereby, all else being equal, tend to be accepted more easily by those involved. Therefore, they can be expected to unfold a stronger motivational effect than absolute goals (cf. Weber/Linder/Hirsch 2004, p. 67). Following this line of thought, relative goals oriented towards benchmarks are recommended in the current discussion on the rede- sign of operational planning as a proposed solution for improving operational planning from the perspective of motivation (for more detail, cf. Weber/Linder/Hirsch 2004).

> Relative goals are said to have a stronger motivational effect than absolute goals.

3.3.4.3 Motivational effect of goal specificity

Clearly defined goals avoid demotivation as a result of misunderstandings and limit opportunistic behavior.

The more clearly goals are formulated, the lower the risk of misunderstandings (cf. Locke/Latham 1984, p. 20), and the less those being managed feel that they might disappoint the expectations others have of them. A lacking degree of precision therefore carries the risk of low motivation and also leaves leeway that can be opportunistically exploited and lead to unsatisfactory performance.

This brings us to one of the core tasks of controllers. They are responsible for ensuring that goals are sufficiently operationalized; general postulates (»We will be the most innovative company on the market«) are not really helpful because they are very much open to subjective interpretation. Controllers have to make sure that specific goals are operationalized in the same way throughout the organization. One business unit's sales targets are not automatically defined the same way as another's. Considering non-financial goals (such as service level or customer satisfaction), heterogeneous definitions are the rule, not the exception, in practice. Finally, controllers have to ensure that goal levels are not manipulated, be it through conscious falsifications of measurements, by changing the measured quantity or through measures which lead to other results in the short term without being materially sustainable. Issuing invoices at the end of the financial year and then canceling them at the beginning of the next year boosts sales on the books, but nowhere else, and even there only for a short time.

3.3.4.4 Motivational effect of goal commitment

Goals which are not linked to any consequences are usually not very helpful.

According to expectancy theory, the motivational strength of a goal, the achievement of which is not linked to appropriate incentives or suitable utility for the employees, is lower than that of a (comparable) goal where the utility derived is high. Accordingly, it makes little sense to set goals without obtaining commitment to the goal or providing incentives to achieving it: If no consequences result from achieving or not achieving a given goal, it is very likely that this lack will be interpreted to mean that the goal is not important and that its realization can be neglected.

Conversely, we are confronted with the problem that goals can rarely be defined in such a way that they can be achieved in every case if the person responsible for them just makes the right effort. Often, there is environmental uncertainty; often, achieving one's own goals (such as profit goals for a product division manager) depends on the efforts of others in the company (e.g. on successful wage negotiations or meeting product development deadlines). Excessive goal commitment (e.g. by creating direct links between incentives/penalties and the outcomes of actions) may therefore lead employees to act in dysfunctional ways from the company's perspective. For instance, they might manipulate performance indicators, documents and invoicing dates in order to achieve their goals after all and avoid the negative consequences of failing to meet them. Controllers come across this dilemma of incentive coupling in most companies. It positively impacts commitment to a goal from the company's perspective, but may also lead to dysfunctional behavior.

Managers are often given a mix of goals, which they can only influence to a limited degree.

Therefore, »mixed approaches« are often selected in practice, where managers are rewarded in two ways: on the one hand, for achieving goals in their area of responsibility (e.g. keeping within a cost budget), on the other hand, for achieving higher-level goals (such as a business unit's profits). Compared with an exclusive focus on higher-level goals, which can only be influenced to a limited degree, this mixture of goals reduces the risk of missing a goal for the person responsible. In the case of a business unit manager, this could mean that her variable pay consists of three components: achieving personal goals (e.g. successfully concluding a training course), achieving the business unit's targets (e.g. a certain increase in value) and the company's goals (e.g. increasing the company's value overall). Whereas achieving the first goal depends to a large degree on her own actions, success or failure are determined partly »from the outside« for the second and even more for the third goal.

The problems just described generate tasks for controllers at the stage of formulating goals as well as at the stage of monitoring goals. Regarding the former, the requirement is to take into account how much a goal can be influenced when setting it. In the context of monitoring goals, the controller's task during variance analyses is to filter external influences on goal achievement from the variance. This is necessary for determining which share of goal achievement can be attributed to the actions of the person responsible for the goal and which share should be ascribed to other influences, be they positive or negative. However, the corresponding causes cannot always be clearly identified. This is the case especially for team efforts (e.g. when a project group develops or launches a new product), where the individual contribution to success or failure is often hard to determine. In such cases, there is a risk that the person being monitored succumbs to the temptations of »free-riding« or »social loafing« (for more detail on the following, cf. Weber/Linder/Spillecke 2003, p. 119):

▸ The concept of »*free-riding*« analyzes group effort as a so-called public good. Producing an outcome is associated with costs (»effort aversion«) for individual members of the group or team. But as it is assumed that it is impossible or exceedingly difficult to exclude group members from the benefits or use of the »public good« (e.g. the reputation of a successful company), there is an incentive for individual employees to reduce their own contribution while still benefiting from the »public good«.

»Free riding« and »social loafing« should be avoided if at all possible.

▸ »*Social loafing*« describes a situation where a group member's willingness to contribute his or her effort to the group's goals declines with increasing group size (cf. Schäffer 2001, p. 99). In this way, the transfer of individual incentive design to a design incorporating a company's overall profits may mean that an individual's contribution is all but impossible to identify or may even simply be lost. Both factors are detrimental to individual employees' levels of effort in the medium term.

In order to assess the likelihood of such behavior, which is dysfunctional from the perspective of the company, controllers need to know individual persons, their attitudes, abilities and behavioral history – in addition to the usual data and figures.

Summary
(see guiding question 6)

▸ The effectiveness and efficiency of coordination based on plans depends to a large extent on being able to define appropriate goals at appropriate levels for all management units of the company.
▸ Companies focus mainly on financial goals. These are, however, being complemented more and more by non-financial goals (e.g. rate of innovation, service level or customer satisfaction).
▸ There are different possibilities for determining the right goal level. Currently, benchmarks are gaining increasing importance.
▸ When defining goals, not only the characteristics of the goals have to be taken into consideration. As goals are meant to influence behavior, motivational effects also have to be taken into account.

3.4 Summary

As shown in the first two chapters, controllers are found in only one management context in practice, which can be described as coordination based on plans or management by objectives. This type of management is characterized by a multistage definition of goals, which specifies the financial and non-financial goals individuals have to achieve at different levels of the organization, but which allows them to choose how to achieve the goals. Such degrees of freedom are then primarily defined by personal instruction and mutual adjustment, accompanied by some general rules.

The requirements of this specific coordination mechanism – »plans« – determine controllers' tasks. They play an essential role in determining which types of goals are specified, and how many. They manage the process by which goals are defined. They are involved in determining goal levels, be it in a preparatory role by breaking down top management goals to other hierarchical levels, be it as critical counterparts when they analyze and question the suitability of suggested goals. They measure the level of goal achievement and thereby create transparency about any action that may potentially be required from those responsible for achieving the goals. They monitor goal achievement, analyze variances and initiate corrective measures. They collect experiences from the goal achievement process and feed these forward to the next round of goal definition. To summarize: Controllers support management in assuring management rationality and thereby play a central role in assuring the effectiveness and efficiency of coordination based on plans. If other coordination mechanisms dominate, the management task focuses on completely other areas. In this case, controllers with their specific set of tasks are not needed.

Management by objectives is a complex task for managers; here, controllers can help in many ways.

Recommended reading ...

... The management cycle
Hahn/Hungenberg 2001, pp. 32–38
Weber/Brettel/Schäffer 1996

... Coordination mechanisms as patterns of management
Kieser/Walgenbach 2003, pp. 108–135
Schäffer 1996, pp. 62–80
Weber 2003

... Goals and the process of defining them
Heinen 1966
Locke/Latham 1990
Locke/Latham 2002
Weber/Linder/Hirsch 2004
Welge/Al-Laham 2003, pp. 111–121

4 How to design controller units

Guiding questions:

1 What do the expressions »controller unit« and »design« mean exactly?

2 What determines the chances of actively influencing the design of a controller unit?

3 Assigning tasks to persons or positions is one of the original problems of organization. What is the problem's basic structure? Which special aspects result from the specific, heterogeneous tasks of controllers?

4 How can one ensure that controllers do not abuse their role? Who monitors the controller?

As before, we will be approaching the key topic step by step. Chapter 4 serves as an introduction that deals in general terms with the question of how to design controller units. Chapter 5, the final chapter, will deal with concrete design questions.

4.1 Terminological basics

In chapter 1, we carefully separated the expressions controller, controllership and controlling from one another. One of the main aims was to clarify the relationships between controllers – the persons carrying out the task – and controlling – the task they carry out. The terminological understanding thus created brings us to a new, somewhat inelegant expression in this chapter: the controller unit. It is hardly used in practice. As noted in the first chapter, companies almost always speak of »our controlling« when speaking of the controllers who work there. In literature, too, the expression is rarely found and not used uniformly – this comes as no surprise at this stage (for instance, cf. Mosiek 2002, p. 1; Horváth 2006, pp. 799–886). In this introduction, we will be following the definition provided by David (2005, p. 12), who defines the term controller unit to mean »that organizational unit within a company which encompasses the employees whose job title is ›controller‹, in other words, all employees organized in a ›controlling‹ department«. There are almost always several such departments in large companies; at the very least, one will find a unit at headquarters and various local units, which may have been formed for specific functions and/or divisions. All such controller sub-units work together within the company; however, sometimes they also compete against one another, as will be shown in greater detail in chapter 5.

> Controller unit is the term we use to describe what in practice is usually referred to as »our controlling«.

We will use the expression »design« to cover all questions dealing with the fundamental orientation of the controller unit. These begin with a question which may at first glance appear somewhat counterintuitive, namely: Do controllers even have any influence on the design of their units? Controller units are part of the hierarchical order of a company and are therefore placed in the organization by management. It is therefore not obvious that controller units should have any influence on their own design. However, the arguments presented below show that they do have some influence (within limits). The following steps will therefore deal with the strategic positioning of the controller unit and with measures for implementing specific strategies. Finally, design also encompasses the way in which controller positions are organized. These elements make up the last two chapters of the book.

Summary
(see guiding question 1)

▸ Controllers usually work in dedicated departments or units in companies. These will be termed »controller units« in the following.

▸ It is assumed that controller units are able to define their tasks and implementation methods actively – within certain limits.

4.2 On the freedom to take design decisions

As indicated, the following discussion is based on the understanding that controllers are generally able to design their tasks actively. This assumption is first explained. Next, two specific framework conditions are discussed which limit the degree of design autonomy: On the one hand, from the perspective of contingency theory, there are internal and external environmental factors influencing the controller unit. On the other hand, we want to link back to some ideas that have been mentioned at various points in the book: The way in which controlling is set up functionally and institutionally within a company depends not only on the work that needs to be done, but also on the development status of the idea of controlling and the controller unit itself in the specific company. For this, we postulate a certain model of development, which concludes section 4.2.

4.2.1 Designing the controller unit: between autonomy and heteronomy

The tasks of controllers are determined by the hierarchy – but they can be influenced by controllers.

Controllers provide management support. To this end, positions are created in the company's hierarchy. Managers determine their type, size and position in the organization. This, the possibility of assigning the many different tasks in a company to the various positions in a coordinated, integrated fashion, is one of the key benefits of hierarchical coordination. However, realizing this benefit requires appropriate knowledge of tasks and persons. This quickly becomes a limiting factor as complexity and dynamism increase (see the sections on coordination mechanisms in chapter 3 of the book). Insofar, there have been efforts for a considerable period of time aimed at transferring market patterns and behavior to internal departments (»internal competition«). From this perspective, controllers offer services to management which they are able to influence to a large extent in respect of design and scope.

4.2.1.1 »Role taking« versus »role making«

There are two contrary perspectives on the question of whether controllers have the authority to design their own tasks (cf. Kronast 1989, pp. 194–196). The expressions describing the perspectives derive from role theory, an area of research in psychology (on role theory, cf. Katz/Kahn 1978).

From the »role taking« perspective, the controller unit accepts the management support tasks allocated to it by management without contributing to questions of design and implementation. Management defines the requirements and allocates sets of tasks to business units and »management support providers«. In the extreme case, the controller unit has no possibilities at all of influencing the process. This perspective corresponds to the classical view of organizations as hierarchies. The executive management level divides and delegates the tasks, which the delegated positions then carry out. In the ideal case, tasks can be divided in such a way that there is no overlap between the tasks of individual actors. Nevertheless, it will not be possible to avoid certain dependencies. In this case, the individual units should ideally cooperate harmoniously with one another in terms of the company. This perspective usually does not take into consideration opportunistic behavior and »silo mentality«. All units follow a consistent goal function which corresponds to the company's objectives. This enables specialization and the division of labor, both of which lead to efficiency advantages.

»Role taking« – controllers do what management tells them to do.

The second perspective is the opposite of the first: It is described as »role making«. According to this viewpoint, it is up to the controller unit itself to define its role and services in the context of management support. In the extreme case, there is absolute freedom to act, limited merely by an approximate specification of an area of work entailing »management support« that provides services and assures rationality. This perspective corresponds to coordination based on internal markets. Each market participant is free to choose which services he or she supplies or demands. There is no hierarchical instruction; services are offered at market prices and satisfy a corresponding demand. Several suppliers produce the same service and therefore compete with one another. Such competition is generally positive for consumers: Competition is a key indicator for the performance of markets. The goals of the different market participants do not have to be the same – they may even be in conflict with each other. Competitive behavior takes the place of »harmonious« cooperation.

»Role making« – controllers determine most of their tasks themselves.

There is no general answer to the question of »role taking« versus »role making«; it can only be answered on a case-by-case basis for each company. Still, one may observe a clear positioning that holds true empirically across companies (cf. Weber et al. 2006, pp. 46–47; Weber 2008, pp. 148–150): Controllers no longer merely play the role of »role takers« because most companies are no longer pure, centralized hierarchies, but rather grant considerable leeway to departments and business units. Within certain limits, controllers are able to define task focus areas and roles autonomously. Depending on the degree of autonomy in the company, they are able to design their »playing field« under their own responsibility. In this way, they enter into competition with other departments and try to enforce their own interests – (hopefully) to the benefit of the company as a whole.

Such competition is reflected in corresponding behavior, for instance when the goal is to obtain the attention of top management, to further one's career or when competing for important new projects or areas of responsibility. Competition may also be generated around human, financial or other resources. Controllers correspondingly try to realize their ideas, to manage projects that appear to be particularly relevant, to place staff from their own unit in important positions and to recruit excellent employees – and are also prepared to engage in conflicts with other areas (»We are the ones compiling the management report, not accounting!«).

However, controllers cannot be »role makers« exclusively. Hierarchies and the principle of cooperation remain dominant in companies: Which CFO would voluntarily give up the responsibility of defining the cornerstones of the relationship between »his« controlling unit and »his« accounting department? There are always directives governing which unit has to carry out which tasks. Within each company, there is also an organically grown image of controllers, and subsequently a basic understanding regarding how controllers should work with managers and how they should work with departments. In this sense, the role of controllers is determined without their input, as »role taking«. From the perspective of controllers, defining their activities takes place between the two extremes: Both »role taking« and »role making« are relevant.

> For controllers, the »role making« and »role taking« perspectives are of equal relevance.

4.2.1.2 »Role making« as a current priority

In this book, we decided to concentrate on the perspective of »role making«, even though it is unfamiliar and has been much-neglected up to now. We view controllers as »entrepreneurs in the area of management services« within the company, as service providers who are willing and able to influence their surroundings, who are obliged to take the initiative especially when it comes to supplementary and constraining tasks, who may not and cannot wait for a manager to request or demand their services. We will maintain this »bias« in the concluding chapters of the book as well. In section 2 of chapter 5, we will show in detail how the controller unit can position itself strategically, taking into consideration its customers and competitors, and how it should define its own role in order to ensure optimum management support. The outcomes of such considerations are concrete strategies as well as a consistent vision and mission for controllers.

This perspective results from changes in the environment of the controller units. Controllers no longer monopolize the services they offer within companies; there are more and more overlaps; internal competitors are appearing and becoming increasingly active. This applies for »less interesting«, routine processes (e.g. monthly information updates) as well as for occasional, »advanced« support services (e.g. business consulting to a manager).

> Controllers are not the only providers of services to management.

Figure 4-1 provides an overview of potential internal competitors of controllers. With regard to routine information supply processes, for instance, financial accounting is taking over ever more basic services. The internationalization of accounting means that many companies no longer have a separate set of books for cost accounting. Internal control, too, is often based solely on financial data to which slight adjustments have been made, and publishing quarterly results is becoming obligatory. In this way, financial accounting and its data are becoming more and more important for internal control – often at the expense of the data traditionally provided by controlling. It is questionable whether controllers will be able to provide sufficient management support without »their basis«, namely cost accounting and financial statements.

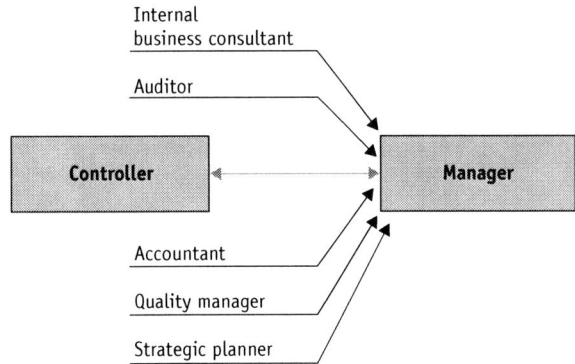

Fig. 4-1

Overview of important internal competitors of controllers (source: Weber/David/Prenzler 2001, p. 10)

The withdrawal from routine processes does offer controllers the opportunity of gaining a foothold in the area of internal consulting; at the same time, however, it increases the risk that they will lose the quantitative information base they need for providing well-founded, competent advice. In other words, they might give up their traditional core business without managing to secure their new business. In many companies, controllers' attempts to expand towards providing consulting and project support services face well-established competition in the form of internal consulting units. External consultants are often used for developing and implementing value-based management concepts. Strategy development is another area rarely covered by controllers. Here, too, controllers face stiff competition. Such developments make it more plausible for controllers to adopt a »role making« position. It holds the promise of a series of benefits, even without such »self-centered« considerations (cf. David 2005, pp. 96–97):

(1) *Motivational effect:* There are two motivational effects: On the one hand, controllers are given the opportunity to carry out tasks which they themselves have prioritized. On the other hand, their own performance level becomes visible on the basis of customer feedback: In the long term, controllers will only be able to present managers with services they want and appreciate.

Benefits of a stronger »role making« position

(2) *Innovation effect:* If controllers view themselves as suppliers of services to customers, this implies they have to review the services offered on an ongoing basis, making adjustments when customer requirements change. For instance, if managers have the choice of obtaining information on the company's performance either from accounting or from controllers, then controllers have to find a way of adding a better complement of additional services to the information, in other words, to provide better explanations, to enable a better interpretation and understanding or to represent the information in a way that makes more sense. As a further example, it would be a tough blow if the initiative for introducing a Balanced Scorecard came from the personnel department instead of controlling. The best way to avoid this is by constantly searching for beneficial innovations and making them attractive for management.

(3) *Resource savings:* The constant comparison between the services being supplied by controllers and those demanded by management improves the focus on concrete benefits. It helps to avoid »free goods being wasted«, a fundamental observation from economics, as well as the continued supply of services in which management is not interested.

(4) *Performance boosts:* When managers participate in designing the services provided to them by controllers, it is reasonable to assume that they will match the needs of managers more closely and provide them with greater utility. This relationship has been shown to exist on several occasions for the relationship between companies and customers.

We will return to internal customer orientation in chapter 5. The following section deals with the internal competitors of controllers.

4.2.1.3 Internal competitors of controllers

The internal competitors of controllers were briefly mentioned in the preceding section. The most important ones will be described in greater detail below. In addition to the individual preferences of managers, they play a key role in constraining controllers' opportunities for »role making«.

Accountants

Financial accounting is a competitor that has been going from strength to strength in recent years. This is illustrated by the following quote from the head of controlling of a DAX 30 company: »There is often a rivalry between the two, and it is one of the key tasks of a CFO to create a sensible balance between financial accounting on the one hand and controlling on the other« (Weber 2008, p. 167). The key task of financial accounting is to supply information to target groups outside the organization. These include providers of capital, i.e. creditors and shareholders, but also tax authorities, customers, and suppliers. Financial data is the basis on which tax payments and dividends are determined. In addition, external recipients can form an impression of the financial status of the company on the basis of the published information. In order to satisfy the information requirements in a form that is generally understandable, financial accounting has to comply with externally specified accounting standards such as those codified in Germany's commercial code, the *Handelsgesetzbuch* (HGB), or in the IAS/IFRS.

> There are now significant overlaps between the tasks of accountants and controllers.

Financial accounting meets its objectives above all by generating annual financial statements. Furthermore, the department is usually also responsible for ongoing bookkeeping and for interacting with external auditors. In small and medium-sized enterprises, it sometimes also prepares tax payments, e.g. sales/value-added or business tax payments.

Controller units and financial accounting departments use the same financial and non-financial raw data, such as payments or quantities, for their respective areas of responsibility. The tendency towards integrated financial and cost accounting systems, which is being fed above all by the increasing use of accounting software, implies that data is becoming more and more standardized across the cost and financial accounting functions. It is usually financial accounting which is responsible for entering data into the computer systems, thereby providing a large part of

> Accounting provides controlling with an essential part of the information it requires.

the data needed by controller units. In this sense, financial accounting can be described as a supplier of information – especially financial information – to the controller unit.

In medium-sized enterprises in particular, cooperation on investment decisions is becoming more common between controller units and financial accounting. Whereas capital budgeting is essentially the controller unit's responsibility, financial accounting has special know-how concerning taxation questions, so that controllers can obtain information about designing investments in a tax-efficient way from this department.

Conversely, controller units are increasingly providing information and tools to financial accounting. This is true especially in companies that prepare their balance sheets according to IAS/IFRS. Whereas controller units (via cost accounting) have for a long time been supplying data for calculating manufacturing costs, preconditions for correct accounting according to IAS/IFRS include information derived from planning processes and knowledge of net present value calculations, for instance when performing impairment tests on goodwill. Financial accounting depends on cooperation from the controller unit in this instance, if one wants to avoid having to capture the existing information in the company a second time.

The financial accounting department represents a (potential) competitor of the controller unit – especially in companies where it generates financial statements more often than once a year. By being provided with the opportunity of explaining the statements to management, it gains increased access to the management level and thereby has more chances of increasing its offering of services. It benefits from the fact that it possesses valuable knowledge of the way the business is developing across the respective companies because it deals with financial information on a daily basis. Such knowledge includes information about segments or subsidiaries as this has to be included in group reporting. Employees who work in the financial accounting department are usually assumed to have strong quantitative skills combined with a high degree of attention to detail. Financial accounting departments can use the skills and knowledge mentioned above to take over management support tasks from controller units, especially in the areas of information supply and planning, as well as carrying out tasks related to assuring rationality. They can also take advantage of the fact that they – in contrast to controller units – do not have to justify their budgets because their work is based on legal accounting requirements.

Nevertheless, controller units do have some important competitive advantages compared to financial accounting departments. Controllers are still seen as »custodians of numbers« and are more likely to have access to non-financial information, the importance of which has increased recently from the perspective of management. Furthermore, financial accounting departments tend to be inexperienced in the areas of strategic and operational planning, whereas controller units make extensive use of planning and monitoring tools. Controllers are also used to making forecasts, whereas financial accounting departments used to focus on historical calculations in the past. This is also why controller units continue to be considered more suitable for capital budgeting.

Accounting has little experience in the area of planning.

In order to become an important competitor of controller units in their role as consultants or sparring partners to management, financial accounting departments would have to catch up in the area of communication skills, which tend to be underdeveloped, and to build up know-how regarding tools as well as detailed knowledge concerning the business model and development of the respective company.

Finally, it should also be mentioned that financial accounting departments have only limited leeway in designing their own work areas (»role making«) as changing external requirements resulting from accounting rules and legislation may require changes in the way financial accounting is organized.

The strategy department

A potential competitive situation also exists between the controller unit and a department that may be referred to by various names in practice, but which is commonly known as the business development or strategy department. In medium-sized and large companies in particular, management often receives support from positions or departments especially created to provide guidance on strategic management issues. Such units, which we will refer to as strategy departments in the following, usually report directly to the CEO and are thus in direct contact with the highest management levels. Strategy departments offer strategic management support and concentrate their activities on providing input – both formally and regarding contents – into planning and decision-making processes, as well as carrying out strategic monitoring. The tasks can be summarized in a similar way to that used for the controller unit as belonging to the activity categories information supply, planning, monitoring, and other tasks (similarly, cf. Pfohl/Zettelmeyer 1987, pp. 151–152):

> ▸ The *information supply task* encompasses the strategic information services provided by the strategy department. As in the case of the controller unit, one may differentiate between system-related and content-related sub-tasks. The strategy department develops and operates the strategic information and early warning system. From a content point of view, it primarily supplies management with market and competitive analyses. However, as a result of the emergence of the resource-based view of strategic management and the growing importance of company-related data for the strategy process, ever more strategy-relevant information from within the company is being processed.

> ▸ The *strategic planning task* can also, analogously to the tasks of controllers, be subdivided into process-based activities relating to managing the planning process on the one hand and to content-related tasks of planning support on the other hand. Strategy departments are particularly likely to take responsibility for strategic planning management. They design the strategic planning system, coordinate the planning process, and provide support for the use of strategic tools. Content-based planning tasks can be subdivided – with reference to the strategic management cycle – into activities of strategy formulation and of strategy implementation. Strategy departments are traditionally involved in strategy formulation in particular. They help prepare decision making and support management in formulating, evaluating and selecting strategic options. As the importance of strategy implementation has increased in companies in recent years, however, operational planning activities are also gaining importance for strategy departments.

> ▸ *Strategic monitoring*, consisting of the sub-tasks strategic early warning, the monitoring of strategy implementation, and the monitoring of assumptions,

Strategy departments usually report to the CEO.

At the strategic level, strategic planners are responsible for many of the same tasks which controllers perform at the operational level.

forms the third area of activity of strategy departments. Based on their market knowledge and ability to identify weak signals, members of strategic staff units are often responsible for undirected strategic monitoring. The area of activity also includes monitoring the assumptions on which planning is based and monitoring the process of strategy implementation.

▸ *Other tasks* include all tasks which strategy departments carry out when the need arises or at irregular intervals. They may include specific projects such as introducing a Balanced Scorecard or value-based management, or consulting activities in the context of strategic acquisitions.

The activities of strategy departments which we have described are similar both structurally and from a content-based perspective to those of a controller unit. Depending on the respective company context, overlaps and potential conflicts between the two units may occur in all four activity fields – information supply, planning, monitoring, and other activities:

There are significant overlaps between the tasks of strategic planners and those of controllers.

▸ Both departments operate an information supply system within the framework of their *information supply function*. Rivalries are more likely when the controller unit's information system includes the strategic level in addition to the operational level. Furthermore, there may be overlaps in the context of providing information content. It is true that the focus of strategy departments traditionally lies on markets and the company's competitive environment, whereas controller units primarily supply company-related information. However, there may be competition when both units try to dominate the supply of strategic information.

▸ In the context of *planning*, there is also the possibility of competition between the two departments. Both controllers and strategists possess the relevant skills for strategic planning management and for designing the planning process. Furthermore, there may be overlaps in the context of content-based planning support. These are likely to occur in cases where the controller unit is included in strategy formulation and evaluation in addition to the strategy department. A competitive relationship is also likely to emerge when the strategy department takes on operational tasks – which traditionally form part of the controller unit's activities – in the context of strategy implementation.

▸ Activities in the area of *strategic monitoring* may also generate competition between the two departments. Owing to their operational monitoring experience, controllers have the opportunity of contributing to the strategy process, particularly by tracking the implementation of strategy. The sub-tasks of strategic monitoring are, however, also carried out by the strategy department, meaning that there is a possibility of overlaps here as well.

▸ Finally, competition between the two departments is also possible in the area of *other tasks*, for instance in the case of occasional consulting services or critical questioning of strategic decisions. As an example, both the controller unit and the strategy department could be involved in introducing and maintaining a Balanced Scorecard. Similarly, a competitive relationship may result in the context of providing consulting services or acting as a critical sparring partner for strategic issues.

Differences between the
skills profiles of
controllers and those of
strategic planners

The competitive advantages and disadvantages of a strategy department in relation to a controller unit can essentially be derived from the skills profiles of the respective employees. In addition, the organizational reporting structure is of importance.

The qualifications of staff members are one of the *strengths* of a strategy department. They are usually recruited from management consulting companies and from among top graduates of business schools and universities. For this reason, strategy departments in many companies have replaced controller units as the prime »hunting grounds« for recruiting top management. Furthermore, many corporate strategists possess detailed market and competitive knowledge – in contrast to many controllers. They are able to identify market trends and their implications for the company from incomplete and mostly qualitative information. From an organizational point of view, the fact that strategy departments are often found at the highest levels of the organization, reporting to the CEO, is another competitive advantage in relation to the controller unit. In this sense, members of strategy departments usually have easier access to the top management ranks when working on strategic issues than controllers, whose work focuses more on the operational level.

Controllers are more
familiar with their
respective company,
strategic planners with
the markets in which the
company operates.

On the other hand, strategy departments also have certain *weaknesses* compared to controller units. For strategic management, the combination of the market- and the resource-based views means that both internal company data and market information are important. Strategic planners do not have direct access to such information. Furthermore, the representation of strategic issues in financial terms is becoming increasingly important in many companies in response to the concept of value-orientation. Both knowledge of the company and the financial perspective are core competencies of the controller unit and enable it to position itself favorably within the company in relation to the strategy department. Furthermore, the latter's high hierarchical position can be seen as a competitive disadvantage (»no contact to the shop floor«). Owing to their separation from the operational level, corporate strategists often find it difficult to develop realistic strategic specifications. The strategic plans developed by strategy departments also risk running aground during implementation. Finally, efficiently monitoring implementation is more difficult because of the great separation from the persons actually involved in implementation. For all these activities, it therefore appears that controller units have a competitive advantage because of their highly differentiated organizational structure, which provides close contact to local units and reliable information flows. This also seems to have consequences for careers, as is illustrated by the following quote from a top controller of a DAX 30 company: »Of course strategic planners have the nicer, more interesting topics, and of course they can always raise their own profile on that basis; of course they have better access to the management board. That is simply the way it is. But at some stage they will have to transfer to an operational function, and then they will have to face the music for everything they have done up to then. So from that point of view, I do not have a problem with it. There is a late revenge. The late revenge will come up at some stage during their careers« (Weber 2008, p. 177).

Weaknesses of strategic
planners in the area of
strategy implementation

Internal auditing

The main purpose of internal auditing departments is to deliver objective and independent audits using a systematic methodology for analyzing business processes. Historically oriented checks of procedural compliance continue to be one of the core services of internal auditing departments. The reason for such checks is to ensure that legal and company regulations are complied with under formal and material aspects. The goal is to prevent harmful activities and protect the company from suffering losses.

However, the spectrum of services offered by most internal auditors has been broadened under the influence of new challenges to include utility checks and efficiency reviews; procedural compliance checks as a share of all internal auditing tasks have been in decline for quite some time now. The optimality criteria which form the basis of utility checks usually have to be developed by internal auditing departments. For efficiency reviews, the economic principle is used to derive planned figures.

Utility checks and efficiency reviews are used especially for evaluating procedures, processes and systems, whereas the internal monitoring system should be viewed as a core system that has to be checked by the internal auditors. Furthermore, internal auditing departments are increasingly used for checking the usefulness and efficiency of management tasks.

By expanding its range of services to include utility checks and efficiency reviews, internal auditing departments are encroaching ever further onto fields traditionally claimed by controllers. In this sense, internal auditing departments use their findings to extend their spectrum of services to include analyses of critical points and of opportunities for streamlining. This means that internal auditing departments act increasingly as internal consultants and sometimes as critical counterparts, implying an overlap between the services of the two units. In addition, internal auditing departments see themselves as responsible for ensuring that the company retains its capacity for ongoing development. This aim also indicates overlaps with the self-image of controller units. It is therefore hardly surprising that the large overlaps between controller units and internal auditing departments are often remarked upon (cf. IIR/IIA/SVIR 2004, p. 34; Berens/Schmitting 2003, p. 363; Heigl 1989, p. 4).

The increasing overlaps place competitive pressure and justification requirements on controller units as well as on internal auditing departments; Peemöller/Richter even speak of a latent threat to internal auditors from controllers (cf. Peemöller/ Richter 2000, p. 66). Apart from the option of internal cooperation between the two departments on the basis of the many aspects they have in common (cf. Birl 2007), controller units could benefit from a competitively oriented strategic positioning vis-à-vis internal auditing departments. To do this requires knowing the key strengths and weaknesses of controllers in relation to those of internal auditors.

As a result of the international trend towards strengthening internal monitoring systems resulting from the recent corporate governance debate (cf. the COSO report by the Treadway Commission, the German corporate governance law KonTraG, the Sarbanes-Oxley Act), internal auditing departments see themselves as being in a strong position. Internal auditing departments are specifically credited with having easier access to top management, a stronger power base and a more positive image in the eyes of management (cf. Peemöller/Richter 2000, p. 52).

Efficiency reviews as the task with the largest potential overlaps

Controllers as a »latent threat to internal auditors«?

Controller units therefore have to take care to defend their access to top management and thereby to financial resources as well as their image and power claims; else, they risk falling behind on dimensions relevant to both units in the long term. The most promising measures from the view of controllers include focusing on the decisive competitive advantages and distinct competencies of controller units compared with internal auditing departments. These include their broader knowledge of business methods, their greater knowledge of quantitative evaluations, their deeper experience regarding future-oriented perspectives on information as well as their better access to information as a result of a broader company-wide network. This specific background in business administration is not available to internal auditing departments in the same form. It is an advantage that controller units have to leverage, especially when providing support for assuring rationality, an area which is of strategic importance.

Competition within controller units

A special kind of internal competition may emerge in large companies between »central« or »group controlling« at headquarters and »decentralized controlling departments« at the local, subsidiary level, which will be referred to as »local controlling« in the following. The relationship between central and local controlling departments is fundamentally a mirror image of the relationship between central and local management. The reporting and authority structures of managers exert a considerable influence on the relationships between controllers. Like managers, controllers need to adopt different perspectives resulting from the respective management problem: The global view with a low degree of resolution is juxtaposed against the local view with highly detailed knowledge. The different perspectives interact; as a rule, they are derived hierarchically from one another. However, there is also sufficient potential for conflict at the boundaries between levels, which can be seen every time operational planning processes are carried out or capital expenditure funds are disbursed by headquarters.

The relationship between central and local controlling mirrors the relationship between central and local management.

This potential conflict between levels affects the controlling function in particular. Controlling has to ensure that results-oriented planning works properly within the company. In the context of corporate planning, the different company units have to be coordinated with one another. Satisfactorily resolving the coordination task becomes difficult when individual units are too intent on promoting and enforcing their own interests. When managers want to instrumentalize their controllers (»Make sure your budget leaves me with some leeway«), controllers are confronted with a classical conflict situation: Should they rather follow the interests of »their« division or adopt the perspective of the company and its overall goals as a whole?

Resolving this specific dilemma is influenced to a considerable degree by the fundamental relationship between central and local controlling. This will now be analyzed more closely for the different activity areas:

▶ *Information supply:*
It is usually central controlling that specifies which results-related information has to be captured and communicated within the company. It is responsible for designing the information system and usually works in close cooperation with

(financial) accounting. Local controllers are then tasked with ensuring that actual data is properly captured in their units, both in respect of volume and quality. There are no degrees of freedom worth mentioning.

These only crop up when it comes to commenting on values such as deviations or variances, for instance. Depending on how much information the local controllers provide, central controllers can offer their managers explanations varying across a wide range. In the extreme case, the »explanation« is limited to simply providing a variance value; in this case, top managers would have to contact local managers if they wished to find out the reasons for deviations. This can strengthen the position of local controllers with their managers because they »gave nothing away«.

Central controllers depend on their colleagues at the local level for information.

Local controllers also possess degrees of freedom in respect of standard planning data, e.g. for operational planning. The format is specified by central controlling in this case as well; but the amount of information communicated beyond the pure planning figures can be interpreted in very different ways. Central controlling may question figures; but the contact persons for such questions are primarily local managers. If they do not want the figures to be harmonized in advance by controlling, the amount of information available to central controlling is significantly smaller than in the case of close information exchanges within the controlling function.

Central controlling depends even more on local controlling in the case of occasional topics, in other words of new questions (ranging from individual requests to complex projects). A corresponding »muzzle« by local management largely has the effect of cutting central controlling off from the required information. One solution could be to obtain external benchmarks.

However, local controlling is also the recipient of information from central controlling. For instance, local controllers need data such as exchange rate fluctuations or economic statistics for their periodic planning. Having knowledge about the standing of a local unit or about current strategic thinking at headquarters can be an invaluable benefit enabling early reactions. In this sense and within certain limits, central controlling does have some leverage over local controlling, although on the whole a (considerable) imbalance exists in the area of information supply.

▶ *Planning:*

The tasks of local and central controlling are clearly divided in the area of periodic planning. Central controlling is in charge of the structure and process of planning. To this purpose, it also specifies – as mentioned in the section on information supply – important planning parameters. Other tasks depend heavily on the type of management in the company.

The relationship in the area of planning depends heavily on the type of management.

If it is highly centralized, central controlling is tasked with breaking down central objectives; central controlling works to ensure that the aims of headquarters are enforced; the local controller tends to be the keeper of local interests, »fighting for her unit«. In this sense, there is a competitive situation: Whoever has the better arguments, wins. On the other hand, if the company has chosen a decentralized management structure, then central controlling tends to play the role of critically evaluating local proposals. They are checked for consistency, plausibility and sustainability and are assessed in conjunction with plans

Whoever has the better arguments, wins.

from other units regarding their suitability for being integrated into the company's overall plans. In this case, cooperative forms of interaction are to be expected. When individual divisions are feeling economic pressure, however, there may be a confrontational relationship in this case as well.

Finally, concepts such as »Beyond Budgeting« mark the outer limits of decentralized structures. In this case, coordination is no longer based on planning, but rather on mutual adjustment. Here, headquarter's only role is to define the context. It determines the »rules of the game«. In this case, there are few points of contact between central and local controllers.

▶ *Monitoring:*
The monitoring task of controllers is closely linked to the two activity areas just mentioned. The following thoughts can therefore be summarized in brief.

If a company delegates substantial authority, then local monitoring will usually be done by local controllers. Central controlling is then tasked with collating and commenting deviations from the overall perspective. Doing this requires understanding the variances. This in turn has to be linked to the right to question local controllers accordingly, otherwise the additional monitoring by central controlling is »toothless« (an accusation one frequently hears in practice). As shown, central controllers usually do not have the right to source information autonomously; they are not allowed to go to the local unit without authorization. At this point, conflicts may emerge between central and local controlling. As local controllers can furthermore distinguish themselves in central management's view, there is reason enough to dedicate some thought to competitive behavior. In the case of planning, such behavior cannot be excluded even in the case of centralized management.

However, the relationship between central and local controlling departments can also be conducted in a very open and cooperative fashion in monitoring activities: Local controllers have the chance of building a strong reputation with central controlling by being open and thereby gaining advantages compared with other units that tend to hold back information from central controlling. Cooperation sometimes makes sense even if it is for very egoistical reasons!

▶ *Consulting:*
Controllers also provide many different consulting services to management. The relationship between central and local controlling departments depends on the type of consulting services offered.

Consulting within specific business units is usually not part of the normal spectrum of tasks of central controllers. If central expertise is required, this tends to be a job for internal consulting departments in large companies. However, it may well be in the interest of local controlling departments to call on central controlling. For instance, when strategic topics appear at the local level, it makes sense to contact headquarters in order to run a preliminary check on the topic, be it to anticipate the views of headquarters or to warn or influence the central controllers ahead of time.

When strategic themes relevant to local units are initiated by headquarters, the central controllers who are involved are often considered with the same suspicions as external consultants – and may be influenced in a similar way with the aim of achieving decisions favoring the local unit. However, such projects can also represent a chance for local controllers to cause a positive impression with management at headquarters, which may be helpful for one's own career. To sum up, there is a varied and somewhat contradictory theme of loyalty for local controllers here.

If one looks at the diverse activities of controllers, the impression one gets is of a tight and heterogeneous network of relationships between central and local control-ling departments. There are many different customer-supplier interdependencies between them. A tight network of tasks and services can be observed as well as areas where the two departments mostly work independently of one another. Overall, there is a clear need for cooperation, without which controlling as a whole would not work efficiently and effectively. However, there are also many areas in which competition between the controlling units is possible and makes sense. These find-ings form the framework for the organizational design of the cooperation between central and local controlling, which we will analyze more closely in chapter 5.

> Both central and local controlling can derive benefits from cooper-ating with one another.

We will conclude this section on the internal competitive situation of controllers by referring back to a finding from the ICV study mentioned in chapter 1. Controllers were explicitly surveyed on their perspective on key competitors and their perceived competitive strength. The first question resulted in the response shown in *Figure 4-2*. Controllers see external business consultants as their main competition. Three of the internal competitors described earlier occupy the next three spots on the ranking (the study did not include competition between a company's controllers). Regarding the question on the intensity of competition with other

Fig. 4-2

Competitors of controller units (source: Weber et al. 2006, p. 48)

Which of the following departments and external service providers would you currently consider to be your competitors?

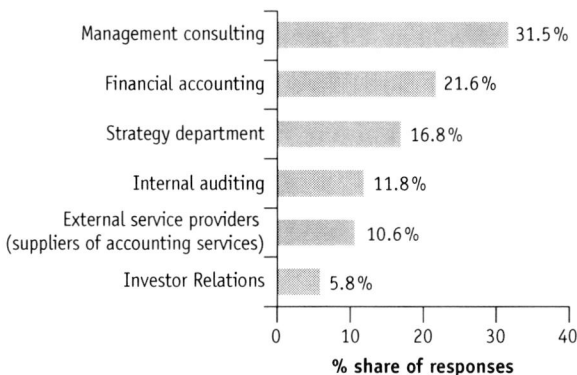

Department	%
Management consulting	31.5%
Financial accounting	21.6%
Strategy department	16.8%
Internal auditing	11.8%
External service providers (suppliers of accounting services)	10.6%
Investor Relations	5.8%

% share of responses

departments or external service providers for management attention, the controllers' answer was very self-assured: The average value was 21.2 on a scale from 0 (complete absence of competitive pressure) to 100 (very high competitive pressure).

4.2.1.4 Risks of excessive autonomy in determining controllers' tasks

Internal markets are not free from disadvantages – otherwise companies would not primarily organize themselves as hierarchies. Such disadvantages also contribute to limiting the »role making focus« of controllers. In detail, they can be described as follows (cf. David 2005, pp. 98–101):

Excessive »role making« by controllers can be detrimental.

▸ *Incurring transaction costs*
Coordinating tasks with managers and continually adapting the schedule of activities to changes in demand requires both sides to invest time. The same applies for negotiating payment for the services provided (e.g. per coaching session or as a flat rate for monthly reporting during an entire year), for measuring performance and for accounting for payments. There are companies whose controllers are able to present service catalogs and price lists for their activities, and who use them. Maintaining such information involves a substantial administrative effort, however.

▸ *Using leeway to pursue one's own goals*
In chapter 1 we already dealt briefly with the risk that controllers may follow their own goals such as effort aversion as well as attempts to gain power and influence or to attain an excellent reputation in the company. The more controllers follow their own goals, the more significant the negative consequences of high levels of design autonomy may be for the company as a whole. This risk is especially great when managers are not well-informed about the basic function of the controller units.

Drawbacks of excessive »role making«

▸ *Redundancy of resources*
Internal markets mean that parallel resources have to be maintained to provide services. Otherwise, internal competition would not be possible. However, this also implies that costs are incurred several times over. When accountants and controllers are able to carry out monthly financial reporting in the same way, this may be an indication that there is room for rationalization.

▸ *Negative impact on cooperation within the company*
Internal competition is seen by many as being good for business, but others see it as a sign of lacking mutual respect and cooperation. For instance, if controllers can keep control of the market for »internal reporting« against powerful competition from the accountants, it is quite possible that they will not be quite as cooperative the next time the controller unit requests additional fundamental data. This aspect also includes building »barriers to market entry« (for instance, when controllers start planning for content in addition to providing process support, thereby expanding their importance for planning in a way that makes them almost invulnerable) and attempts to develop and maintain an information advantage compared with customers and potential competitors. This is something

one may frequently observe in the way tools are used: Instead of training managers to use them appropriately, thereby enabling them to do their work without the controllers' assistance, the training task is systematically neglected. It is also hard to argue against the impression that some of the tools used by controllers are purposefully made complicated to ensure that controllers become indispensable.

The scope within which controllers can design their own units should therefore be limited. This does not change the recommendation to promote »role making« – the concept of actively influencing tasks is still very underdeveloped in many companies.

4.2.2 Influences of the external and the internal environment on the design issue

If managers provide controllers with more or less extensive scope for designing controller units, controllers are nevertheless not completely free within this scope; the design task is instead influenced even more strongly by some context factors, as implied by the fundamental observation of contingency theory.

Zünd's typology as the most widely known study on the context dependency of controlling

The best-known contribution in German-language controlling literature to deal with context dependency is Zünd's controller typology (cf. Zünd 1979). Depending on the relevant environmental situation, Zünd differentiates between three types of controllers: »In a relatively stable environment, controllers work as registrars; their activities make them bookkeepers rather than controllers. In somewhat dynamic environments, controllers appear as navigators, whose most important control tool is the integration of planning and monitoring. Finally, in highly dynamic environments, controllers act as innovators who participate in the problem-solving process and are responsible for introducing early warning systems« (Zünd 1985, p. 32). These hypotheses leave no leeway for influencing design. The environmental situation allows no choices. According to Zünd, the three types of controllers often exist simultaneously in reality because the three environmental situations commonly appear in combination in companies, and controller units should keep the different types available to ensure a fast reaction capability to environmental changes (cf. Zünd 1979, p. 8).

Further insights concerning possible environmental influences on the design task of controller units can be gained from empirical studies (for an overview, cf. Bauer 2002, pp. 53–84). Factors internal to companies that were researched include company size, internal organizational structures, management expectations and attitudes, and the management style practiced in the company. The study by Bauer finds that of all these factors, »constructive transparency« as »an individual attitude, i.e. the behavioral predisposition of the respective managers in relation to the basic principles of controlling« (Bauer 2002, p. 111) is the most important by far.

Constructive transparency and environmental munificence as additional context factors

Typical external factors to be analyzed include environmental complexity and dynamism. Bauer also includes the construct of »environmental munificence«, which expresses »how strongly the company environment penalizes less than optimum behavior by management in certain areas« (Bauer 2002, p. 102). This factor is especially important from the perspective whereby controlling is seen as being responsible for assuring rationality. One may deduce from this approach that the importance of controllers increases as the munificence of the environment decreases because mistakes become ever more »costly« for the company. This is exactly what this study confirmed (cf. Bauer 2002, p. 251).

From the source

In the most widely known work on the context dependency of controlling, Zünd identifies three types of controllers:

»It is apparent that in a relatively static environment, where management behavior is primarily reactive, there is no real need for a control function. The ›controller‹ merely plays the role of registrar; he bears his job title without justification. The controller-registrar only carries out a documenting function. His orientation is towards past events and bookkeeping. Henzler describes him as the ›top cost accountant‹. The tools used by this controlling type are primarily traditional, namely cost accounting with financial and operational bookkeeping. Management receives routine periodic reports on the results recorded in the accounting systems. The image of the controller-registrar corresponds to that of a conventional bookkeeper, for whom compliance with accounting rules is the highest law.

...

The increasing dynamism and complexity of the environment leads to uncertainty in management decision making. This uncertainty results in a need for better adaptation to accelerating environmental changes and for better management of internal coordination problems.

For adaptation and coordination to take place, a company has to be controlled, i.e. planning and monitoring have to be integrated. The organizational institutionalization of this integrating function is the controller as navigator. This controller type is today seen as the controller in the true sense of the word, a person responsible for providing methodic planning and monitoring tools in a way that supports decision making and is user-friendly, as well as providing analyses of planned-vs.-actual comparisons that compel others to take corrective action. This controller works on the principle of ›control means action‹ or – as formulated by Wilson – ›information without action is curiosity – not control‹. As some-

body who provides warnings that are often inconvenient, he contributes to decision making and thereby carries out line functions in addition to staff functions. He therefore does not fit very well into the hierarchical model of companies. A large dose of diplomacy is needed to avoid becoming a permanent conflict party. Controller-navigators who know the potential conflicts associated with their control tasks are, on the other hand, predestined to becoming conflict managers who know how to handle conflicts between third parties.

...

It is obvious that the controlling concept has to be particularly future- and action-oriented when the relationship between a company and its environment is extremely dynamic. The controller turns into an innovator who not only moves within the system like the controller-navigator, but who also has to question the existing system on an ongoing basis because of the rapid environmental changes while searching for new, better solutions. Participating in problem-solving processes is therefore an important activity for this controller type. The task of planning, which is the focus of controller-navigators' attention, loses importance compared with the early warning task of controller-innovators. The controller's reporting is characterized by aperiodic special reports. The environmental dynamism is thereby transmitted to management and therefore also to controlling.

In his function as system-changer, the controller-innovator runs the risk of becoming a disturbance within the company, with frequent special analyses acting as a brake on operations. He has to take care not to demotivate others and create conflict through his constant suggestions for improvements, the innovative effect of which is lost when they exceed a certain level of stimulation.

The innovator function of controllers is one of the most stimulating, but also one of the most difficult tasks of future controllers« (Zünd 1979, pp. 19–23).

Considerations of this type, motivated by contingency theory, should not lead one to assume that the influences analyzed describe straightforward cause-effect relationships that always hold true. Companies can react in very different ways to different environmental situations. Assuming determinism would thus clearly be a mistake. But similarly, it would be just as foolish to ignore the influences mentioned above as a general principle. Controller units have to be designed to match each individual company. There is no »single best way«, just as there are not unlimited degrees of freedom for the design task.

4.2.3 The development status of controlling as an influencing factor

Finally, there is another factor that influences the design of the controller unit. This factor takes us to controllership and from there to the functions of controlling – thereby leading back to the topics discussed in chapter 1. There, we traced the development path of controllers in companies as well as the term »controlling«. The core statement of the following discussion is that the question of how to modify the design of a controller unit depends essentially on its pre-existing design, i.e. that the design depends on the development status of the controller unit or the understanding of controlling. We will support the plausibility of this statement on the basis of the development of controlling terminology, as well as on the basis of a description of the development of controller tasks, which results in a developmental model of controllership.

4.2.3.1 Different development phases as reflected in the terminology of controlling

In chapter 1, we introduced three different terminological approaches to controlling, which preceded the perspective whereby controlling assures rationality. These can be derived on the basis of different bottlenecks that hinder rational management (cf. Weber/Schäffer 2001, pp. 38–42):

The three traditional perspectives on controlling address different rationality bottlenecks.

- ▸ Rational management depends on the availability of sufficient knowledge. This includes both knowledge of methods and knowledge of facts. If there is no knowledge of facts, then it is not possible to make a decision on the basis of reflection, and correspondingly it is not possible to influence others and enforce a decision. Therefore, supplying management-relevant information is of vital importance for assuring that management is rational. This is the basis underlying the perspective of controlling as an information supply function (bottleneck: information relevant to management).
- ▸ Approaches that view controlling as a special form of management emphasize the need for systematic planning of objectives on the one hand. This is equivalent to reflexive decision making. On the other hand, the integration of planning and monitoring is emphasized. This also strengthens the reflexive component of management (bottleneck: systematic planning and monitoring). The availability of corresponding information is either implicitly assumed as part of this perspective or explicitly mentioned as part of the concept.

▸ The coordination-based approach emphasizes that the (core) bottleneck of rational management lies in linking planning, information supply and monitoring. The extensions of this coordination-based view to organizational and incentive aspects was described at an earlier stage and can be explained through the pressure to change resulting from dynamism: The more strongly the company is subjected to changes, the more strongly the function of assuring rationality also has to apply to the relationships between planning, information supply and monitoring on the one hand and organization and personnel management on the other.

In this way, the three terminological approaches are built upon one another: Systematic planning and monitoring is not possible without the corresponding information; coordination problems only become apparent when the sub-systems which are to be coordinated are already sufficiently developed. Whoever tries to introduce controlling as a coordination function in public administration will come across a fundamental lack of understanding on the part of the affected managers – and will not be able to avoid having to implement information supply and, on top of it, planning and monitoring.

Controlling goes through various phases in its development.

4.2.3.2 The development of controllership in Germany

Taking a look back to the 1970s and 1980s shows that controllership in (large) companies often followed a similar development path.

Information supply as the basis

Controllers' work starts with an intensive engagement with internal cost accounting. Controllers often emerge from cost accounting or from »*betriebswirtschaftliche Abteilungen*« (business administration departments) which support management through methods such as capital budgeting. Controllers as »number crunchers«, as custodians of profit-relevant information, are the typical »starting pattern« of controlling. This applied not only to large companies in the 1970s, but continues to be true when controlling is introduced nowadays. In public administration, the first aim is generally to create transparency about services and costs – just like in a medium-sized company which used to be managed without formal business data, but instead on the basis of the owner-manager's intuition and experience. Setting goals requires information. If it is not available, this becomes the core bottleneck for rational management.

Controllers cannot work without reliable information.

Building systematic planning and monitoring as a consequence

Once there is sufficient transparency, systematic planning and monitoring systems can be introduced as a next step. Launching planning and monitoring systems without first having a broad information base makes as little sense as producing information without anticipating what it could be used for.

Building systematic planning is not a trivial problem. It begins with the question of which objectives should be pursued. The most obvious ones are the ones represented in internal cost accounting (operating profits, contribution margins). If further goals are to be added (as is the case in a Balanced Scorecard, for instance), then planning and monitoring cause feedback effects to the information supply function of controllers. They then either have to ensure that the required data is

Planning and monitoring are only possible if adequate information is available.

available (extension of the obligation to transparency) or they have to capture the information themselves.

Designing planning also means answering the question of the appropriate level for the objectives. Here, too, cost accounting provides some assistance: Defining planned costs, for example, is an integral part of standard costing. If certain functions are not available (e.g. for overheads or revenue), the data that is captured still makes it possible to derive experience values. Experience offers a good base when things do not change much. However, this is becoming ever less common. As a consequence, target levels in companies are obtained increasingly from other sources such as benchmarks. Again, there is a feedback from planning to information supply.

Systematic planning makes little sense when compliance is not monitored; only with systematic monitoring is it possible to commit management to predefined goals and to ensure systematic learning. Reliable information is needed to enable monitoring to take place. Such information is supplied especially by cost accounting.

Consulting for coordination problems as the third level

Whoever is involved in planning and monitoring is automatically in close contact with management. Organizing and moderating the planning process requires personal contacts, as does the discussion of deviations from the goals. Every (good) controller knows his or her managers and knows how to deal with them. Based on the solid knowledge of facts, tools and persons, it is only a small step for controllers to provide comprehensive business advice to management. There is a demand for such a service especially when management is confronted with frequent changes. The problems that controllers help solve are of a complex nature in this case.

For instance, if a company wants to introduce a value-based management concept, this superficially appears to relate only to issues of how to define and capture the required information and how to adapt planning to the new concept. But during implementation, it quickly becomes clear that managers have problems understanding the concept (either because they do not want to or because they are not able to) and that the goals formulated in the context of the system are not immediately understandable or connected to the existing incentive systems. Aspects of motivation and acceptance become important. Controllers working on implementation will also find that fundamental questions of organization are affected. Controllers therefore not only have to learn new lessons in their traditional fields of competency such as information supply, planning and monitoring, but also have to chart unknown territories (and departments!): financial accounting, human resources (incentive systems) and organization. Controllers turn into internal consultants, work on a project basis and carry out overarching coordination functions.

The fact that managers seek their support for such issues has two main reasons: On the one hand, they are highly competent in the classical areas of information supply, planning and monitoring, i.e. in areas affected by most change projects. On the other hand, controllers are anchored at almost all levels and business units of the organization; they are therefore more capable than other potential candidates (such as the business development or internal consulting departments) of accessing broadly-based knowledge and are able to participate on a large scale in implementation.

Different management problems within the company thereby lead to different tasks for controllers. On the one hand, they depend strongly on the respective

Different management problems in companies lead to different tasks for controllers.

Fig. 4-3

How corporate practice views controlling, as shown in the ICV study
(source: Weber et al. 2006, p. 31)

Please indicate which view most closely matches controlling the way it is seen in your company.

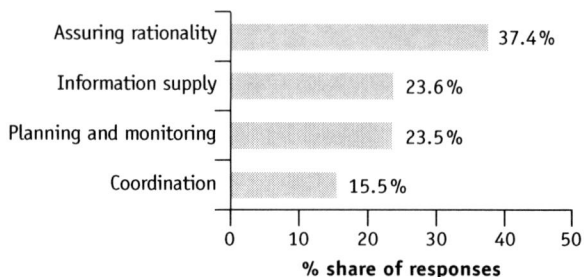

Assuring rationality	37.4%
Information supply	23.6%
Planning and monitoring	23.5%
Coordination	15.5%

0   10   20   30   40   50
% share of responses

context. On the other hand, they also highlight certain development states which enable more general statements to be made about designing controller units.

In the ICV study mentioned previously, we asked how important the different controlling conceptions developed and discussed in theory were. With a score of 37.4 percent, the conception whereby the function of controlling is to assure management rationality is the viewpoint most widely accepted by ICV members in practice; in other words, more than a third of the ICV members who responded to the survey indicated that this understanding matches controlling practice in their companies most closely. 23.6 percent of respondents stated that information supply was what controlling was most concerned with in practice. An almost identical share of respondents, namely 23.5 percent, considered planning and monitoring or results-oriented control to be the most characteristic controlling function. The controlling conception that focuses on coordination came in with a significantly lower score of 15.5 percent for both subgroups. These findings were recently confirmed by a further empirical study (the »DAX 30 study«), which surveyed the top controllers of the DAX 30 companies (cf. Weber 2008, p. 61). This shows that there is clear discrepancy between the high importance of this controlling conception in the theoretical discussion and its relevance and acceptance in practice.

Summary
(see guiding question 2)

▶ Recognizing the controller unit's role in internal competition means having to think about actively designing tasks. Pure »role taking« has to be complemented by active »role making«.

▶ A number of factors influence design. Two of the most important are managers' attitudes and the development status of the controller unit.

▶ Consequently, and in spite of all agreement concerning the basics, controller units have to be custom-designed for each specific company.

4.3 Basic structure of the design task

4.3.1 The organizational problem of assigning tasks

Assigning tasks to persons is the core problem of organization theory. It defines tasks as obligations to carry out certain actions. If one adds the insights gained in chapter 2 during the discussion on rationality levels, a task can be defined as consisting of the object of the action, the action itself and the result of the action. Persons – either individually or as a group – are provided with certain resources for carrying out the task. Tasks and the persons with the responsibility to carry them out interact as follows from an ideal perspective:

The starting point is that certain actions have to be carried out (e.g. evaluating a capital budgeting proposal), which results in a need for production factors (persons, calculators, pencils and paper). These can be described in terms of quantity (one employee), deadlines (»this afternoon«) and the suitability of the factors (knowing how to calculate net present value). Depending on the specific actions, such needs may vary greatly in terms of volume, heterogeneity and specificity. Also, it is not always possible to describe them accurately (e.g. a controller's level of integrity). Such factor requirements specify which concrete production factors are selected and made available (»controller Smith«). Their characteristics have to meet the requirements. However, characteristics are not sufficient for carrying out the action; the factors also have to be physically available. Potential constraints may result from temporary »physical« obstacles to deployment (»Smith is off sick«) or – in the case of persons – from differences between basic skills (ability) and the willingness to contribute these skills (motivation – »Smith doesn't feel like it«).

Required actions are the starting point.

Companies consist of an enormous number of different, interconnected actions. Organizations therefore have to deal with many interdependencies between tasks. *Figure 4-4* outlines the additional dimensions of the organization problem resulting from these factors.

First, »quantum effects« may play a role with respect to a specific factor. Not all factors can be provided exactly in the required amount at a given moment. This applies both to managers and controllers. For instance, the demand for controller services may mean that only 60 percent of a local controller's capacity is used on site on certain days, whereas on other days, even working overtime for many hours is not enough to finish all the tasks on schedule. That is why one should try to use under-utilized capacity for other activities. In this way, some controllers carry out »pure line activities« from time to time. This, however, is not always smooth going: The more controllers get used to line activities, the more difficult it is for them to maintain their neutrality and independence.

A further aspect is the specialization of factor demands. Organizational literature understands specialization to mean the subdivision of a heterogeneous bundle of tasks into more homogeneous sub-tasks. The economic importance of specialization can hardly be overestimated. Without it, the current level of industrial development could not have been achieved. Specialization starts by focusing on individual types of actions: Consider Adam Smith's famous pin-manufacturing example or the image of a cost accountant who spends all day assigning invoices to cost centers. Later, it

Specialization can lead to considerable efficiency gains.

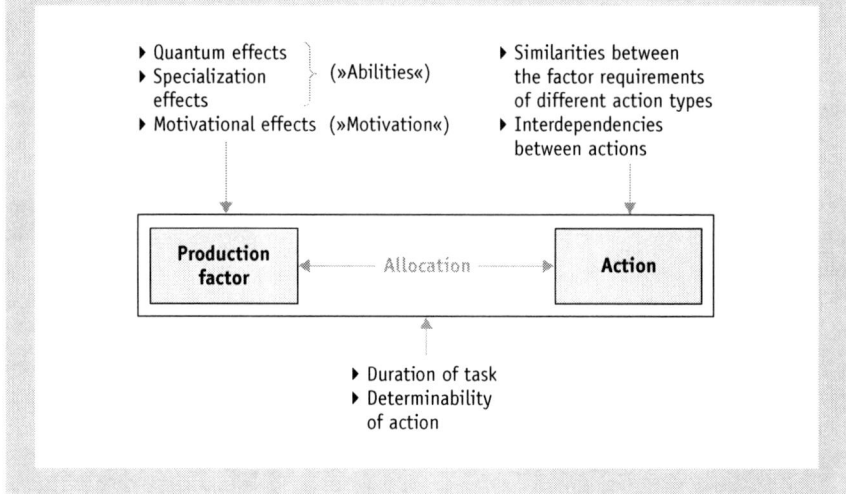

Fig. 4-4

Factors influencing the problem of organization

- Quantum effects
- Specialization effects } (»Abilities«)
- Motivational effects (»Motivation«)

- Similarities between the factor requirements of different action types
- Interdependencies between actions

Production factor ←——— Allocation ———→ **Action**

- Duration of task
- Determinability of action

was extended to include object specialization (giving a controller responsibility for the production department) and spatial specialization (»central controller for Latin America«).

There are a number of strong arguments in favor of specialization, including the benefits of experience effects resulting from constant repetition and the possibility of recruiting special talents for a position. Many cost accountants love ensuring data consistency and enjoy dominating every aspect of a cost accounting system. They attain a high level of skill in their areas.

However, these benefits are counterbalanced by disadvantages. Specialization creates a need to coordinate the separate tasks. This causes costs and may result in lacking coordination between tasks. What is the benefit of a highly advanced system of cost allocation when the quality of the data fed in from data capturing systems is poor (and cost accountants do not deal with the problem because it is the responsibility of a completely different department)? A high level of specialization makes coordination more difficult. On the one hand, it narrows the perspective of the persons involved. At the same time, it reduces the ability of those receiving the results of the activity to assess its quality properly. For instance, a cost accountant may generate certain analyses and provide them to a manager as a report; the manager has to accept the results without being able to question how they were arrived at or what they mean. In order to avoid such a situation, cost accountants need to understand the manager function sufficiently to be able to assess the results and coach the manager accordingly.

In addition to quantum effects and specialization, motivational aspects also have to be taken into account when analyzing the organization problem for the human production factor. Different combinations of requirements affect the »willingness to

High degrees of task specialization make coordination more difficult.

work« of diverse individuals in different ways. A very low range of tasks (as epitomized by a specialist who focuses on one subject to the exclusion of anything else) can be just as demotivating as a range that is too broad, which may stress a person or prevent him or her from concentrating on the things that are »really fun«. If one considers how broad the spectrum of tasks of individual controllers may be (from »number cruncher« to management consultant), this motivational effect becomes very important when recruiting controllers; there is no single controller who can carry out all tasks involved in the activity of controlling with the same level of motivation. Furthermore, it should also be noted that the same motivational problems that were described at various stages for managers may apply to controllers: Controllers, too, may behave opportunistically. For instance, they may not do their work properly (avoiding »work suffering«), avoid necessary conflicts (thereby neglecting their counterpart function) or exercise undue influence over management (»éminence grise«). The motivation of controllers and the problem mentioned previously – »Who monitors the controller?« – will occupy our attention in greater detail soon.

The motivation of employees also has to be taken into consideration when addressing the issue of organization.

From the source

In his most well-known book, »The Wealth of Nations«, Adam Smith illustrated the benefits of the division of labor using the manufacture of pins as an example:

»The greatest improvement in the productive powers of labour, and the greater part of the skill, dexterity, and judgment with which it is anywhere directed, or applied, seem to have been the effects of the division of labour.

The effects of the division of labour, in the general business of society, will be more easily understood by considering in what manner it operates in some particular manufactures. ... To take an example, therefore, from a very trifling manufacture; but one in which the division of labour has been very often taken notice of, the trade of the pin-maker; a workman not educated to this business (which the division of labour has rendered a distinct trade), nor acquainted with the use of the machinery employed in it (to the invention of which the same division of labour has probably given occasion), could scarce, perhaps, with his utmost industry, make one pin in a day, and certainly could not make twenty. But in the way in which this business is now carried on, not only the whole work is a peculiar trade, but it is divided into a number of branches, of which the greater part are likewise peculiar trades. One man draws out the wire, another straights it, a third cuts it, a fourth points it, a fifth grinds it at the top for receiving the head; to make the head requires two or three distinct operations; to put it on is a peculiar business, to whiten the pins is another; it is even a trade by itself to put them into the paper; and the important business of making a pin is, in this manner, divided into about eighteen distinct operations, which, in some manufactories, are all performed by distinct hands, though in others the same man will sometimes perform two or three of them. I have seen a small manufactory of this kind where ten men only were employed, and where some of them consequently performed two or three distinct operations. But though they were very poor, and therefore but indifferently accommodated with the necessary machinery, they could, when they exerted themselves, make among them about twelve pounds of pins in a day. There are in a pound upwards of four thousand pins of a middling size. Those ten persons, therefore, could make among the upwards of forty-eight thousand pins in a day. Each person, therefore, making a tenth part of forty-eight thousand pins, might be considered as making four thousand eight hundred pins in a day. But if they had all wrought separately and independently, and without any of them having been educated to this peculiar business, they certainly could not each of them have made twenty, perhaps not one pin in a day; that is, certainly, not the two hundred and fortieth, perhaps not the four thousand eight hundredth part of what they are at present capable of performing, in consequence of a proper division and combination of their different operations« (Smith 1776/1952, p. 3).

In the abstract view, action-based influences on the organization problem result from the similarity of factors required by different action types and from their inter-dependencies regarding content and time:

▸ A person who is able to evaluate capital budgeting proposals can also explain the underlying calculations and methods. Combining both tasks in the activity profile of a controller makes sense from the perspective of abilities.

▸ When new capital investments lead to changes in cost structures, there is poten-tial for substantial savings on coordination costs by ensuring that the same controller makes the necessary adjustments to cost accounting (e.g. changed cost splittings) after participating in the capital budgeting process.

▸ Periodic planning processes are characterized by considerable time pressure in practice. The tight deadlines can best be met by enabling controllers to manage both the generation of individual plans and their coordination (including multi-stage feedback and adjustment processes).

In analyzing the allocation of tasks to persons, there are two further aspects that need to be highlighted. Firstly, the expected duration of the assignment influences the allocation problem. For instance, the same tasks may exist in a project struc-ture as would usually be carried out by a controller in the course of his »normal work«. However, a high degree of specialization is not worthwhile for the (short) project duration, meaning that including a controller would make no sense. Secondly, the allocation of existing knowledge is determined by the tasks and the requirements placed on the persons responsible for their execution. Whenever we approach areas of creative activity, such determinability is limited. Creativity is required not only in R & D or strategic planning. It is also needed for identifying improvements and innovations in existing areas of activity. This also affects controllership. In this sense, it is beneficial to create change potential purposefully by making allowances for corresponding capacities: We already came across the usefulness of such options in a different context, when discussing Zünd's controller types.

The outcome of a process of organization is to assign rights and duties to persons. Duties may relate to

▸ *Factors*
The spectrum ranges from free decision making (»You'll have to leave it up to me to decide which consultant I use for this project«) to exogenous specifications (deploying a standard PC).

▸ *Processes*
Travel expense guidelines are a popular example for standard processes. Conversely, controllers are almost completely free in deciding how to carry out variance analyses.

▸ *Results*
On the one hand, controllers have to keep to strict deadlines for reporting; on the other hand, the outcome of a coaching process is up to those involved.

Defining duties always requires the simultaneous definition of rights or competencies (abilities and motivation are complemented by rights). These relate to the same
objects or situations as the duties and include rights of disposition and information.
For instance, the former includes the right to use an allocated budget completely; an
example for the latter is the right to participate in managers' planning meetings
without express invitation. One of the core rights of controllers, which often has to
be »earned in battle«, is the right to take the initiative in contradicting managers.
The right to comment on important management decision papers is a further
important right. Such commenting rights range from formal hearings (»All capital
budgeting applications have to be processed via a controller's desk«) to veto rights.
They provide controllers with influence over managers; it has been shown empirically that this type of influence has a positive effect on company success (cf. Bauer
2002, p. 253); the most extensive right, the right of veto, had a lower influence than
obligatory hearings (cf. Weber/Schäffer/Bauer 2000, p. 31).

> A key right of controllers is the right to contradict others without being requested to do so.

Finally, rights and duties are linked to consequences which are triggered by the
outcomes of the monitoring process. Consequences may take the form of rewards
(such as paying a bonus) or of penalties (punishment ranging up to dismissal). For
controller tasks, one of the core problems is that their outcomes are hard to measure
or were usually not measured in the past. For this reason, there was no performance
monitoring in the strict sense of the expression. Consequences for controllers were
therefore based on an unstable foundation (global personal assessment by the
manager). We will discuss possibilities of making changes in this area at a later
stage.

> Usually, controllers' activities are subject to few direct penalties.

4.3.2 Specific aspects of the design task resulting from the function of assuring rationality

The previous section provided a basic framework for the organizational design of
controller tasks relevant for all activities within the company. Next, we will add
specifics resulting from the character of controller tasks as a special form of management support, which controllers have to provide in different forms. Their share of
the function of assuring rationality specifically requires controllers to be close to
management. Supplementary and constraining tasks have to be matched to each
specific case; rationality cannot be assured as »one size fits all«. However, it also
requires sufficient separation between the manager and the controller: If the
controller adapts too much to the manager, there is a risk that he will lose his independence and autonomy. The interaction between managers and controllers has to
follow a kind of dynamic equilibrium. Deviating from it in one direction means
losing the counterpart function; controllers then turn into pure service providers
»without any opinion of their own«. Deviations in the other directions result when
controllers increasingly play the role of *éminence grise*; if this happens, they take
over core management roles.

> Controllers simulta-neously have to maintain sufficient closeness and distance to »their« managers.

For a dynamic equilibrium to result, certain conditions have to be fulfilled which
we will sort into three groups relating to abilities, rights and motivation. First,
aspects relating to abilities:

▸ On the one hand, controllers need to know enough about the rules of managers' activities to understand their actions. On the other hand, they have to avoid knowing managers so well that they end up thinking like them. This would reinforce the internal models of managers instead of complementing and challenging them, a fact which is also highlighted by the following quote from the top controller of a DAX 30 company: »In controlling, having a profound knowledge of the business can sometimes be an impediment because one becomes too understanding of the other party. ... On the one hand, understanding the business is very helpful because one is able to analyze issues and identify relationships very quickly. On the other hand, dealing with a topic in too much detail can create an excessive level of understanding for the problems that exist in the other unit. In this case, one may not be able to demand solutions with the same firmness as if one were not as familiar with the details of the problems« (Weber 2008, p. 108).

▸ Controllers need to develop an appropriate level of »intuition« regarding what is going on in »their« business units. This is essential for arriving at a level of situational awareness that permits the actions of managers to be evaluated. It depends on having a broad personal network on the one hand and a high degree of sensitivity on the other. However, controllers should not lose their ability to assess situations objectively. Understanding situations must not lead to judgment being clouded.

▸ If controllers are supposed to comment »professionally« on decisions and plans of their managers, they need to have sufficient knowledge of each individual decision and its context: No investment project can be assessed solely on the basis of the figures contained in the costing. Controllers would then only be able to discover inconsistencies and errors in calculations. This means having to interact more intensely with capital budgeting decision makers and participating in the process of preparing the investment proposal. If controllers are included at the early stages, however, this should not make them lose their neutrality towards the project. One cannot avoid their becoming a fixed part of the project team and being dominated by the objective of wanting to bring the project to a good conclusion, i.e. implementing it.

▸ Finally, another ability controllers need to have is that of taking a minority position and defending it. We have described the elements of diverging from established positions on several occasions previously: A consciously risk-averse way of analyzing decisions in advance is as much part of this attitude as is emphasizing reflective elements over intuitive ones in the decision-making process. Conversely, controllers also have to ensure that they do not influence decision making too strongly in their own direction, thereby making managers rely excessively on numbers or making them too risk-averse.

The aspect of participation rights was already addressed in the previous section: In order for managers to take their controllers seriously as counterparts, the controllers need sufficient power to influence processes, ranging from information rights to the possibility of expressing a veto in the decision-making process. Without such participation rights, controllers potentially become »toothless«: If the owner-manager of a medium-sized company employs a controller primarily to be a personal business assistant, then the only way for the controller to exert an influence would be by

If controllers have insufficient influence on managers, they risk becoming »toothless«.

»force of the stronger argument«. The effectiveness of the counterpart function would thereby be (severely) compromised. On the other hand, the rights of controllers should not be so far-reaching that they become a bottleneck for the business. The following quote from practice provides a good example of misdirected influence: »Whenever we managed to get a project through controlling, the champagne flowed freely!« In such a situation, controllers quickly play an exaggerated holding-back role.

Controllers can also overdo their holding-back role.

Finally, there is the motivation of wanting to act upon managers. Two aspects are of core importance for the dynamic equilibrium:

▶ The first concerns the willingness to play an active role as a counterpart. As discussed previously, the inclusion of controllers in decision-making processes curtails managers' perceived scope of action, which may lead to negative behavioral effects. Even when managers are fundamentally convinced of the importance of controllers' activities, it may still bother them if controllers »have a finger in every pie« and keep on »rubbing salt in open wounds«. Perfectionism on the part of the controllers, an approach of »only 100 percent is good enough«, can be detrimental; a certain degree of »laissez-faire« often helps to »clear the air«. Controllers should therefore aim to focus their counterpart function on core topics. Usually, the limited resources available to controller units are helpful in this respect. On the other hand, they should try not to emerge as »winners« from all conflicts. Nothing creates more backlash than always being right. At the same time, controllers should not be too lenient; defensive behavior can quickly be interpreted as a weakness. This would imperil the counterpart function considerably.

▶ The second motivational aspect to be addressed essentially only concerns local controllers not working at headquarters. They are expected to identify with their business unit. Otherwise, they are quickly labeled as »spies from headquarters«. Effectively working together with the unit's management in an atmosphere of mutual trust is placed at risk, as is getting access to the different types of information needed from the unit. However, such identification and team spirit can again go too far. This becomes clear when a manager mentions that she will be sending »her« controller to headquarters for negotiations. Controllers should not lose their overall company perspective just because they work for a subsidiary. They should also not forget that those on whose behalf they carry out the constraining function sit further up in the management hierarchy.

The specifics of the mixture of controllers' tasks result in a tension described in the literature as a conflict between »involvement« and »independence« (cf. Sathe 1982, pp. 17–38). Fundamentally, this tension cannot be resolved, certainly not with structural tools. However, it is helpful to be aware of it and to address it explicitly – e.g. by creating a corresponding mission statement or launching discussions when there is a specific cause (for instance, when a controller has been holding managers back too much). On the other hand, »potential problems associated with active controller involvement [can be overcome] if controllers and other managers are able to create and maintain interpersonal trust and respect while challenging each other to excel« (Sathe 1982, p. 38).

Creative tension between involvement and independence

Excerpts from the article »Controller Involvement in Management« by Vijay Sathe (1982):

»In addition to the responsibility for assisting management in the running of the business, requiring some degree of involvement in the decision-making process, the controller is responsible for accurate reporting of financial information to stockholders and government agencies and is also responsible for protection of the company's assets. ... The last two responsibilities are of a custodial and monitoring nature and require a degree of controller independence from management. ... Without the opportunity for active involvement in business decision making that the service role provides, the controller may not be privy to sensitive management accounting information and deliberations in progress. Thus, the controller's role becomes one of checking compliance with corporate policy and procedures after the relevant decisions have already been made, that is, *after-the-fact or reactive control*. In contrast, a controller actively involved with management in business decision making has an opportunity to put an early stop to ill-conceived, ill-advised, or illegal courses of action being contemplated, that is, *before-the-fact or anticipatory control*. More responsive control is therefore possible with a broadened definition of the controller's areas of responsibility, *provided that the controller's involvement in management does not impair the controller's sense of objectivity and independence, or vice versa*« (Sathe 1982, pp. 17–19).

4.3.3 Problems of motivation specific to controllers

Finally, there are also issues concerning the design of incentives for controllers that influence the design of controller units. These result from the special characteristics of controller tasks and have been neglected in the relevant literature up to now. Even in practice, the topic does not seem to generate much interest currently. However, a closer look seems to indicate – as a working hypothesis – that a considerable part of the problems many companies experience with their controllers (»wet blankets«, »number crunchers«) may be related to the lacking engagement with the issue of motivation.

Controllers' motivation is often neglected.

Two theories of motivation are cited most frequently in the relevant literature. On the one hand, there is Maslow's hierarchy of needs (which has become common knowledge); on the other hand there is the differentiation between motivators and hygiene factors that resulted from a study by Herzberg. The findings of the latter are summarized in *Figure 4-5*. Specific problems of designing incentives for controllers immediately become apparent: Managers are effectively motivated by their performance output. As shown previously, however, measuring the performance of controllers is difficult. Where controllership is expressed in its most typical form, the key challenge for controllers is to ensure that line managers act in a way consistent with the company's goals. The success of their activities is not visible externally: The company's results are subject to so many internal and external influences that controllers' contribution to company success cannot be measured comprehensively or accurately. When controllers stand out (e.g. when engaging in conflicts), this is usually a sign of friction, i.e. of mistakes. A similar observation applies to the second-strongest motivator according to Herzberg's studies, namely recognition. Only with regard to work itself as a facet of intrinsic motivation are there no specific negative influences for controllers.

The performance of controllers is hard to measure.

There are two solutions to this unsatisfactory state of affairs, which can also be used in combination. The first addresses the possibility of making one's own performance visible to managers. If controllers manage to find a way of making core aspects of their services measurable with sufficient validity and reliability, and if they can set objectives for their services together with their internal customers, the managers, this makes their performance visible and provides a sufficient basis for recognition by management in the form of planned-vs.-actual comparisons.

The measurement of performance can, however, only apply to specific parts in the case of services. Furthermore, systematic distortions of managers' assessments have to be expected – especially for constraining tasks: It would be asking a bit much of managers to welcome their own »defeats«! It therefore makes sense to create additional incentives matching the tasks. Career planning appears to be particularly suitable and will be described in greater detail.

Generally, individual career motivation can range across a very wide spectrum. One of the many different attempts to provide some structure was proposed by Schein (1977, pp. 49–64). In his often-cited basic differentiation, he identified five so-called »career anchors« on the basis of empirical studies:

Concept of »career anchors«

▸ *General managerial competence*, i.e. the legitimacy of carrying out management actions. Power and status as well as satisfaction derived from accepting responsibility play an important role in this case.
▸ *Security*, i.e. the need to establish and protect a satisfactory position in the long term. Employees thus motivated would prefer job or pension guarantees to hierarchical promotion.
▸ *Creativity*, i.e. the opportunity to try and make new things.
▸ *Technical-functional competence*: this career anchor is similar to managerial competence, but focuses on a different aspect: In this case, motivation is derived from making the most of specific abilities and from achieving recognition for these abilities. This form of motivation is often found for specialists (e.g. development engineers).
▸ *Autonomy and independence*, i.e. the opportunity of having maximum freedom in designing and carrying out one's job.

Fig. 4-5

Herzberg's two factor theory of motivation (1968, p. 57)

Motivators	Hygiene factors
▸ Achievement ▸ Recognition ▸ Work itself ▸ Responsibility ▸ Advancement ▸ Growth opportunities	▸ Company policy and administration ▸ Supervision ▸ Relationships with supervisors, peers, subordinates ▸ Work conditions ▸ Salary ▸ Personal life ▸ Status ▸ Security
Factors that lead to extreme satisfaction	*Factors that lead to extreme dissatisfaction*

Controller positions primarily offer technical-functional competence and autonomy and independence as career anchors:

▶ *Technical-functional competence*
Controllers have to be able to familiarize themselves with the fundamentals of their unit's business. Only individuals who understand the structures and processes of production are able to participate in managing them. Further competence aspects relate to the tools of planning, information supply and monitoring, as well as to the need for compensating a lacking positional authority with persuasion and consensus-building skills.

▶ *Autonomy and independence*
Controller activities are characterized by their considerable degrees of freedom. In addition to the usual, standardized »daily business« (e.g. monthly discussions of variances), planning tasks and consulting activities provide sufficient space for implementing one's own ideas and for finding one's own way of completing tasks in accordance with individual preferences. Furthermore, independence is – in addition to involvement – a key characteristic of controller positions.

Managerial competence is, however, not something that controller positions can teach. If one withholds this from controllers in the long term, there is the risk that they will acquire the skills in spite of their role (»éminence grise«). It therefore appears not only sensible, but even desirable, to view controller positions as an essential career step for managers, which they should, however, take not once, but several times. Such job rotation could make a significant contribution to overcoming the formation of fault lines between controllers and line managers, to creating mutual understanding and to assuring that controller tasks are executed (even) more effectively and efficiently than before.

4.3.4 Assuring the rationality of controllers

Amongst other things, controllers are tasked with assuring their managers' rationality. But who assures the rationality of the controllers themselves? Or, to put it more simply: Who monitors the controller? This type of question is common in business practice, but one hardly ever comes across it in the relevant literature (an exception for the area of accounting is the study by Weißenberger 1997, whereas the study by Herzog 1998, pp. 218–223 addresses the issue for the area of controlling; cf. also the most recent study by Paefgen 2008).

First, one has to ask the question of whether there is even a need for assuring the rationality of controllers. According to the structure usually used in this book, such a need could result either from deficits in the abilities or deficits in the motivation of controllers. We mentioned possible deficits in the area of abilities various times in the previous sections and chapters:

▶ Controllers could be immersed too deeply in the world of financial indicators and therefore lack a complete understanding of the business, its success factors and strategic potential.

▸ Controllers might also lack knowledge of the business as well as the corresponding experience since they remain only briefly in a given unit or department.
▸ Controllers often underestimate the value of intuitive assessments. They reduce decision problems to hard data and thereby risk ignoring important information.

Furthermore, controllers carry out tasks whose quality managers are often unable to assess correctly. Whether a cost allocation really corresponds to the state of the art in cost accounting or whether a controller really knows the nitty-gritty of how to break down overheads thereby remains an unanswered question. Gaps in the technical abilities of controllers often remain undiscovered.

We have also come across arguments on the side of controllers' motivation several times, and dealt with the question in greater depth in the previous section. To summarize important aspects of the problem:
▸ Controllers are also not free from being tempted to reduce their work suffering. There are opportunities to do so in the context of all supplementary and constraining tasks (at least), i.e. whenever the manager is unable to assess the quality and quantity of the controller's performance satisfactorily. The possibility of limiting one's effort is already given in standard information systems. Even a cursory inspection of the cost accounting of large companies reveals problems with out-of-date information. Changes are not captured or captured too late (for more detailed information, cf. Weber/Weißenberger/Guth/Spieker 2000). Higher quality standards in combination with a greater effort would help prevent this. As managers in their role as customers often do not see the problems, however, there is no extrinsic incentive for controllers to put more effort into their work.
▸ Controllers also want to have a successful career. As mentioned above, there are different ways of achieving this goal. For instance, a controller could try to discover extensive management problems as often as possible, e.g. regarding faulty budget proposals (such as those that contain too much slack), regarding overly optimistic or badly prepared capital budgeting requests, or by detecting problematic business behavior. Such an approach is based on the expectation: »The first controller to be promoted is the one with the most scalps«. On the other hand, controllers can act in collusion with managers, i.e. cooperate with them even when they really should be steering in the opposite direction. In the sense of »scratch my back, then I'll scratch yours«, the underlying idea is to be able to switch to »the other side« – namely that of the managers – at a later stage without too many problems.
▸ A further cause could be unpleasant personal attitudes on the part of controllers. For instance, one hears stories about controllers who enjoy making life difficult for other people or who try to achieve a sense of greater self-worth by exercising power. Controllers have lots of chances to do so. The boundary between assuring rationality (a desirable action) and arbitrary hindrances is not clear in each case and therefore hard to prove.

The arguments shown above indicate that there is some justification for inquiring about how to assure the rationality of controllers. Managers are the most suited for this task. They have a great deal of influence, particularly in the case of unburdening tasks, and are able to test their controllers' willingness and ability to

Managers usually have sufficient opportunity to address the rationality deficits of their controllers.

perform. As managers are usually hierarchically superior to controllers, they have a broad range of escalation options available to them, ranging from giving bad performance evaluations to the detriment of the controller's career planning to working towards having the controller removed from his or her position. In other words, managers fundamentally find themselves in quite a strong position in relation to their controllers – in this sense, we have pointed out various times that controllers need to find ways of performing their counterpart function successfully in spite of the strength of managers.

Controller units can also limit the risk of inappropriate behavior by controllers by designing their work context accordingly. This begins with the formulation of a mission statement describing a desirable standard of behavior for controllers – we will be dealing with mission statements in greater detail in chapter 5. Another avenue of influence is the fundamental orientation of the controller positions: By providing controllers with a perspective that includes the chance to join management instead of remaining professional controllers, the time they are likely to spend in the controller unit is limited from the time of recruitment. This eliminates long-term strategies aimed at accumulating and exercising power. Furthermore, concrete designs for normative controller career paths are an even more direct approach. These include rules governing typical periods spent in specific controller positions (often less than three years) and the desired job change into management. The risk of having to deal with deficits of controllers' abilities and motivation can be dealt with very effectively at the recruitment stage. On the one hand, the image presented to candidates by a controller unit has a self-selecting effect; if the monitoring and counterpart aspect is exaggerated, there is a risk of getting inappropriate controllers. On the other hand, potentially critical personality aspects can be checked and questioned during the recruitment process. Finally, there are also opportunities for limiting potential rationality deficits of controllers in the context of interactions within the controller unit. An intensive information exchange between controllers provides the opportunity of recognizing potential misconduct of individual controllers and of reacting swiftly and appropriately. Changes to personnel can also be made – proactively in a sense – by the head of the controller unit.

Overall, as shown by this short section, the topic of »Who assures the rationality of those responsible for assuring rationality?« is of fundamental relevance. The spectrum of possible causes for controllers' rationality deficits is wide. Nevertheless, it is not necessary to dedicate a special position within con-

Summary
(see guiding questions 3 and 4)

▶ A key part of designing a controller unit consists of assigning tasks (»controllership«) to persons (»controllers«). This is a typical problem of organization.

▶ Controller-specific quantum, specialization and motivational effects impact on the solution to this problem. Interdependencies and similarities between tasks are additional factors. Finally, the duration and describability of the assignment task have to be taken into account.

▶ Particular features result from the specific function of assuring rationality. Controllers need to find a dynamic equilibrium between involvement and independence. Too much independence can be as damaging as excessive identification with management and its problems.

▶ Special conditions for controllers' motivation result from their specific situation between involvement and independence. There are only very limited chances for extrinsic incentives. One of the strongest potential incentives is career planning.

▶ Incentive problems may cause unprofessional, opportunistic behavior on the part of controllers, but this can be prevented or limited sufficiently by management.

trolling to solving this problem. The influence of managers over controllers is suffi-ciently strong for them to penalize clear misconduct. Still, the topic should be taken into consideration when designing controller units, and addressed with the appropri-ate measures. Furthermore, recognizing potential risks often helps to avoid them.

4.4 Summary

The share of controllers exceeds one percent of total staff in some companies. This can lead to up to four-digit figures of the number of employees holding controller positions. In spite of their large numbers, however, the relevant literature has not dedicated much attention to the question of how to design the composition of all these positions, i.e. the controller unit. This may also be because there is a percep-tion that there is little leeway for active design within the hierarchical structure of a company. However, a more detailed analysis, as started in this chapter and continued in section 2 of the next chapter, quickly shows that there are considerable degrees of freedom for designing a controller unit even within hierarchical contexts.

Internal (e.g. management's attitude towards controlling) and external (especially environmental munificence) context factors influence the solution to this design problem. The development status of controlling in the specific company needs to be taken into account as a key factor. Also, the special character of the task of assuring rationality within the bundle of controllers' management support services has to be taken into consideration. This factor especially requires a dynamic analysis of the design problem. Apart from that, designing a controller unit should be identified and solved as a »normal«, albeit complex and challenging, problem of organization. The following, concluding chapter of the book will begin with the steps that can be taken to address this issue.

Recommended reading...

... Terminological basics
David 2005, pp. 12–18

... On the freedom to take design decisions
David 2005, pp. 28–43
Kronast 1989, pp. 184–196
Weber/David/Prenzler 2001, pp. 7–18

... Basic structure of the design task
Berthel 1991, pp. 481–498
Frese 1996, pp. 3/1–3/15
Jost 2000

5 The strategic positioning of controller units

Guiding questions:

1 Which basic aspects have to be taken into account when designing controller units in companies?

2 Which role do mission statements play in the strategic positioning of controller units and how can such mission statements be designed?

3 Can corporate strategic planning tools be applied to the strategic positioning of controller units?

4 Which aspects have to be taken into account when defining the hierarchical structure of a controller unit? Depending on the context, which options are there – and how are controller units structured in practice?

In chapter 4, we dealt with fundamental aspects of designing controller units. Now, in the final chapter of the book, we will focus our attention on the strategic positioning of the controller unit. In doing so, we will be referring back to the discussion on »role taking« vs. »role making« that was started in chapter 4 and which will now be considered in greater depth. This is then extended to include tools that help to identify and implement the most suitable basic strategic position. Afterwards, we will deal in greater detail with the question of what can be said about the organization of controller units – »structure follows strategy«. This is the design aspect that has received the most attention in the relevant literature, and it is also of considerable importance in practice. The chapter concludes with a short summary and outlook on the future development of controlling – linking up with the historical past that was described in chapter 1 of this book.

What to expect in this chapter

5.1 Basic aspects

Strategic planning deals with success factors and the skills required to activate them. Transferring this perspective to controller units, which form part of a company's hierarchy, means having to abandon the pure »role taking« perspective. Viewing controller units strategically presupposes the option of »role making«, at least in some areas. The following is based on this assumption (see the corresponding section in chapter 4).

What are the key success factors for a controller unit?

Potential success factors are a good point for starting the discussion. It is not immediately apparent what this means in detail. Therefore, the first question has to be how the success of a controller unit or of controllers' activities can be measured.

5.1.1 Controllers' contributions to company performance

Asking managers about their impact is one of the basic pillars of controllers' business:

▸ New investment proposals have to meet profitability targets.
▸ New products are only included in the product range if they promise to improve results.
▸ If managers do not achieve their targets, they have to face unpleasant questions from controllers about the variances.

Conversely, it is a very unfamiliar concept for controllers to ask themselves about their own contributions to company performance. Whether company profitability increases if an additional controller is employed – or whether the salary he or she draws lowers profitability – is a question no controller is able to answer properly in practice. Seeking comparisons with other companies is therefore very important in deciding on the size of a controller unit; having many more controllers than one's competitors is a weak negotiating position internally. If one is close to the industry standard, there is no need for justification. Finally, there is also the efficiency hypothesis. It states that a given behavioral pattern has to be efficient if most companies apply it in the long term in a competitive environment. If it were not efficient, companies would suffer competitive disadvantages and disappear from the market at some stage.

The relevant literature is aware of the question concerning controllers' contributions to success, but the topic has not been intensely debated to date. There is not even any agreement on how to measure their contribution to success (cf. Bauer 2002, pp. 137–145, and the sources provided there). One often finds approaches which used the degree to which the objectives of controlling are achieved as a yardstick: The better controllers fulfill the goals their managers or they themselves have set (e.g. as derived from the literature), the more successful they are considered to be. However, this is still quite a long way off from the kind of statement that is really required: Even if controllers execute the information supply function for managers flawlessly, for instance, this does not necessarily mean they contribute a single additional euro to profits. There is a large gap between transparency concerning decisions and their actual impact.

On the other hand, there is one effect on a company's profitability that is immediately apparent: Controllers cause costs. Making do without controllers provides substantial, immediate and direct savings on payroll costs. In searching for financial benefits to counterbalance these costs, one might think of saved costs for managers: Controllers unburden managers, meaning that the same amount of work can be done with fewer managers. As has been mentioned previously, controllers are considered to be effective cost cutters: The costs they save could be offset against their payroll costs. Apart from questions of allocation (can one really allocate the cost reductions to controllers alone?), this would, however, only cover a small facet of controllers' activities.

The problem of having to take into consideration different factors influencing an outcome and placing them into a relationship is discussed in the Balanced Scorecard concept. The realization that different leading and lagging indicators have to be

Measuring the costs caused by a controller unit is easy – but the same cannot be said of a controller unit's performance.

used simultaneously led to the decision to form four measurement perspectives and to establish cause-effect relationships between them. Similar observations can be found in the research on how to measure companies' success (cf. Bhargava/Dubelaar/Ramaswami 1994 for an overview). It is very often not only measured in financial terms. Instead, three measures of success are used, as suggested by Walker/Ruekert 1987:

The problem begins with the question of how to measure company performance »properly«.

▸ The starting point is the *adaptability* of a company to environmental changes caused by external shocks or other events, be it on the resource or market side. A higher level of adaptability makes it possible to exploit opportunities faster and to react more quickly to risks or detrimental developments. In both cases, this results in competitive advantages, which in turn are related to better profits in the long run.

Adaptability

Controllers can support their companies' adaptability in many ways, e.g. by supplying early warning indicators, continuously questioning strategic assumptions and promoting projects that increase the organization's adaptability.

▸ *Market success* is a further measure of success. It may result from factors such as achieving a high level of customer satisfaction, considerable customer benefits or strong customer retention. In addition to such customer-related aspects, there are also market-related measures such as the company's market share. Greater success on the market provides possibilities such as earning higher margins, incurring lower costs for attracting new customers and registering higher sales, thereby contributing to financial success.

Market success

Controllers can achieve market success especially by providing support to marketing and distribution, e.g. by determining profitability per customer and by acting to assure rationality in the process of new product design. Initiating and encouraging a higher degree of process orientation can also be helpful as this contributes to greater customer satisfaction.

▸ Finally, the third measure of success is *financial performance*, which is usually the center of attention when measuring commercial success. It is not really necessary to justify this measure any further. Controllers are used to working with this outcome measure. Potential influences of controllers on this dimension – such as their own payroll costs – have already been mentioned.

Financial performance

The three measures of success provide a highly comprehensive description of company success, both in terms of content and in terms of time. Adaptability can be seen as an early leading indicator for success. Its significance only becomes apparent over time. Market success is already situated closer to financial success, but is still a leading indicator. Finally, financial success is a lagging indicator. Investing into adaptability is likely to worsen financial results in the short term, and the crop of this planting can only be harvested much later. This applies in a similar way to market success, although the seed will bear fruit sooner in this case.

These thoughts on the components of company success help to identify and structure potential ways in which controllers can impact success more clearly. Still, there remains the problem that controllers usually only have an indirect effect on the measures of success. They are able to influence their own costs; these are subject to the usual budgeting processes, just like other units. But a large part of their impact on financial success and all of their contributions to enhanced market success and stronger adaptability are in fact only realized through the actions of managers. If managers do not use the information they are given to make better decisions, if they cannot generate better coordinated activities on the basis of systematic planning organized by controllers, if they do not implement the results of monitoring by improving processes and activities, if they choose to ignore the warnings of controllers regarding impending decisions, then there will be no effect on the different measures of success. If the owner-proprietor of a medium-sized company employs a controller, but then continues to manage his company just as before, the company's results will suffer and its competitiveness will not be boosted. Therefore, managers are essential for the success of controllers.

> Controllers can only be successful »through their managers«.

Measuring the success of controller activities thus requires a kind of »triple jump«: Good work on the part of the controllers increases the quality of work of managers, which in turn impacts the company's success positively. In other words, we are confronted with a highly complex set of relationships which cannot be measured with sufficient precision in most companies – although their conceptual effect should not be underestimated. What is possible, however, is to check the set of relationships across many companies. Cross-sectional empirical studies with large numbers of respondents are an ideal way of doing this. One such study, which was based on the above considerations, will be outlined in the following (cf. Spillecke 2006). It extends the »triple jump« mentioned above to a four-level relationship: The first level consists of the quality of controller services. It influences the way management uses these services (the higher the quality, the stronger the usage). The usage of these in turn has a positive impact on the quality of management, which is measured using a management cycle consisting of decision making, influencing, and monitoring. Finally, the quality of management affects company success positively (cf. Spillecke 2006, p. 164). This is measured, as described above, using the three components adaptability, market success, and financial success. This multilevel relationship was confirmed impressively in the survey. Therefore, controllers not only have to believe in the efficiency hypothesis (all companies have controllers, therefore it cannot be uneconomical to have them), but can actively postulate an impact on success – and work on improving the level of success. The study by Spillecke also provided interesting information on this question: For instance, it confirmed that there is a danger of negatively impacting a company's development capacity by assuring rationality too zealously. More specifically, the study found that there was a weak, negative influence of controller services on company adaptability, which did not, however, change the overall positive impact on company success. Another valuable finding of the study was how strongly controllers' internal customer orientation influences the quality of their services as perceived by managers. In other words, this is a key lever for influencing controllers' impact on company success. For this reason, we will be dedicating some more attention to internal customer orientation in a separate section.

> Empirically, controllers can have a positive impact on company performance.

The relationships between the determinants of success of controller activities are largely defined by the context within which controllers do their work. As mentioned several times previously, the type and characteristics of controllers' activities depend heavily on the context. This context dependency is determined both by (1) the characteristics of the managers with whom controllers work and by (2) the environment within which the managers themselves operate.

▶ Regarding (1): Controllers' activities are expected to have the greatest »leverage« when management functions poorly, e.g. when it is spoilt by success, focused on power or not responsive to market forces. Assuring rationality is only necessary if there are significant rationality deficits. Professional management does not render controllers ineffectual, but it essentially limits their impact to the benefits derived from unburdening management.

▶ Regarding (2): If the market is lenient when it comes to management mistakes, in other words, when the competitive environment is munificent, then one would expect controller activities to have only a small impact on company success. For instance, being a controller in a regulated environment, where cost increases are automatically »rewarded« through price increases, quickly leads to controllers becoming ineffectual. Conversely, if the environment is highly competitive and therefore punishes management mistakes mercilessly (e.g. through sales losses), then the blessings of controllers' work can show up very clearly in the companies' profits.

> **In the spotlight**
>
> The last-mentioned aspect has been confirmed empirically. In the study by Bauer, the construct of »environmental munificence« was used, as mentioned in the previous chapter (cf. Bauer 2002, pp. 102–104). It reflects how easy it is for management to obtain the required resources on the factor markets, how easily it can build or maintain the required skills and how identifiable weaknesses of the company (e.g. delivery problems, wrong pricing etc.) affect demand (cf. Bauer 2002, p. 182). The findings of the study were as expected. Environmental munificence does indeed act as a moderator on controllers' contribution to success: Controllers' activities have a greater impact on company results when the external environment is miserly than when it is munificent (cf. Bauer 2002, p. 255). In other words: The more inhospitable conditions are in the marketplace, the more important it is to have controllers.

5.1.2 Internal customer orientation: a key factor influencing the success of controlling

The expression »customer orientation« is originally a marketing term. It is of key relevance to the field of marketing; one could even say that orienting a company towards the needs of its customers is the essence of marketing. It appears to be only a small step from orienting one's activities towards external customers to viewing other departments and their employees as customers and behaving accordingly. However, this step means turning one's back on the classical understanding of hierarchy, whereby departments work closely and smoothly together because that is how it is organized. Viewing individuals, groups and units within the company as customers means that one possesses degrees of freedom in the way one designs one's activities, in other words, having the freedom to engage in »role making« to a certain degree – and with reference to controllers, this is exactly the situation on which we have based our arguments in this chapter.

Internal customer orientation is the key lever allowing controllers to work effectively.

Both the expression and concept of internal customer orientation were also developed by marketing. An »external« construct (the relationship between companies and market customers) was transferred to the relationship between different persons and/or departments within the companies themselves. The literature on marketing typically differentiates between three perspectives of internal customer orientation (cf. Spillecke 2006, pp. 30–43):

▸ From an *information perspective*, internal customer orientation relates to knowing the needs of one's customers. For controllers, this means knowing the skills (»astute business man«, »inexperienced scientist«) and characteristics (»loyal mercenary«, »power-hungry careerist«) of managers. Otherwise, it is not possible to focus appropriately on the internal customers; only when controllers possess the required information can they decide whether a specific service involves unburdening, supplementing or constraining their manager's activities. Classifying activities according to this scheme is something we have addressed before. Furthermore, controllers have to know which services their managers want; this allows them to coordinate the mix of tasks and to align their focus areas with the managers' interests. Knowledge about internal customers also has to be developed within each task type. It requires asking about the respective needs (»more graphics, fewer tables«) and taking them into consideration when designing and implementing services. Finally, if controllers want to be customer-oriented, they also have to know how satisfied the managers are with their performance, and have to ask the appropriate questions to find out. They need this information in order to be able to critically analyze and improve the services they deliver.

▸ From a *cultural perspective*, the key aspect is the basic attitude, which should focus on delivering the best services to internal customers and achieving the highest rate of customer satisfaction. In this sense, internal customer orientation in a certain way forms a »genetic code« which determines behavior. For controllers, this could mean anchoring internal customer orientation in their mission statement (on which we will focus in more detail in section 5.2.1) and communicating it actively to managers as a type of performance promise. Furthermore, this philosophy can be a key selection criterion for employing new controllers (»a special kind of controller«).

▸ Finally, the *strategic perspective* emphasizes translating the idea of internal customer orientation into concrete designs and activities. In this sense, »customer orientation in the area of controlling can be seen as a strategy for asserting oneself in the context of the company by providing a unique benefit, thereby strengthening one's position within the organization« (Mosiek 2002, p. 46). This benefit is the point of reference for controller units and the yardstick for their work.

Of the three perspectives, it is the first which is the most interesting for our purposes: Internal customer orientation as a »genetic code« cannot be prescribed and is a result of customer-oriented behavior rather than its cause. Internal customer orientation as a strategic perspective requires accurate knowledge of the needs, characteristics and abilities of managers. Knowing the customer is the »enabler« of customer-oriented behavior and will therefore be analyzed in greater detail in the following. We base our approach on Spillecke 2006. The benefit is that it allows us to present the corresponding empirical findings instead of having to rely exclusively on conceptual argumentation.

In his model, Spillecke differentiates four elements determining internal customer orientation of controller units:

▸ *Formal generation of information*
»Formal generation of information encompasses ways and means of discovering managers' information needs in official or formal ways, using techniques that controllers apply in their functions and activities as members of a controller unit. Some examples of formal methods of information generation are written surveys or qualitative, narrative interviews« (Spillecke 2006, p. 113). Based on such formal methods, controllers can – on the one hand – gain essential information about the services required by managers in the sense of instrumental use of information. On the other hand, using information conceptually, they can signal to managers that they consider it important to know the needs of their internal customers.

▸ *Informal generation of information*
This »encompasses ways and means of discovering managers' information needs by using informal channels that lie outside the usual set of controller activities. Some examples for informal generation of information« are conversations in a hallway or personal meetings after business hours« (Spillecke 2006, pp. 114–115). The better controllers are networked in an organization, the more information they can obtain about their internal customers using such informal methods. This channel is an abundant source of information on attitudes (»he really doesn't care about the figures«) and abilities (»she never understood what a net present value is«).

▸ *Distribution of information*
It is important to ensure that information concerning internal customers does not remain isolated with individual controllers – especially against the backdrop of the coordinating activities of controllers. »Only by sharing knowledge about customers' information needs widely can controllers ensure that they have a common basis from which to react in a coordinated way to the wishes of the customers of controlling« (Spillecke 2006, p. 116). Some of the tools that can be used for this purpose are newsletters, reports and formal presentations, but also strong informal communication between controllers.

▸ *Reactions of the controller unit*
The first three characteristics of internal customer orientation serve to achieve a better awareness of the services required by managers. However, knowledge alone does not add value. It has to be translated into concrete actions. »The reactions of the controller unit can be defined as a set of measures aimed at reacting to the information that has been acquired, in other words, to the information needs of the customers« (Spillecke 2006, p. 119). In this sense, controllers have to check the assumptions underlying their services (e.g. low knowledge of analytical business tools amongst managers) on an ongoing basis; if there are changes, they need to reconsider the spectrum of services they are offering. The same applies for the individual services offered, where new, innovative products can be used to react to changes in customers' needs.

Information-based internal customer orientation can be represented using four aspects.

This model was recently analyzed empirically. Overall, it was found that all four elements have a strong and significant influence on the internal customer orientation of controllers (cf. Spillecke 2006, pp. 122–134). Not surprisingly, the strongest effect was found for the reaction of the controller unit. This is where managers see the closeness of their internal suppliers most directly. The second strongest influence was found for formal generation of information. Here, too, we are confronted with an area where managers directly perceive the efforts of their controllers aimed at providing appropriate services. The remaining two elements also had a positive impact on the internal customer orientation of controllers.

With these elements, the playing field on which controllers can positively influence their contribution to company results has been outlined: As has been shown, a higher level of internal customer orientation improves the quality of controller services, which makes managers use the services more extensively, which boosts the quality of management, which in turn improves company results.

5.1.3 Content-related influences on the strategic design of controller units

In chapter 4, we described the development of controllership in terms of a multi-stage model. The starting point was the need to supply management with relevant information. Next, a planning and monitoring context had to be built on the information and management had to be trained to use the necessary tools. Finally, the third development phase included management in its entirety and thereby integrated questions of organization and personnel management. We will use this development concept to discuss key influences on the strategic design of controller tasks.

As regards the *focus on information*, there are two key developments to which controllers have to react nowadays – as has been emphasized previously:

▸ *The increasing importance of information describing quantities, time and quality:*

Growing importance of non-financial information

Controllers are seen as the »custodians of business data«. This perspective corresponds to a view still prevalent in companies whereby business administration is truncated to mean only accounting and capital budgeting. As this focus becomes less sustainable for various reasons, controllers have to ask themselves whether or not they can also enter into the field of non-financial information. Such information was traditionally supplied by »technical« units and was the responsibility of line functions. Controllers first have to recognize the importance of non-financial information themselves – only then can they explain to management why it makes sense to give controllers the task of supplying such information. Empirical findings provide a strong argument: In an empirical study on the practice of metrics, managers who received their metrics in a report from a single source were significantly more satisfied than those who did not (cf. Weber/Sandt 2001, p. 26). However, this also means that controllers need to upgrade their skills considerably.

▸ *The increasing importance of data from financial accounting:*
We have also come across the observation several times before that »classical« controller data derived from cost accounting is currently losing importance compared to the figures from financial accounting. Quarterly reporting require-ments and growing demands derived from investor relations are important reasons for this development. However, controllers have traditionally had no influence on financial accounting. The area where relationships were most likely was that of stock valuation. But if managers obtain their metrics mainly from financial accounting, this begs the question of whether they still need information from controllers or whether it would be better to get it from financial accountants, from a single source – we have addressed this competitive situation in chapter 4 previously.

Data from financial accounting is also increasingly important.

Let us next consider the *models* which individual managers use to do their work and for which they receive support from »their« controllers. Here too, there are two important developments which create a considerable need to change for controllers:

▸ *Emphasizing an outside-in perspective:*
The model most firmly anchored in controller units and also most commonly used by controllers is that of operational cost planning and monitoring. In most companies, introducing and implementing standard costing and the subsequent construction of systematic cost planning and monitoring form a central part of the development of controlling. However, the standard costing tool has certain conceptual effects, as has been shown at various points in this introduction: It directs attention inward, into the company. The focus lies on using existing capacity as effectively as possible. Change is as alien to standard costing as including markets is to the management role. However, it is becoming increas-ingly clear through ever tougher competition that a purely inward-directed perspective is no longer sufficient, not even for operational management. For controllers, the resulting challenge is to become familiar with outward perspec-tives and to link them to inward perspectives. Benchmarking is a helpful tool for achieving this goal. For controllers, it is not only important as a part of their »toolbox«, but also helps them adapt to the outside-in perspective. Controllers have to develop a sense for the critical thresholds where questioning the capac-ities of a company as they are reflected in existing structures too rigorously may have detrimental effects on the further development of the company – truly a daunting challenge.

The outside-in perspec-tive is becoming more and more important for controllers.

▸ *New market-oriented tools:*
The need for new tools is closely linked to the need for new perspectives. For instance, the concept of real option valuation, which reflects the ever more important aspect of a company's flexibility, shares close bonds with the tradi-tional set of controller instruments. On the other hand, there are tools which necessitate skills going far beyond what controllers usually do. For instance, determining a customer lifetime value requires not only knowledge about customer-related costs, but also intimate familiarity with the workings of customer satisfaction and customer retention. Few controllers feel at home in this

Many controllers are currently not sufficiently familiar with their company's markets.

area. Both tools demand a sufficient understanding of how markets work. If controllers do not build up the appropriate knowledge, they will not be able to help managers with important decision problems. If the support role is thus compromised, there is a danger that managers will look for other persons to do the job. Controllers have to be leaders in the area of innovative business tools; else they are voluntarily giving up the field of decision support.

The final area of impending challenges for controllers and resulting developments for controller units is somewhat more abstract. It deals with new »*management patterns*«. There are two groups which can be differentiated:

▸ *Content-based management patterns:*
In the past, companies were always required to keep on developing their capacity as a result of market competition. As shown in *Figure 5-1*, different levels can be identified for the development of skills. The origins of the focus on functional, production-related specialization – linked to the image of a conveyor belt – lie at least a hundred years in the past. About half a century later, companies started specializing increasingly on the demands of their customers. The fact that these efforts have not yet ended is shown by the development of Total Quality Management, which can be seen as a concept for systematically implementing customer orientation in all process steps of the value chain. In the 1960s, logistics emerged as a further form of specialization. In its current incarnation as Supply Chain Management, it focuses on processes with the aim of designing value chains reaching across companies. A concept that did not achieve such a wide distribution was Time Based Management, which aims to increase companies' flexibility by minimizing action and reaction times. *Figure 5-1* shows change processes (Change Management) as a final content-based topic; companies are increasingly recognizing the importance of being able to manage change professionally.
If one tries to place the current tasks of controllers into this framework, one finds them predominantly on the lowest level: Controllers are performance optimizers »at home«. Even specializing on customers causes them some trouble, as has been mentioned before. The same applies for logistics. Time Based Management passed controllers by completely, and to date they have hardly dealt with Change Management either. If controllers really want to provide support to managers for all essential management issues, they have to increase their level of knowledge in this area as well. On the one hand, this affects the basic understanding of the direction of specialization. On the other hand, controllers also have to know the preconditions for the efficiency and effectiveness of the patterns individually and in terms of their interaction – truly a broad field.

▸ *Process-based management patterns:*
We have also mentioned many times previously that the diverse activities taking place in a company are coordinated using different mechanisms and instruments. The development of controlling and controllership was defined by coordination based on plans. Complex »planning bureaucracies« have, however, been increasingly criticized in recent times. Demands for more freedom to act within the com-

Controllers usually work only at the lowest level of the skills pyramid.

pany (»intrapreneur«), local responsibility, more flexibility and improved innovativeness were decisive in this area. From the perspective of coordination mechanisms, this meant an increase in the use of coordination based on personal instruction and on mutual adjustment. This results in a series of far-ranging questions for management: In which contexts are which coordination mechanisms successful, how can they be used efficiently and effectively (for instance, when does a team work?), how can they be combined in a sensible way (e.g.: within a framework based on plans, how much personal instruction makes sense, and when?), how should units that are managed in different ways be coordinated (a question many companies are currently asking themselves in the context of their subsidiary controlling)? All of these questions would benefit from management

Fig. 5-1

Content-based specialization of management – a learning model

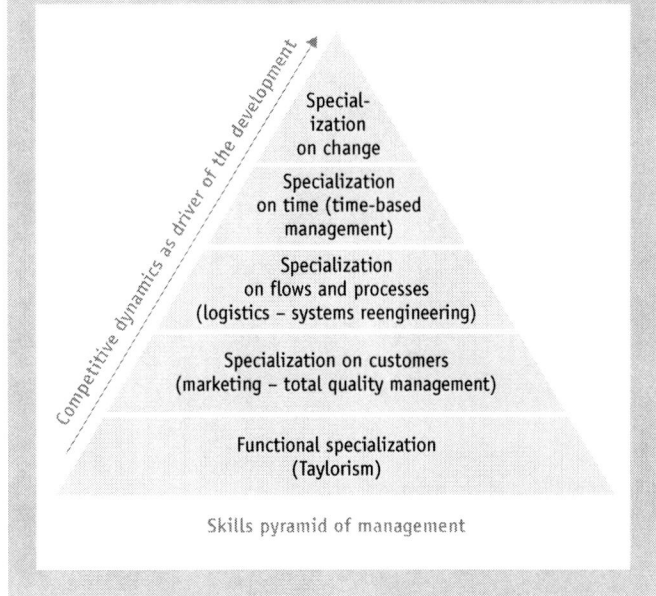

Specialization on change

Specialization on time (time-based management)

Specialization on flows and processes (logistics – systems reengineering)

Specialization on customers (marketing – total quality management)

Functional specialization (Taylorism)

Competitive dynamics as driver of the development

Skills pyramid of management

support provided by controllers. However, most controllers do not have any answers to such questions at present. This situation is unsatisfactory; not least because it is to be expected that this type of question will become increasingly important in the future, and because this is exactly where a new constraint on rationality will occur – or has occurred already, with hardly anybody noticing.

5.1.4 Controllers' abilities

In the previous sections, we described the strategic playing field of controllers from the perspective of the services to be delivered and the relationships to internal customers. There were frequent references to how controllers should adapt their abilities to such challenges. In the following, we will deal with the aspect of abilities in greater detail. Here, we will be differentiating between the abilities of individual controllers on the one hand and those of controller units on the other hand.

5.1.4.1 Analysis of an individual controller's abilities

It is not only the functions of controlling and controllers that are often described as being multifaceted in the relevant literature. The same applies for controllers' abilities, extending to the somewhat exaggerated formulation that controllers should be all things to all people (or, in the German idiom, an »*eierlegende Wollmilchsau*«, an egg-laying, wool-providing pig that also gives milk) in order to carry out all required tasks according to the company's wishes.

Controllers should also be familiar with coordination contexts that are far removed from the planning context type.

This lack of clarity is also reflected in empirical analyses. *Figure 5-2* shows the findings of the analysis of job advertisements mentioned in the first chapter of the book (cf. Weber/Schäffer 1998, pp. 230–231). The professional and personal requirements listed reflect one specific aspect: They represent the only characteristic of a pure controller which is essentially the same for controller-like positions. This is an indication that companies themselves are not clear about the profile of required skills. This impression is reinforced by other research findings.

The requirements profile by Deyhle, which is shown in *Figure 5-3*, has gained widespread popularity in extant literature. This system of professional and behavioral requirements is built on Deyhle's comprehensive training experience, which was already mentioned in the first section of this book. The list of requirements

Fig. 5-2

Requirements for controllers as reflected in a longitudinal analysis of job advertisements
(source: Weber/Schäffer 1998, p. 231)

Period	1949–1959	1960–1964	1965–1969	1970–1974	1975–1979	1980–1984	1985–1989	1990–1994
Professional skills requirements								
University studies	20.0	8.3	18.8	16.3	14.9	21.9	24.3	22.5
Studies at a university of applied sciences *(Fachhochschule)*	–	–	6.3	6.5	11.0	9.7	8.3	12.1
Vocational training	–	8.3	–	1.1	1.6	0.9	1.4	4.8
Practical experience	20.0	25.0	24.9	25.0	24.4	21.1	22.9	21.7
IT	–	16.7	10.4	4.3	8.3	10.7	11.7	12.0
Cost accounting/costings	20.0	16.7	8.3	9.8	10.2	8.8	7.5	8.1
Finance	–	–	2.1	3.3	3.9	4.8	1.7	1.4
Technical know-how	20.0	8.3	4.2	1.1	2.0	1.7	1.4	0.9
Knowledge of foreign languages	–	16.7	20.8	23.9	15.8	14.5	16.1	12.7
Other	20.0	–	4.2	8.7	7.9	5.9	4.7	3.8
Personality requirements								
Ability to coordinate	–	–	8.3	–	3.0	0.9	1.2	0.7
Communication skills	–	14.3	–	19.2	6.0	4.9	11.5	14.2
Assertiveness	50.0	–	8.3	23.1	22.0	18.9	16.2	15.2
Analytical skills	50.0	14.3	33.4	11.6	9.0	17.9	21.6	19.3
Leadership skills	–	14.3	8.3	34.6	25.0	24.4	18.1	14.4
Autonomy	–	14.3	25.1	–	14.0	9.4	8.2	14.4
Willingness to cooperate/ team player	–	14.3	8.3	3.8	10.0	17.9	15.4	17.3
Innovativeness	–	14.3	–	7.7	6.0	5.7	3.6	2.1
Integrity	–	14.3	8.3	–	5.0	–	4.2	2.3

Fig. 5-3

Catalog of requirements for a controller (source: Deyhle 1980, p. 40)

Professional and technical requirements	Behavioral requirements
▸ Intimate familiarity with accounting systems ▸ Ability to think holistically and systematically ▸ Ability to think in abstract terms ▸ IT skills, enabling controller to order systems solutions ▸ Good at explaining ▸ Strong training abilities ▸ Communication skills ▸ Learning ability ▸ All-round talent ▸ Analytical curiosity ▸ High degree of familiarity with problem-solving approaches and procedures ▸ Ability to use communications tools and devices (flipcharts, pens, overhead projectors, pinboards, conference equipment)	▸ The patience required to keep on interpreting the same kind of issue again and again ▸ Friendly pushiness ▸ Broad tolerance ▸ Knack for vivid expressions (visualization) ▸ Ability to sense whether one's counterpart twitches (or gulps) ▸ Courage not to publicize every issue at the drop of a hat ▸ Ability to act as a court jester, being able to communicate inconvenient truths in a way that makes people laugh about themselves ▸ Not taking oneself too seriously ▸ Indefatigability

Deyhle strongly emphasizes behavioral requirements.

appears very convincing because of its vivid language and strong emphasis on behavioral requirements. However, readers cannot identify the reasons for the specific combination of items on the list.

The assessments of the controllers surveyed in the ICV study underscore how important technical and behavioral abilities are for the professional success of controllers – especially the behavioral requirements, which are often neglected (see *Figure 5-4*). Professional or technical skills occupy positions three, four, seven and nine in the ranking. In addition, the top ten requirements for the controller role include six characteristics related to behavioral requirements and social competencies of controllers, especially their communication skills (54 percent). These skills are trailed by teamworking ability (16 percent), persistence (16 percent), persuasiveness (12 percent) and managerial competence (9 percent). The first position in the ranking is, however occupied by a key ability of controllers that combines professional and social skills very tightly: the ability to ask critical questions and recognize weak points.

The requirements for controllers have only rarely been derived in a deductive manner, i.e. by starting with certain controlling conceptions and the controller tasks derived from them. Küpper 1990 represents an early approach which can still be found – without any significant changes – in the current fourth edition of his textbook (Küpper 2005, pp. 536–540). The resulting task profile is shown in *Figure 5-5*.

If one analyzes the problem from an organization perspective, the required skills of controllers have to be derived from the tasks they have to perform, or, to be more

Fig. 5-4

Requirements for the controller role (source: Weber et al. 2006, p. 56)

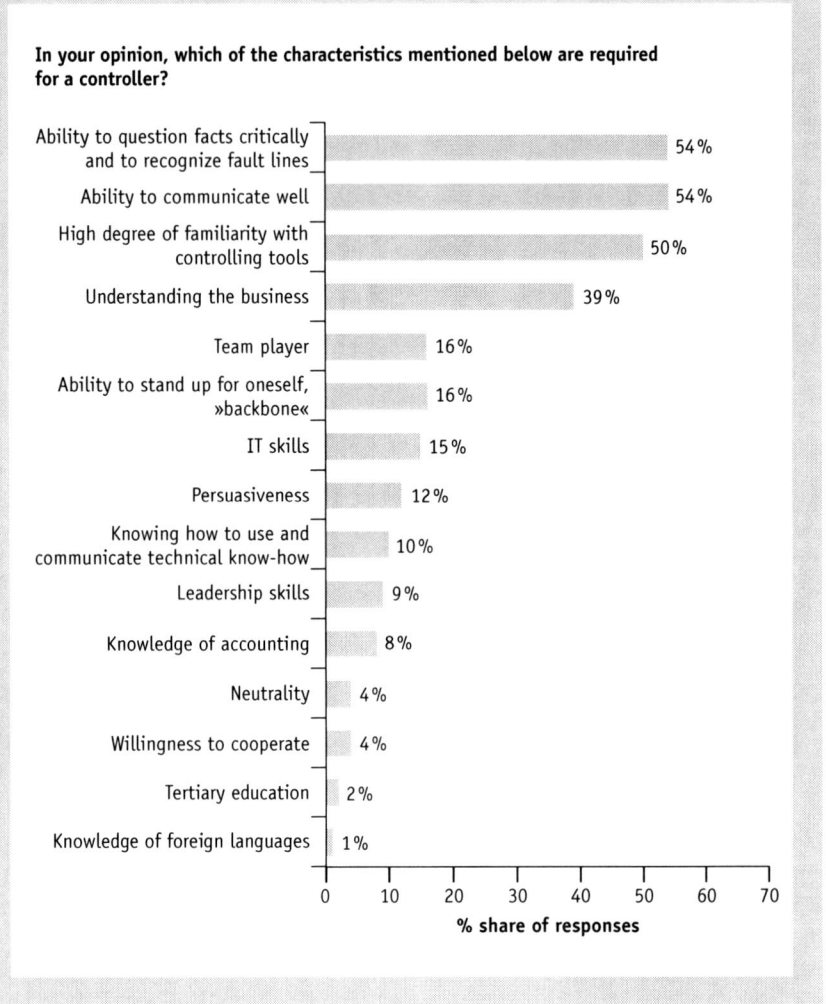

In your opinion, which of the characteristics mentioned below are required for a controller?

Characteristic	%
Ability to question facts critically and to recognize fault lines	54%
Ability to communicate well	54%
High degree of familiarity with controlling tools	50%
Understanding the business	39%
Team player	16%
Ability to stand up for oneself, »backbone«	16%
IT skills	15%
Persuasiveness	12%
Knowing how to use and communicate technical know-how	10%
Leadership skills	9%
Knowledge of accounting	8%
Neutrality	4%
Willingness to cooperate	4%
Tertiary education	2%
Knowledge of foreign languages	1%

% share of responses

specific, from the individual tasks and their contexts. The following basic themes can be identified for the support role on the basis of the differentiation discussed in chapter 2, namely into management support in the strict sense and the counterpart function:

▸ For solving *specific business-related problems*, an intimate knowledge of cost accounting, planning and monitoring procedures as well as the corresponding decision-support calculations (e.g. capital budgeting) and increasingly of financial accounting is required. Controllers work as specialists in business administration, which is also how they are perceived by management. Know-how deficits regarding these tools make it more likely that they will fail to be accepted. In the

Controllers need to cover a broad spectrum of skills.

end, controllers have to know everything about such tools – or should at least know where they can find the information quickly if needed.

▸ For the *management of interaction-related problems*, it is typically »social skills« which are required. Controllers need to be able to assess the know-how and characteristics of their managers. They have to know how to address their internal customers correctly and how to sell their services. They have to know how to behave in a customer-oriented fashion. They need a high degree of sensitivity in dealing with managers and should also have some teaching skills to enable them to communicate their services, which are often highly complex and abstract.

Further behavioral skills are needed to manage the tasks summarized under the term »counterpart function« (for empirical evidence cf. Weber 2008, pp. 109–124). The ability to manage conflicts is particularly important. Controllers can only perform their supplementary and constraining functions if they have sufficient »backbone« and persistence. If a controller is easily intimidated and influenced by hierarchical displays of power (»Think carefully about what you are doing. I'm still the one responsible for your performance assessment!«), he will not really be able to act as a counterpart to the manager. Controllers really fail in their role if they join forces with managers. (Almost) every controller can tell stories about corresponding

The counterpart function in particular places high requirements on a controller's personality.

Fig. 5-5

Overview of important requirements for controllers (source: Küpper 2005, p. 536)

Technical requirements		Personal requirements
Type of skills and experience	Areas of application	
Theories of the relationships between the management and operational system	**Information system** Cost and performance accounting Capital budgeting (Financial accounting) (Social accounting) (Human capital accounting) IT	**Intelligence** Analytical thinking Mental flexibility
Coordination tools Measurement systems Budgeting systems Transfer pricing systems		**Social behavior** Networking skills Persuasiveness
Methods for performance planning	**Planning and monitoring** Systems Processes Tools	**Dependability** **Leadership skills**
Behavioral theories		
Motivation techniques	**Goal systems** Resolving conflicts between goals Defining goals	
Early warning tools		
Creativity tools	**Human resources management** Management styles Incentive systems Determinants of human behavior	
	Organization	
	Interdependencies within the operational system	

Fig. 5-6

Job advertisement for a Business Line Controller

Saltigo – a young company in the LANXESS Group – is a leading, globally oriented supplier of custom manufactured fine chemical products. Our customers are located all over the world and are active in innovative markets. We see ourselves as a »full service« vendor offering comprehensive solutions to our clients. Our primary point of reference are the needs of our customers and we offer complete services in three business lines: pharma, agro and specialty chemicals.

Saltigo is ready to take off – are you?
We are searching for a

Business Line Controller

in the Specialty Chemicals business line.

The challenge: you will support business line management in managing the business. Apart from providing controlling services to the business line, this also includes writing business plans and discussing opportunities and threats. You feel at home in the realm of strategic analysis and cost effectiveness studies and have a keen sense for numbers. You are able to measure the business situation of the business line objectively and critically against its objectives. Through your analyses, you confidently contribute to the strategic development of the business.

We will prepare your way: after a comprehensive orientation you will roll up your sleeves with a great deal of autonomy in order to support the management of the business line with your analytical and conceptual skills. In doing so, you are service-oriented, consistent, communicative and are not afraid to think and act unconventionally.

Here is what we expect from you: you hold a university degree in business administration *(Diplom Betriebswirt or Kaufmann)* with several years of experience as a controller. You enjoy using SAP R/3 and MS Office applications. You are fluent in English and also display above-average commitment and a sense of personal responsibility.

Are you interested in enthusiastically joining a dynamic, innovative company? Then convince us with your application.

saltigo
customized competence

Saltigo GmbH | Human Resources | Daniela Gans | Building Q18 | 51369 Leverkusen, Germany | daniela.gans@saltigo.com

A company of the
LANXESS
Group

Fig. 5-7

Job advertisement for a Head of Central Controlling

International business development

Our client is an innovative and highly successful group of medium-sized companies in North Rhine-Westphalia. The company has a presence in many European countries and is expanding its market position through an aggressive corporate growth policy. It employs approximately 1,300 staff world-wide and offers customers a comprehensive, innovative portfolio of products and services.

Head of Central Controlling

You will be reporting to the CFO and can rely on the support of a highly qualified team in executing your duties. You are responsible for the ongoing development of existing reporting structures and controlling tools as well as for providing a transparent and capital market-oriented management information system. Your task profile is completed by participating in and directing cross-sectional projects (e.g. M & A, due diligence, restructuring, planning processes).

Our client expects you to have successfully completed studies in business and to have relevant practical experience, preferably in the controlling function of a group, combined with exceptional competency in the area of project management. You are as familiar using SAP R/3 as with applying IFRS. Your strengths are above-average analytical skills as well as the ability to communicate the results of your work in a concise manner. You have already gained experience managing a team. Your profile is rounded off by excellent English language skills.

If you are interested in the challenges and growth opportunities offered by a dynamically growing company, please send us your application (CV, copies of your degree(s), information about your salary expectations, and a photo), quoting MA .... as a reference. Ms Cornelia Lentge (Tel. +49 221/20506...) and Ms Regina Bolz (Tel. +49 221/20506..., e-mail regina.bolz@ifp-online.de) will be happy to provide you with further information if needed.

We will respect any non-disclosure requests.

International Search Group

ifp | Personalberatung
Managementdiagnostik

Postfach 10 31 44
5 0 4 7 1 K ö l n
www.ifp-online.de

attempts made by management. Controllers who are unable to resist become susceptible to blackmail. In other words, *incorruptibility* is a core skill for controllers, without which they cannot perform their counterpart function.

Taking into consideration that controllers usually have not one, but several managers as internal customers, further requirements can be derived. Controllers should not let themselves be instrumentalized by individuals, in other words, they have to maintain their independence and show that they are not spineless. When controllers create the impression that they are taking sides, their ability to act as referees is lost. This is clearly illustrated by the following quote from the top controller of a DAX 30 company: »Well, you can just forget it if you are seen as being politically biased. In the end, it is just like a collective bargaining process. It is not about ensuring that everybody wins, but rather about making sure that everybody suffers the same loss. In fact, from time to time you have to kick your »best friend« – the one who always performs best – in the backside because otherwise it will look as if you are only really making an effort with all the others« (Weber 2008, p. 117). This is problematic because the ability to mediate is an essential condition for being able to balance and coordinate the various interests of individual managers. It is also helpful to have a self-assured, confident communication style and strong negotiation skills.

In the end – as shown by the short descriptions above – it is not that difficult to derive requirements for controllers in a clear and logical way. As long as controllers' tasks are clearly defined, deriving their abilities is no more difficult than deriving those of managers. Deficiencies in describing the tasks have a direct impact on the formulation of requirements for the persons responsible for carrying out the tasks. Placing different requirements on controllers is not a problem as long as they result from different aspects of controllership. A local controller at a subsidiary has to fulfill other requirements than a corporate controller who works in business development.

In spite of all the different aspects described above, a common set of core requirements can be identified: In order to perform their duties well, controllers have to be highly qualified leaders who in principle meet the same quality standards as line managers. Anyone who is unable to converse competently on management issues will not be accepted by managers requiring management support. The key difference between controllers and line managers is that the former are not authorized to issue instructions. Controllers always have to rely on their ability to persuade others. They cannot impose solutions they consider to be right without support from others. Having to avoid detrimental developments and supporting promising paths without having any direct authority, i.e. by working »through others«, makes controllers ideal candidates for assuming direct management responsibilities at a later stage. At the same time, this combination of facts makes the controller role an ideal qualification position for future leaders. They can learn about management without having to learn how to impose solutions from the start. That is why controller positions – similar to executive assistant functions at the highest levels – are typical entry positions for top managers.

Controllers have to be highly qualified managers.

5.1.4.2 (Core) competencies of the controller unit

Up to now, we have followed the tradition of organization theory and only looked at the abilities an individual controller should have in order to be well-equipped for his duties. In doing so, we adopted a rather operational perspective. When dealing with abilities from a strategic perspective, one has to focus on the big picture instead of details, and to identify the fundamental aspects and relationships that matter in a competitive environment. There is a broad-based and intensive discussion on such topics in the literature on strategic management, which is usually based on the so-called »resource-based view« (cf. Prahalad/Hamel 1990, which is probably the best-known publication in this area). This perspective sees the key source of competitive advantages in the development and combination of a company's resources. Competitive advantages are also known as strategic competencies. Of all competitive advantages, the most important are those which competitors cannot imitate at all or only with great difficulty. These are known as »core competencies«.

Core competencies are a well-known aspect of strategic planning.

Introducing such a perspective for a controller unit as an internal department is essentially a novel approach in the literature on controlling. In this context, we would like to present an approach developed by David 2005 in greater detail. The author identifies five different competencies and analyzes their suitability as *potential* core competencies for controller units.

Competency of data ownership: This consists »in having access to quantitative information relevant to management as well as the right to determine the methods used for generating the information, such as the cash flow or operational results of a business unit. The competency includes the authority to define the systems for recording and communicating data« (David 2005, p. 149). Controllers usually have data ownership for cost accounting. However, there are also companies which have a separate cost accounting department in addition to the controller unit. In this case, controllers »only« have the authority to demand information. Data from financial accounting, which is becoming ever more important for internal control as well, is administrated by the accounting department. Most operational data is also not administrated by controllers, but rather by the different line functions (e.g. logistics). Gathering and aggregating all the required management-relevant information is a key competency of the controller unit. But it is not unique. At the very least, the accounting department starts from a comparable competitive position. Therefore, the competency of data ownership is not a core competency of controller units.

Competency of financial valuation: Within controllers' spectrum of tasks, performing financial calculations plays a key role. It is also perceived by managers as being important and useful. Controllers are usually particularly suited for financial valuations for two reasons. On the one hand, they possess deep knowledge of the methods needed for this purpose. On the other hand, they also have access to a (large) part of the data needed for such calculations. However, there are competitors in both areas. First, there is the accounting department, which has already been mentioned several times as a potential competitor of controllers. Accountants possess knowledge of methods and also have direct access to accounting data. However, such data is usually only historical, i.e. oriented towards the past. Management itself could also be seen as a kind of competitor. Firstly, this applies when managers themselves have technical business knowledge. Secondly, management is getting ever easier access to financial data via data warehousing solutions and similar IT concepts. Therefore, financial valuations should usually not be a core competency of controller units.

Competency of »creating transparency«: According to David, this is the competency of the controller unit to »ensure that customers achieve a shared, clear understanding of the relevant business situations by supplying management-relevant information« (David 2005, p. 152). Three abilities are essential for this competency: (1) a structured approach to obtaining the required information, (2) preparation of the information in a way suitable for managers and (3) »the ability of controller units to communicate this information clearly to management in order to ensure that management uses it« (David 2005, p. 152). Specifically, the combination of these three abilities is an area where controllers possess clear advantages compared with potential internal competitors. For instance, accountants are also able to prepare information in a structured way. However, they were not accustomed in the

Competency of data ownership

Competency of financial valuation

Competency of »creating transparency«

past to supplying it in a user-friendly format to management because they followed external accounting requirements (»compliance with regulations«) rather than ensuring that every manager understood the importance of specific figures. Although it is likely that accountants will increasingly address management's requirements, there is still a lot of ground to cover until a point is reached where they start thinking from the receiving side and ask which information a manager really needs to achieve sufficient business transparency. There is also little risk of strong competition from other potential suppliers of information – e.g. from technical line functions – because the comprehensive overview of an entire company as well as the independence and neutrality of controllers cannot be compensated. The competency of »creating transparency« therefore qualifies as a potential core competency.

Competency of acting as a critical sparring partner a critical sparring partner: »The competency of the critical sparring partner is built on the resources of independence, a profound understanding and experience of the business, behavioral abilities and acceptance from management. ... It enables controller units to discuss business topics with the responsible managers and to add an independent perspective. ... This should help ensure a higher quality of solutions for problems by bringing together two independent viewpoints« (David 2005, p. 154). This competency hardly requires further explanation at this stage of the book. This is a key element of controllers' function of assuring rationality, which they are able to perform in a unique way because of a combination of reasons mentioned frequently earlier: Controller positions are present throughout the entire company, ensuring that a complete overview exists throughout the company and that the perspective is balanced. As a result of their information supply function, controllers achieve a profound understanding of all business aspects. Their involvement in the planning and monitoring function has the same effect. Controllers also unburden managers in many different ways, which helps them attain the acceptance needed for performing a counterpart function. Controllers, as a result of their specific role, have to view the business from a different perspective than managers, which also increases their usefulness for management. If the role of the critical sparring partners is at risk, then the competition would be coming from the managers themselves, who have the opportunity of introducing appropriate discursive and monitoring routines for themselves. In a group-based management structure, there is always a different manager who can take on the role of sparring partner. However, the awareness of the need for such a role has to be deeply anchored and the groups have to be sure that they can avoid groupthink and similar phenomena. For »normal, continental European« management structures, controllers can therefore hardly be replaced as counterparts. This leads to the reasonable assumption that this is a core competency of controllers.

Competency of acting as a business partner: »This [competency] shows itself in the ability of controller units to supply advice for improvements on the basis of their planning, monitoring and information-related activities« (David 2005, pp. 155–156). Here we see the second part of controllers' function of assuring rationality. Controllers should use their know-how to suggest improvements, and not only to avoid management mistakes. The argument supporting their suitability is similar to that used for their role as a critical counterpart and does not need repeating.

Competency of acting as a business partner

The competency of acting as a business partner can therefore also be seen as a core competency of controller units.

On the whole, the strategic discussion of controller units' competencies generates insights that go well beyond analyzing the abilities required for individual controllers. This approach shows vulnerabilities towards internal competitors; at the same time, it shows areas where there are competitive advantages and which should therefore be strengthened in the future.

Summary
(see guiding question 1)

▶ If one accepts that controller units have the possibility of engaging in »role making«, it makes sense to discuss their positioning from a strategic perspective.

▶ The starting point for this discussion is the underlying question of whether or not controllers contribute to company performance, and how. Their contribution can be identified conceptually and confirmed empirically. The fact that companies have created positions for controllers is therefore neither coincidental nor inefficient.

▶ Controllers' contribution to success increases the more they orient their activities towards their internal customers, the managers. Customer orientation should therefore not only be a key objective for marketing and sales, but also for controllers.

▶ Changes in tasks influence the strategic orientation of controller units. A stronger orientation on markets and processes is a challenge for most controllers, as is covering a wider range of management issues.

▶ The competencies of controller units are key for their strategic orientation. Core competencies of controller units are the competency of »creating transparency«, of acting as a critical sparring partner and as a business partner.

5.2 Selected strategic positioning tools

Section 1 of this chapter has shown that controller units also need strategic orientation if they do not want to be limited to pure »role taking«. In the area of strategic management, a broad spectrum of tools has been developed to enable such orientation. One might reasonably assume that they can also be applied to controller units. However, in order to keep the size of this textbook within acceptable limits, we had to choose carefully which tools to include. Four examples will be presented in the following.

Four examples to clarify the points being made

To begin with, controller units can develop a mission statement. Mission statements should serve as a fundamental point of reference for actions; in the sense of being the verbal expression of a controller culture, they should determine behavior in controller units. Next, we will review Porter's five forces model, which is very commonly used in strategic planning, as a basic approach for determining the strategic positioning of controller units. Technology portfolio analysis, the next approach to be presented, is a strategic planning tool that can also be applied to controller units. Finally, a Balanced Scorecard will be developed which serves as a tool for defining selected strategies of controller units more precisely, as well as helping with implementing them.

5.2.1 Designing a mission statement for controllers

If one asks controllers about their strategic orientation, controller images – in the sense of overdrawn, metaphorical self-descriptions – are usually first to be mentioned; the most commonly used are those of the internal consultant, the pilot and the economic conscience. These idealized images refer to certain desirable core services and behavioral patterns of controllers, which are summed up in just a few words. However, they carry the risk of being concretized with very different properties. Following the assessments of the controllers who took part in the ICV study, the images just mentioned play an important role in management's perception. More

Fig. 5-8

Controller images in companies (source: Weber et al. 2006, p. 44)

Which of the following role images corresponds most closely to how management perceives controllers?

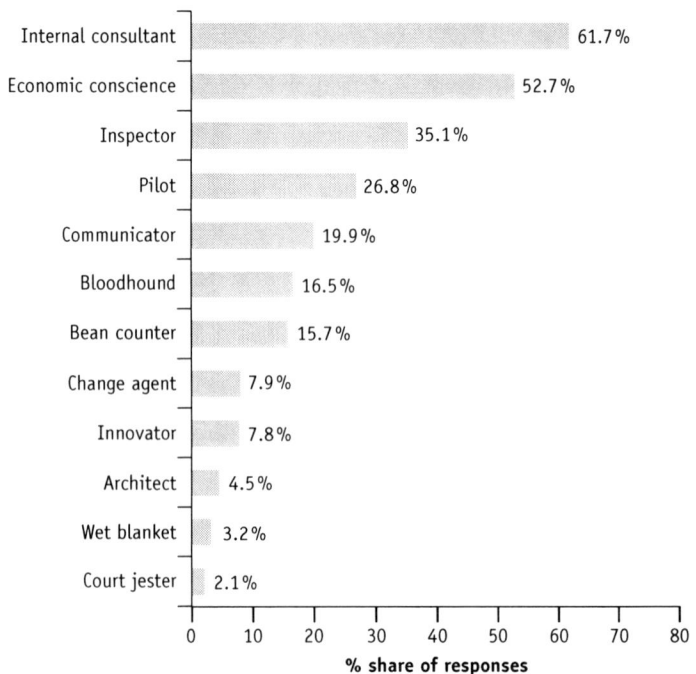

Internal consultant	61.7%
Economic conscience	52.7%
Inspector	35.1%
Pilot	26.8%
Communicator	19.9%
Bloodhound	16.5%
Bean counter	15.7%
Change agent	7.9%
Innovator	7.8%
Architect	4.5%
Wet blanket	3.2%
Court jester	2.1%

% share of responses

than half of those surveyed stated that »their« managers saw controllers as internal consultants (62 percent) or an economic conscience (53 percent). According to participants, 27 percent of controllers were perceived as pilots by managers. Nevertheless, controllers also confirmed that images with a more negative connotation – inspector (35 percent), bloodhound (17 percent) and bean counter (16 percent) – are still rather widespread.

Conversely, written mission statements provide controller units with the chance of aggregating conceptions about their own strategic orientation and making them more precise. Having a consistent vision and mission – as described in a mission statement – can therefore potentially play a very important role. There are two likely benefits:

A mission statement provides two key benefits.

▸ On the one hand, controllers themselves need a certain (high) degree of uniformity in terms of their thinking patterns and use of language. Every controller should understand clearly why he or she is performing certain tasks and should know the criteria for constantly checking whether or not tasks are useful and whether they are being performed correctly. Furthermore, the intensive discussion processes needed to create a mission statement also require considerable knowledge of the many, widely distributed task areas of controller units. Such knowledge is a precondition for communication and coordination across diverse units and job roles.

▸ On the other hand, a mission statement for controllers is also a basis for active communication to external stakeholders, i.e. the business departments and functions that the controllers are responsible for. The lack of understanding or even purposeful misinterpretation of the role of controllers (»wet blanket«, »inspector«, »number cruncher«) – which is often found in practice and has been mentioned throughout the book – can also be actively engaged using a mission statement.

In the following, we will provide a couple of examples of such mission statements. The first is »theoretical« in nature, meaning that it addresses the key basic positions that need to be defined and specified within a company to promote understanding of the roles and functions of a controller unit. The second example comes from the IGC (International Group of Controlling), an association of key European training institutions for controllers.

The »theoretical« mission statement contains four key statements (see *Figure 5-9*). The first addresses the coordinating role of controllers, which they carry out in contexts primarily coordinated through plans. For various reasons, ever more companies are being managed in a decentralized fashion. Decentralization enables full use to be made of decentralized management know-how, but it also entails the risk of uncoordinated or opportunistic behavior – in complete agreement with the motto »At

Fig. 5-9

»Theoretical« mission statement for a controller unit

▸ We assume co-responsibility for ensuring that the desired decentralized form of management leads to the intended company profits as a result of a shared, mutually agreed-upon focus.
▸ We see ourselves as offering a service function with active design tasks.
▸ We have only fulfilled our task when managers need us instead of just tolerating us.
▸ Our business is built on trust.

the end of the day, the sum of departmental interests is the bankruptcy of the company!« Decentralized units are usually kept together by the coordinating bracket of budgeting. This is where controllers play a key role in terms of both process and content. It is often unclear how great the extent of this influence should be. The first key statement takes a clear position. The expression »co-responsibility« is far-reaching. Being co-responsible means influencing decision making actively and some-times also countering the interests of individual local decision makers (»*Contre Rôle*«). The target level is ambitiously high, particularly for local controllers. They can easily run the risk of losing the trust placed in them. By pointing out their potential constraining role from the beginning, almost as a kind of rule of the game, and not following the business unit's interests in all cases, controllers can make their lives much easier in case of conflicts. If there is no such key statement, there is a risk that managers will only make use of controllers' management support for as long as it serves their own interests. One of the ways in which controllers contribute to company performance would therefore be neglected.

> Controllers have to balance the specific interests of different functions.

The second key statement reflects the uncontested requirement that controllers should provide management support. Addressing the role of »salesperson for numbers«, which Albrecht Deyhle has been demanding for a long time, and trans-forming controller units into real service centers, shows in which direction changes need to happen. This need for change is rather large in most companies. Even though the aspect of management support is not contested verbally, customer orien-tation can be described diplomatically as offering substantial room for improvement in real life. Only in exceptions do systematic talks take place between customers (managers) and suppliers (controllers). It is also unusual to find controllers who can tell their customers how much their products cost (»What does a monthly report cost – and what would it cost if it were delivered three days earlier, containing only half the information?«). If controllers want to provide a service function, they need to know the requirements of their customers, have to follow changes in requirements and establish a constant, tight interaction with their customers. Few controllers could state with a clear conscience that they fulfill these conditions. This illustrates the importance of this key statement.

> Deyhle has been calling for controllers to be »salespersons for numbers« for a long time.

But there is a second part to it. The »active design tasks« indicate that it is not enough just to react to customer demands in the sense of »role taking«. Controllers have to possess sufficient know-how to be able to offer new »controller products« to managers on an ongoing basis: For instance, if a manager does not know the concept of target costing, she will not be able to request it from her controller. There is another aspect implicit in the active design tasks in the sense of »role making«: Service orientation must not be allowed to make controllers follow every whim and wish of their managers. This is something we have addressed previously: Controllers have the right and obligation to contradict manager's wishes, not only during the process of creating plans (monitoring of plan creation), but in general. Contrary to sales to an anonymous market, controllers should not be indifferent to what a manager does with the services rendered. Owing to the constant and tight interac-tion between controllers and managers, controllers have to ensure in their own interest that managers derive the greatest possible benefit from controllers' work. If controllers see potential problems in the application of the services received, they have to take appropriate measures to make sure they do not occur.

The third key statement is intimately related to the service aspect. Anyone who acts in a service-oriented fashion is probably needed and not just tolerated. Still, it may make sense to formulate the third key statement separately because it emphasizes the user perspective more than the second one does. If controllers formulate such an objective for themselves, they also have to measure up to it. Consequently, they periodically or permanently have to talk to managers about their level of satisfaction. Some companies have been doing this for some time already for all administrative and operational units, including controller units, whereas others have no experience at all in this area. Controllers can be role models – and have considerable room for improvement (at least, most of them do). Taken together, both key statements promise to increase the effectiveness and efficiency of controllers as much as their acceptance. The paths leading towards this goal are easy if one commits to them.

Controllers should systematically investigate how satisfied managers are with their performance.

The fourth key statement is that »Our business is built on trust«. It addresses a topic whose impact on controllers' efficiency and the way they work can hardly be overestimated. The efficiency of management which is predominantly based on plans depends essentially on the ability and willingness of the managers responsible for planning to generate, coordinate and implement alternatives corresponding to the company's goals. In the process of creating plans, controllers are involved in or responsible for managing and monitoring the planning process. If the relationship between the managers who are responsible for planning and the controllers themselves is based on trust, there is much less need for applying checks and balances to the process and content of planning:

Trust is of essential importance for the work of controllers.

- ▸ Line managers do not have to invest their time and intelligence in »padding« their plans to allow controllers to make unavoidable cutbacks at a later stage in the planning process.
- ▸ Consequently, controllers do not have to spend time on searching for the padding and trying to detect at which point the manager »gulps or twitches« (Deyhle 1980, p. 40).

Within certain limits, there is a tradeoff between the costs saved on planning and those saved on monitoring and checks:

- ▸ If there is a high degree of certainty in planning, controllers can easily check the validity of plans submitted to them; the monitoring costs are comparatively low. However, the additional planning costs are high if the manager responsible for planning insists on having his or her own goals implemented.
- ▸ If planning is characterized by a low level of certainty, the relationship is reversed: In this case, it is easy for managers »to hide« their own goals in plans; for controllers, it is difficult to detect them.

The actual degree of trust is limited by the risk of trust being betrayed: »Whoever trusts another person ... has to keep his own willingness to take risks under control. He has to understand clearly, even if it is just for purposes of self-assurance, that he does not trust unconditionally, but only within limits, and subject to specific, rational expectations« (Luhmann 1989, p. 31). The risk of a breach of trust is determined by several factors:

▸ *The effectiveness of symbolic checks:*
»Exercising so-called symbolic checks enables the person placing trust in another
... to obtain self-assurance. Trust in the sincerity and motive structure of the
partner makes detailed checks of facts redundant. A symbolic check of personal
trust – and not of facts – replaces them, in other words, a constant checking of
whether the integrity and sincerity of the partner also warrant trust to be placed
in him in the future« (Krystek/Zumbrock 1993, p. 9). Such checks have to differ
from person to person, i.e. they have to develop uniquely from the specific relationship between a controller and a line manager.

▸ *Penalty options:*

The risk of a breach of
trust can be assessed
particularly on the basis
of three factors.

Every controller has to formulate relevant limits of trust-critical behavior on the
part of line managers and appropriate penalty expectations, and to make them
clear using verbal or non-verbal communication. Again, the limits are specific to
individuals. Penalties can range from reducing the service level to imposing
system-compliant obstacles (e.g. returning plans several times if they are not
absolutely correct) and to open conflict (e.g. reporting incidents to higher authorities).

▸ *The benefits of breaking trust:*
This is essentially determined by the timeframe within which a controller and a
line manager cooperate. As shown by game theory studies, opportunistic behavior
becomes more likely if the expected time of cooperation between partners is
short. Building trust requires an investment that is only worthwhile when its
period of use is long enough.

Fig. 5-10

**Controllers' mission statement
(International Group of Controlling, as of 2002)**

▸ Controllers design and accompany the management process
of defining goals, planning and controlling and thus have a joint
responsibility with management to reach their objectives.

▸ This means that:
 – Controllers ensure the transparency of business results,
 finance, processes and strategy and thus contribute to higher
 economic effectiveness.
 – Controllers co-ordinate secondary goals and the related plans
 in a holistic way and organise a reporting-system which is
 future-oriented and covers the enterprise as a whole.
 – Controllers moderate and design the controlling process
 of defining goals, planning and management control so that
 every decision maker can act in accordance with agreed
 objectives.
 – Controllers provide necessary company management data
 and information.
 – Controllers develop and maintain controlling systems.

If trust is postulated as the foundation
of the business of controllers in their
mission statement, this can lead to a
discussion that should help eliminate
(justified?) preconceptions (e.g. associ-
ating controllers with distrust), but
which can also become the starting
point for a company-wide debate about
the concept of trust in itself, which is
economically interesting and has the
potential to boost performance. It is
only fair to point out that controllers
should have a considerable interest in
this discussion: As planning certainty
drops because of an ever more dynamic
environment, there are ever fewer
opportunities for controllers to double-
check planning properly if they cannot
reach a high level of trust in cooperation
with line managers.

The second concrete mission statement (see *Figure 5-10*) was, as mentioned above, developed by the IGC (see also section 1.4). It covers the core areas of responsibility of controllers. The way it is formulated also makes it suitable for use as a template for designing a mission statement in a given company.

Summary
(see guiding question 2)

▶ The role of controllers needs to be clearly defined. Mission statements are an effective way of defining and communicating controllers' roles and functions.

▶ Mission statements have to address the central aspects of controllership. These include statements on the degree to which controllers are integrated with managers (involvement vs. independence) and on the relationship between unburdening, supplementary and constraining tasks.

▶ Mission statements only fulfill their function if a lot of effort is put into developing them and if they receive continuous review.

5.2.2 Applying Porter's five forces model

According to Porter's well-known industry analysis (»Five Forces«), the success of a company is based on the attractiveness of its environment and the product and market positioning in relation to the competition (cf. Porter 1980). The five competitive forces are the relative strength of existing competitors and potential entrants, the bargaining power of suppliers and buyers, and the existence of substitute (or complementary) products. This perspective is based on the assumption that outside forces affect all firms in an industry and that the key is found in the differing abilities of firms to deal with them. Thus, the essence of formulating a competitive strategy is relating a company to its environment. The environmental factors listed above are systematically analyzed for this purpose:

▶ Who are the key customers, what do they require from the company and its products and how much bargaining power do they have?
▶ What is the role of existing and new competitors; are they of a similar size and is the market segment growing?
▶ Are there dependencies on specific suppliers or is there a risk that substitute products will make the company's own product redundant?
▶ Are there new markets which the company can enter?

Porter's approach offers many thought-provoking insights for designing controller units.

Figure 5-11 transfers this framework to the internal competitive environment of controllers and thereby uses the approach we mentioned in chapter 4. The search for existing internal competitors quickly brings up the strategy department, internal consulting, but also management itself (»self-controlling«). New competitors who are »knocking on the doors« include members of the financial accounting departments, who are busy giving controllers a run for their money in several companies.

Fig. 5-11

The competitive environment of controllers according to Porter's five forces model (source: Weber/David/Prenzler 2001, p. 25)

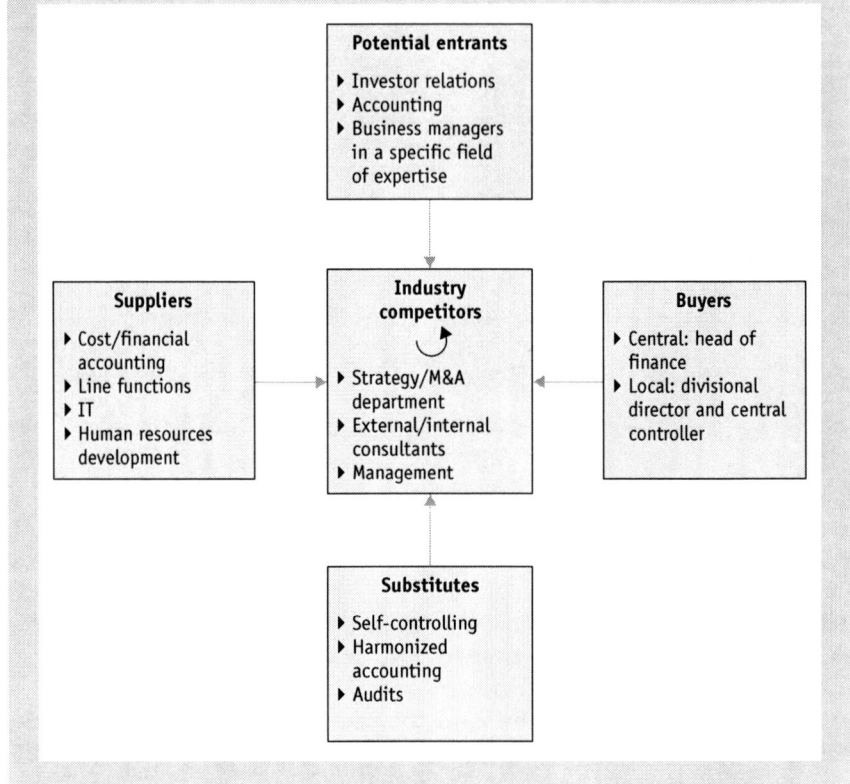

Potential entrants
- Investor relations
- Accounting
- Business managers in a specific field of expertise

Suppliers
- Cost/financial accounting
- Line functions
- IT
- Human resources development

Industry competitors
- Strategy/M&A department
- External/internal consultants
- Management

Buyers
- Central: head of finance
- Local: divisional director and central controller

Substitutes
- Self-controlling
- Harmonized accounting
- Audits

On the customer/demand side, one has to analyze which managers express needs for certain services at which levels of the company and how customer needs may develop in the future. In respect of tasks (i.e. »products«), the competitive potential of substitutive services (e.g. operating income vs. EBIT) has to be monitored. Finally, the supplier perspective focuses attention on the risks and opportunities of IT innovations that deliver data to controllers and on areas such as recruitment (»Will the controller unit be able to keep its function as a recruitment pool for high potentials?«). The examples provided illustrate that Porter's approach can offer valuable input for strategically positioning the controller unit. On the basis of such knowledge, special strategies for different »business areas« (e.g. taking responsibility for introducing value-based management, transferring cost accounting to the accounting department) and functions can be developed (e.g. generating knowledge about facilitation and human resources development).

5.2.3   Applying technology portfolio analysis

As a second example, we would like to present technology portfolio analysis. If one interprets »technology« in its broader sense as a competency for solving certain problem areas, then technology portfolio analysis becomes usable for the strategic orientation of customary controller activities. This is illustrated using the example of cost accounting, an area of know-how that is supplied as a service for achieving company objectives. It is therefore permissible to ask about its attractiveness and the ability of the company to flesh out this attractiveness.

Determining the attractiveness of cost accounting

The potential benefits of cost accounting determine its technological attractiveness. They are in turn determined in the first instance by the possibilities of lowering costs by using cost accounting tools. On the one hand, cost reductions can relate to the »going concern«, as exemplified by standard costing. On the other hand, there are also (increasing) opportunities for reducing costs in the area of fundamental decisions that are binding in the long term. Two typical examples are the fields of product development (»cost-effective design«) and plant automation. Technology portfolio analysis requires first estimating the potential for cost savings and then determining their importance for the company's competitiveness. For instance, cost benefits are much more important for companies aiming to achieve cost leadership as a competitive advantage than for those striving for differentiation on the basis of high product quality. Cost accounting in its instrumental use can therefore not be designed independently of the fundamental competitive orientation of a company.

The attractiveness of cost accounting is derived from its usefulness for costing purposes.

The attractiveness of cost accounting has the potential to go beyond cost savings, however. In borderline cases, cost accounting is similar to a secondary condition for specific types of business and/or customers. Public tenders, although well-known cases in point, are not the only example. The trend towards long-term supplier partnerships is currently forcing many companies to calculate prices on a cost-plus basis, as required by their customers. In addition to calculating prices, cost accounting can also be used to justify prices. At present, there are examples for such a use in the retail and wholesale sector during negotiations to determine a »fairer« allocation of logistics costs. Also, price increases are often easier to implement when they can be »excused« on the basis of corresponding cost increases.

Determining the resource strength of cost accounting

Once it has been established which are the most important areas in which cost accounting will be used in the future, the next step involves determining whether it is even possible to develop these areas. This identification should also take into account the criticism that is often directed at traditional cost accounting:
- an excessive focus on production,
- a lacking focus on the consequences of plant automation,
- a kind of speechlessness when trying to determine the costs of product-related (calculation of variants) and production-related flexibility (short throughput times),

▶ the neglecting of service processes and – in concluding this list without completing it –
▶ the short-term nature of the approach.

The status of the company's IT systems is also of key importance (in addition to the actual cost accounting system, data capturing systems – such as those that register material flows – play an important role). Furthermore, cost accounting know-how is essential. Here, »absorption costing vs. marginal costing« is only part of the focus. Cost accounting departments also need to possess profound knowledge of real processes, e.g. logistics, the activities involved in the product lifecycle or the conditions for computer-aided design. In many companies, there are considerable deficits in these areas in particular.

Cost accounting portfolio

By contrasting the attractiveness of cost accounting or certain of its instruments or partial accounting systems against resource strength, one can derive a cost accounting portfolio as shown in *Figure 5-12*. As mentioned earlier, such a structuring approach is not an exact, incorruptible measurement. It is not possible to determine whether capital asset accounting, for instance, should really be positioned in the middle quadrant or whether it should be moved a bit to the right in a way that everybody would agree on. But this is not what is important. Instead, the idea of the portfolio is to motivate controllers to think about their activities systematically – and to search systematically for new activity areas. On the other hand, building the portfolio will cause controllers to ask many questions and thereby launch discussions into which the »customers« of cost accounting necessarily have to be included. This increases the acceptance of cost accounting and therefore its benefits.

The basic challenge of any portfolio analysis lies in achieving the right balance. In respect of the cost accounting portfolio, this means striving to reach the equilibrium path between attractiveness and resource strength. For instance, if standard costing becomes ever less important (e.g. because of greater plant automation), then the portfolio indicates that it, and the costs associated with it, should be scaled back significantly in the long term. Conversely, the analysis implies that product lifecycle accounting, which does not fit into the usual periodic framework of traditional cost accounting, should receive much

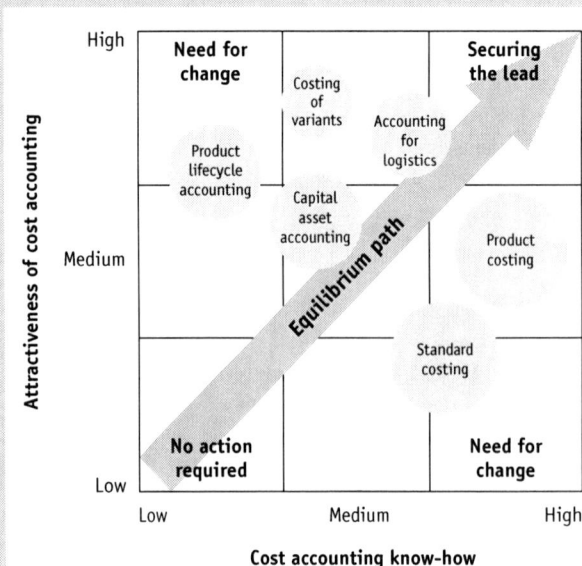

Fig. 5-12

Applying technology portfolio analysis to cost accounting as an example

more attention in terms of a build-up of know-how and instruments. Starting from these recommendations, the next step would be to elaborate strategic plans for developing and/or adjusting cost accounting, which can be the objects of strategic monitoring in combination with concrete milestones, e.g. installing an IT system for collecting all costs per plant and across various periods.

5.2.4 Applying the Balanced Scorecard

The Balanced Scorecard (BSC) can be used first as a measurement system and then as an instrument for reliably linking strategy to operations. This instrument can be applied for the same purpose to a controller unit. We will show this on the basis of a practically-oriented, but fictional example (cf. Weber/Schäffer 2000b).

The controller unit's mission and strategies are the starting point. *Figure 5-13* shows the concrete specifications. The concretizations within the different perspectives of the Balanced

Fig. 5-13

Vision and strategy of the controller unit

Controller vision
We are the market leaders in providing business coaching to our managers – at all management levels.

Strategies for implementation
▸ Separation of consulting functions from accounting functions within the controller unit
▸ Strengthening consulting activities
▸ Controller product-related innovation program
▸ Image and education campaign
▸ ...

Fig. 5-14

The controller unit from an internal customer and market perspective

▸ Ratio of budget for controller-consultants to budget for external management consultants: +10 % year on year
▸ Time spent working on new controller task introduced in previous two years as share of total time: >10 %
▸ MSI (Manager Satisfaction Index) target: > 70 %
▸ Cut throughput time for capital budgeting proposals by 10 %
▸ Train non-controllers in controlling: > 1,250 participant man-days

Scorecard are built on the basis of the strategies. For reasons of simplicity, we will stick to the »standard perspectives« in this case.

For the customer and market perspectives, the aim is to identify goals and metrics which can be measured precisely and which are directed at the core of the respective strategies. As required by the concept, the catalog of goals has to be kept at a manageable size. In the example (see *Figure 5-14*), the following relationships between goals and strategy apply:

▸ The budget relationship metric relates to the goal of winning market share from external consultants.
▸ The time dimension relates to the innovation strategy.
▸ The target value for managers' satisfaction with their controllers relates to a strategy of customer retention.
▸ The reduction of throughput times relates to an improvement of the quality of controller products.
▸ Finally, the training dimension relates to the strategy of spreading knowledge about controlling and thereby strengthening the reputation for being the »repository of competence in business administration«.

In terms of the process perspective, it is especially important to work out two aspects of strategy: ensuring that processes or controller products are as up-to-date as possible and that the level of quality is raised. Both aspects become clear in the five metrics listed (see *Figure 5-15*):

▸ The shorter duration of the operational planning cycle relates to an aspect that is currently highly relevant: Planning for a period of significantly more than half a year makes little sense if one takes into account the ever more rapid changes.
▸ The greater timeliness of reporting enables management to react faster.
▸ Broadly speaking, the process perspective deals with issues of system integration in many companies.
▸ Finally, the last two goals relate to an aspect which in our experience is only addressed proactively in a few cases: the issue of the quality of controller services.

Fig. 5-15

The controller unit from a process perspective

▸ Throughput time for operational planning: reduce from 32 to 24 weeks
▸ Timeliness of monthly reports: 2 working days after month-end cut-off date for urgent reports, 5 working days after monthly cut-off for complete report
▸ Systems integration: complete linkage of sales information system with cost accounting
▸ Cut number of corrective accounting entries by 25 %
▸ Unconditional audit certificate by internal auditing

As a result of the strong pressure to change felt by controller units, the training and development perspective is especially important. In the list shown in *Figure 5-16*, there are none of the person-related metrics otherwise commonly used for this perspective. Instead, all the metrics shown relate to key aspects of building up knowledge in the controller unit and transferring knowledge to management.

Fig. 5-16

The controller unit from a training and development perspective

▸ Training for controllers: 8.5 days per controller per year on average
▸ 1,250,000 hits on controller homepage per year
▸ Up-to-dateness of controller handbook: average age of a page in the handbook < 6 months
▸ Share of innovative projects as percentage of controllers' working time > 10 %
▸ Interpersonal exchange of knowledge: number of presentations per controller > 2 per year

The final perspective to be covered is the financial perspective, which is also needed for the controller unit. *Figure 5-17* shows an example of how to complete it. This example is based on the following ideas:

▸ In most companies, controllers bear a large part of the effort and responsibility for operational planning, but often they do not know the costs (not to mention the benefits) resulting from it. Including planning costs in the BSC focuses controllers' attention on simplifying planning itself and improving the process of planning.

Fig. 5-17

The controller unit from a financial perspective

▸ Planning costs: reduce costs of operational planning, currently at 0.05 % of total costs, by 10 %
▸ Introduction of R3: keep within budget (while cutting project duration by three months)
▸ Consultancy performance: pay-off time projections in consultancy projects performed by controllers accurate to within +/– 1 quarter
▸ Total costs of controller services: reduce controller costs as share of overall costs by 5 %

▸ A significant part of controllers' activities takes place in projects. If one of them is especially important, the project goals are a potential candidate for the BSC.

▸ Controllers provide a specific type of support services to management. That is why it is very difficult – as shown at length in this chapter – to ascribe independent successes to controllers. Still, it is not completely impossible. The example uses a case that could be implemented in most companies: Controllers want to perform internal consulting services and do so. Consulting projects mostly deal with efficiency improvements that quickly offset the costs of the consulting project. This expectation can be converted into concrete goals. In this way, they and their attainment can become the object of the BSC's financial perspective.

Introducing a BSC for a controller unit allows controllers to experience the opportunities and restrictions of this tool at first hand.

▸ Finally, there is a metric that is an obvious candidate for a controller unit's BSC: the total costs of the department, expressed in absolute terms or put in relation to the total costs of the company. Not many companies are currently aware of such figures.

The examples have shown that the Balanced Scorecard represents an instrument in the hands of controllers which they not only apply to other business units, but which they can and should also use on their own activities to their own benefit. Apart from the direct benefits of implementing their own strategies, controllers also learn valuable lessons about using the instrument. On the other hand, there is also the observation that recommendations tend to be accepted more willingly from people who can prove that they follow these themselves.

Summary (see guiding question 3)

▸ If there is a mission statement for the controller unit, this is a suitable basis for developing business unit strategies. Controllers should know the corporate strategic planning tools which can be used for this purpose.

▸ When using strategic planning tools, there should not be any major problems if the possibility of »role making« is perceived and accepted. The tools can be adapted throughout.

▸ Applying a strategy process to a controller unit contributes to greater efficiency and effectiveness, as well as allowing controllers to learn about the pitfalls and opportunities of strategic planning at first hand. This experience can be applied profitably in the strategic planning processes of the company.

5.3 Organization of the controller unit

5.3.1 Preliminary comments

The question of choosing the most suitable form of organizational structure for a controller unit already becomes relevant in medium-sized companies with just a few controllers. However, it only becomes really important in large companies, which the following explanations address implicitly.

The starting point and aim of every organizational design process is to distribute controller tasks. This includes (1) dividing up tasks between central and local controller units, (2) dividing up tasks within controller units at the same level and (3) dividing up tasks between controller units and other management service providers (such as the auditing or business development departments). The distribution of controller units' competencies is derived from the tasks they perform and encompasses their position in the hierarchy as well as the reporting structures, both within the controller units and in relation to management (cf. Welge 1988, pp. 408–412; Küpper 2005, pp. 524–535).

Let us begin by defining central and local controlling as basic units. For the purposes of our example, and unless noted otherwise, we understand them to mean controlling at headquarters on the one hand and controlling in the subsidiaries on the other (for further details on the following, cf. Weber/Hunold/Prenzler/Thust 2001). We will also be making use of a differentiation between three types of corporate groups. They reflect different management philosophies and therefore also have a considerable influence on the organization of controllers' activities:

Integrated group of companies

▶ The original form of a large company is the integrated group of companies. This form usually emerged when international subsidiaries became necessary (emancipation of sales offices) and when the company grew as a result of acquiring other businesses. Integrated groups of companies are characterized by the fact that their business is mostly homogeneous. This makes it possible to exercise direct management from headquarters.

Strategic holding

▶ The wave of diversification in the 1970s and early 1980s created groups involved in diverse types of business. For them, central management of all business activities from headquarters was not possible because of knowledge deficits. The answer to this dilemma was to split the management task: The strategic or management holdings remain responsible for integrating the various parts of the business, i.e. for unlocking synergies; the individual business units have a large degree of operational freedom.

Financial holding

▶ If achieving strategic integration at headquarters becomes too complex, meaning that it cannot be done effectively and efficiently because of knowledge deficits, then the role of the holding can be limited to financial control. Financial holding companies view their subsidiaries as »normal« investment objects from a risk-return perspective. The subsidiaries are subjected to the same portfolio analyses as other investment objects on the capital market. The advantage compared with completely dissolving the company, i.e. a total integration with the capital market, consists in the possibility of leveraging information advantages and selective synergies. Group-wide human resources development serves as an example for the latter aspect.

Before starting, please note we will be making greater use of sources and empirical findings below. This requires an adjustment to different types of language usage, depending on the context. When mentioning »controlling« in this chapter, this is taken as being synonymous with »controller units« (unless otherwise indicated).

5.3.2 Basic structure of controller units

The progressive decentralization of controller units has mirrored the trend seen in companies over the past few years whereby more responsibility is delegated to local units. Consequently, »local controlling ... [is found] mainly in group organizations« (Küpper/Weber/Zünd 1990, p. 287; for empirical confirmation, cf. e.g. Steinle/Thiem/Dunse 1998, pp. 140–149). Local controlling can be assigned to functional or

Fig. 5-18

Two examples of different types of local controlling

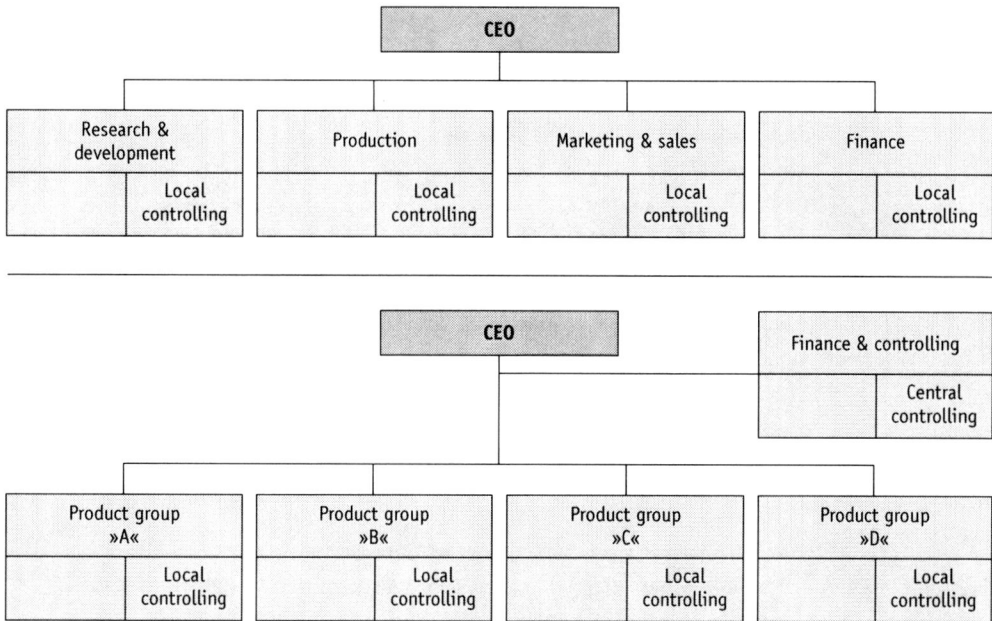

divisional units, depending on the way the company is structured (see *Figure 5-18*). Combined forms are often found, whereby controlling is subdivided by functional and divisional units. One example is an integrated group which started with a functional structure and then sold or outsourced certain activities or integrated other companies. In management and financial holding companies, divisional structuring approaches for local controller units are more common because the group companies report directly to headquarters.

The task of designing an organizational structure for controller units may become even more complex if the controller organization is deeply structured, with functional and regional controllers reporting alongside or to the local controllers of the various group companies. The tasks and competencies of controller units are always designed against the background of how to delimit central and local controlling, as will become clear shortly.

The way controllers are organized can be very varied and highly complex in large companies.

5.3.3 The tasks of central and local controlling

5.3.3.1 Introductory remarks
Even though central controlling is viewed in the literature as an indispensable task at the group level, the general recommendation is to have »as much local controlling as possible, as much central controlling as necessary« (Reiß/Höge 1994, p. 219).

Central controlling which is too dominant may cause a variety of problems of acceptance among managers: On the one hand, it may duplicate work when working on checking and interpreting information from the group's companies. Local controllers would be tempted, for instance, to include buffers in their proposed operational budgets. On the other hand, there might also be a re-delegation of local decision-making rights if, as a result of its informational dominance, only central controlling reports on business developments in the group companies while those actually responsible are not heard. Finally, a constant flood of new information requests from central controlling can lead to the local controllers drowning in their reporting requirements.

Interaction between central and local controlling

Therefore, the centralization of controller tasks should be minimized and activities close to the business – such as operational planning discussions – should be delegated to local controllers. In spite of the delegation of tasks, however, central controlling has to maintain the capacity to create a uniform understanding of controlling, to achieve an objective view on the business and to intervene in exceptional cases. Apart from the different management concepts, the relevant literature assigns certain group-wide, methodological and supervisory tasks to central controlling (cf. Hahn/Hungenberg 2001, pp. 927–934):

▸ Tasks related to consolidating group planning; accounting for group operating income,
▸ predominantly strategic planning and monitoring tasks,
▸ coordinating between business units (e.g. setting of transfer prices),
▸ special overarching analyses (e.g. restructuring activities),
▸ controlling culture, personnel development for controllers, and
▸ developing and maintaining management information systems and uniform methods and guidelines.

The purpose of local controllers, in contrast, consists of performing all activities that are close to the actual business. Typically, the tasks of local controllers are considered to be (cf. Vellmann 1990, pp. 551–553):

▸ Consulting on business issues/special analyses on site,
▸ operational controlling, such as planning for cost centers,
▸ cooperating with headquarters on strategic issues relating to strategic areas of business, and
▸ adjusting tools to meet business requirements.

5.3.3.2 How the allocation of tasks depends on the type of corporate group

The highest degree of centralization of controller tasks can be found in the central controlling of integrated groups of companies: Their main aim is to ensure that the group adheres to a common orientation and that the group's management is provided with the necessary transparency. This is why the task focus of central controlling lies on designing and managing operational planning processes, monitoring developments across business units and within them (e.g. monitoring »normal investments«) as well as designing and maintaining uniform IT systems with a high degree of detail, such as cost accounting (cf. Botta 1994, p. 30). Local controllers mainly serve to provide information and planning support on site.

In strategic holding companies, on the other hand, central controlling focuses on designing strategic planning (e.g. the technical management of M & A projects), on defining the use of operational management tools (e.g. by establishing guidelines on profit and loss accounting), and on participating in capital budgeting. Central controllers limit their role to specifying systems, but still need to have a medium-resolution information system independent from the subsidiaries in order to be able to make adjustments to business activities when necessary (»focal controlling«). For the subsidiaries, central controlling serves mainly as a resource for business administration tools and a mediator in cases of conflict; the local controllers are usually responsible for operational planning and special analyses focusing on their business.

The tasks of central controlling depend (to a large extend) on the group type.

The central controllers of financial holding companies work within the framework of detailed guidelines for planning and reporting structures and limit themselves to low-resolution monitoring of ongoing results reporting and to evaluating and monitoring strategic business areas (regarding a typology of planning aspects, cf. Großeibl 1994, pp. 590–592).

5.3.4 Internal structure of controller units

Regarding the internal structure of controller units, two questions receive the greatest amount of attention in the literature on controlling:
▸ Which is the dominant structural aspect of the subdivisions of controller units: functional, divisional, or a combination?
▸ Are the tasks of cost accounting, financial accounting and strategic planning integrated into the controller unit or organized in separate units? Which special functions do controllers perform?

The dominant approach to organizational structure

When central controllers have to possess detailed knowledge of the markets and business or are often contacted by subsidiaries for information, it is recommended to use a divisional structure for the central controller unit. When specialized knowledge in the areas of planning, reporting or special projects (e.g. tools skills) is at the focus of attention, a functional structure is more suitable for central controlling. A general broadening of the controller unit's perspective takes place when central and local controller units are not structured according to the same criterion (cf. Eschenbach 1994, pp. 113–115).

Functional or divisional structuring of central controlling

For an integrated group, a multidimensional structure may be the most suitable because subsidiaries have to contribute to operational planning and have to make available detailed reporting and planning knowledge. The same applies for strategic holding companies: Here, the authority to define planning tools and methods is contrasted with the shared development of strategies for business areas and operational framework setting. Finally, financial holding companies would usually follow a functional approach to structure because they do not work in detail on the businesses themselves.

The integration of other areas

As a consequence of the harmonization of financial and cost accounting, there are two conceivable developments that could take place: Either overall accounting is allocated to central controlling to ensure a uniform design and tight linkages to the planning function, or financial accounting takes over some responsibilities in the area of internal reporting. Owing to the required level of detailed knowledge about operational business processes and the fact that subsidiaries are managed from the parent company in an integrated group, integrating accounting into the central controlling function appears to make more sense here than in the case of the other management concepts, where sufficient knowledge of the assumptions is all that is needed.

There is also controversy concerning the question of whether or not to integrate strategic planning or its elements into the controller unit (see the corresponding sections in chapter 4). Integrating strategic planning has the advantage of creating tight linkages to the controllers' skill and experience in planning and monitoring. On the other hand, there may be disadvantages resulting from lacking know-how of controllers in the area of innovative strategy development.

Nevertheless, »strategic controlling« is a topic dealt with in all the relevant textbooks on controlling. Such a view is most likely to make sense in the case of a strategic holding: This is where the task of formulating and implementing group strategies or strategies for business areas is the characteristic element. Conversely, in integrated groups of companies, the role of controlling would usually be limited to numerical representations of strategies because of the considerable time needed to carry out operational, routine tasks.

5.3.5 Hierarchical placement of central and local controlling

5.3.5.1 Assignment to a level of hierarchy

There are contradictory statements concerning the organizational placement of central controller units: On the one hand, the controllers should be as close as possible to the top management level in order to exert a sustainable influence; on the other hand, their placement depends on context factors such as their neutrality or participation in decision making (cf. Welge 1988, pp. 408–411). However, there is a widespread consensus that controller units have to be placed at the first or second level of management to ensure that they are sufficiently independent and have enough clout to ask critical questions. The same statement can be applied to local controller units.

Placing controller units at the first management level provides them with significant authority, maximum information transparency – placing them at board level usually implies that accounting reports to them – and usually considerable decision-making rights, which have to be balanced against the tradeoff of less independence in such a small circle of top managers.

By placing controllers at the second management level, their focus on management support is emphasized. This placement reduces their influence on ongoing decision making, but allows a more independent perspective to be taken. The most frequent case in practice, whereby controlling reports to the CFO, ensures that there is a shared buildup of competence between the related functions controlling, financial accounting and finance, which also helps create a critical distance to ongoing decision making. The influence of the controller unit then depends largely on its ability to enforce its views vis-à-vis the other financial disciplines.

Finally, placing the central controller unit as a staff function to the board or the CEO reduces pure financial department thinking on the one hand, but on the other hand it increases the unit's dependency on the reporting manager's position in the company and may limit the controllers' authority vis-à-vis the line functions.

5.3.5.2 Reporting relationships to management

For a long time, the staff/line function nature of controller positions and the authority of controller units to issue instructions dominated the discussion on the optimum controller organization. Today, there is near-unanimity that controllers – in addition to their pure service and consulting functions (staff nature) and decision-making competence for controller-specific issues (e.g. cost accounting) – have to possess additional competencies, such as the right to make suggestions, impose vetoes and have a say in discussions (cf. Küpper 2005, p. 526, for example). Such rights are the basis of the controllers' role as critical counterparts and proactive advisers: As critical counterparts, controllers challenge their managers, for instance by critically questioning proposals and plans. As internal consultants, controllers not only unburden managers from specific tasks, but also proactively complement them. In the context of monitoring, they are responsible for carrying out content-based variance analyses and making suggestions for adjustments. The right to make suggestions and impose vetoes should be conferred especially in cases where management is confronted with strategic uncertainties (e.g. divesting). The obligation to offer advice unasked and to contradict other viewpoints is of key importance for the work of controllers (cf. Weber/Schäffer/Prenzler 2001, p. 33).

Because of the diverse nature of controllers' tasks, it makes little sense to divide controller units into staff and line functions. The service and counterpart natures of controllers have to complement each other: On the one hand, intervening in decisions requires transparency, which controllers can only create, for instance, through their service activities in planning. On the other hand, controllers often lose managers' attention if they concentrate exclusively on routine processes.

These relationships apply to all forms of corporate groups, but relate to different tasks. In the case of holding companies which are characterized by an increasing delegation of controller tasks to subsidiaries, authority and intervention rights are particularly important in order to limit the individual interests of units and to enforce a uniform, group-wide approach if necessary. In contrast to integrated groups of companies, such rights are, however, limited to a few tasks, such as reporting structures or strategic specifications for plans. The same applies for the service and information rights of controller units, which in integrated groups of companies relate to operational planning and information systems, whereas they are also applied to consulting subsidiaries and – where necessary – to strategic questions in the holding companies (cf. Scheffler 1992, pp. 90–98).

5.3.5.3 Reporting relationships between central and local controlling

If one distinguishes between functional and disciplinary reporting, one can derive three basic forms in which local controllers can report to higher levels.

The first option is to build an enclosed controller unit and have the local controllers report functionally and from a disciplinary point of view to central controlling. The benefit of using this approach is that it creates tight linkages within controlling and establishes a common »language«, but this is counterbalanced by the risk of being perceived as an alien body by the line functions. This solution also contradicts – at first glance – the decentralized structure on which large companies are usually based. At second glance, extensive decentralization can be enabled by the fact that top management receives comprehensive insights into local activities through central controlling in the sense of monitoring.

The second option – almost the opposite – is to have the controller unit report in a functional and disciplinary sense to the head of the local operation or subsidiary. This creates a basis for ensuring that the local controllers are accepted by local management, which in turn enables a level of controller involvement that is needed to unburden and supplement management. However, this option also implies a risk of »departmental egoism« as well as a departure from uniform group standards in itself, which could endanger group-wide management of the company. Completely assigning controllers to the local line function can mean that they will lose their independence, and thereby their ability to constrain local managers who neglect the overall objectives of the group.

In order to avoid this outcome, the third option is to separate functional and disciplinary reporting structures (»dotted line«), which is postulated to be the standard case in large companies (cf. Küpper/Weber/Zünd 1990, p. 285). This solution aims to achieve an equilibrium between central framework setting and local business autonomy. A more extensive weighing of benefits and disadvantages can be found in *Figure 5-19*.

A dotted line is not the only possibility for taking into account the interests of both local management and central controlling when placing local controllers within the organization. A further organizational option is to select an undivided reporting line, but »reversing« it from time to time, i.e. switching the solid line at times. If local controllers have been placed under local management and are »drifting« away from headquarters, then they should be required to report to central controlling again. If, as time goes by, they start adopting the position of headquarters too often, they should switch back to reporting to local management. A precondition for this type of organizational solution is that there has to be a certain level of constancy in local controlling's staffing. If the reporting line is switched and most local controllers are also replaced, then the model does not work.

Finally, there is the option of distributing the rights, competencies and responsibilities of local controllers between central and local controlling less rigidly than when assigning functional vs. disciplinary responsibility to them: Fixed or »complete« authority allocations can be supplemented by partial or temporary ones, or a combination of both. An example of a partial allocation of central issues to local controllers occurs when local controllers are in the best position to deal with a certain topic because they know local conditions and possess the relevant technical competencies. A case in point: In order to obtain experience in performing customer

---

Reporting in both functional and disciplinary aspects ... to the central controller.

... to local management.

»Dotted line« solution.

Tasks can also be shared temporarily or on a case-by-case basis between central and local controllers.

Fig. 5-19

Advantages and disadvantages of different organizational placements of local controlling (source: Schüller 1984, p. 210)

Reporting to line manager		Reporting to central controller		Dotted line concept	
⊕	⊖	⊕	⊖	⊕	⊖
▸ Ability to work closely and on a basis of trust with line manager ▸ High degree of acceptance by line staff ▸ Good access to formal and informal sources ▸ Chance to provide decision-making support to line manager ▸ Capacity to match line's needs closely	▸ Overall controlling concept is neglected ▸ Strengthens particularism ▸ Reporting to central controller is neglected ▸ Risk of lacking distance and objectivity regarding line activities	▸ Uniform implementation of controlling concept ▸ Counterweight when participating in decision making by the line ▸ Strong emphasis on integrative aspect of coordination ▸ Rapid implementation of new concepts ▸ Greater independence from line managers ▸ Quick supply of information to headquarters	▸ Special controller = spy from headquarters ▸ Information blockade by line ▸ Special controller is isolated ▸ Low level of acceptance ▸ Not used in decision-making support ▸ Line-specific particularities are insufficiently taken into consideration	▸ Compromise between two extremes ▸ Opportunity to combine the line's needs with the requirements of controlling ▸ Flexible exertion of influence on special controllers	▸ Reporting to two bosses = permanent conflict ▸ Is accepted neither by the line nor by central controlling ▸ Objectivity and neutrality not ensured

lifetime value calculations, a business unit should be used that has a suitable customer structure, i.e. one which has different customer groups which make use of services at distinct levels. Corporate governance topics provide another example: For a German company, Sarbanes-Oxley issues could best be resolved by its U. S. subsidiary. In both cases, it would probably make sense to allocate technical responsibility for the topics to the local units for an extended period of time.

Allocating central controlling tasks to local units temporarily is a case that occurs most often with project work. If the best controller for a specific industry segment works locally, it makes sense, for example, to give her responsibility for participating in an M & A project that is being prepared by central controlling if it relates to the same industry segment. Again, it is the specific competency of local controlling that justifies this measure.

Both of the possibilities mentioned may result from specific events or causes, but can also be a concrete organizational strategy followed by central controlling: It ensures that there is a tight interaction between local and central controlling, enabling local controllers to stay focused on »the big picture«.

When it comes to the details, such arrangements can become quite complex. *Figure 5-20* shows a concrete example borrowed from practice.

Fig. 5-20

Practical example for an arrangement of competencies between managers and controllers at different levels of the hierarchy

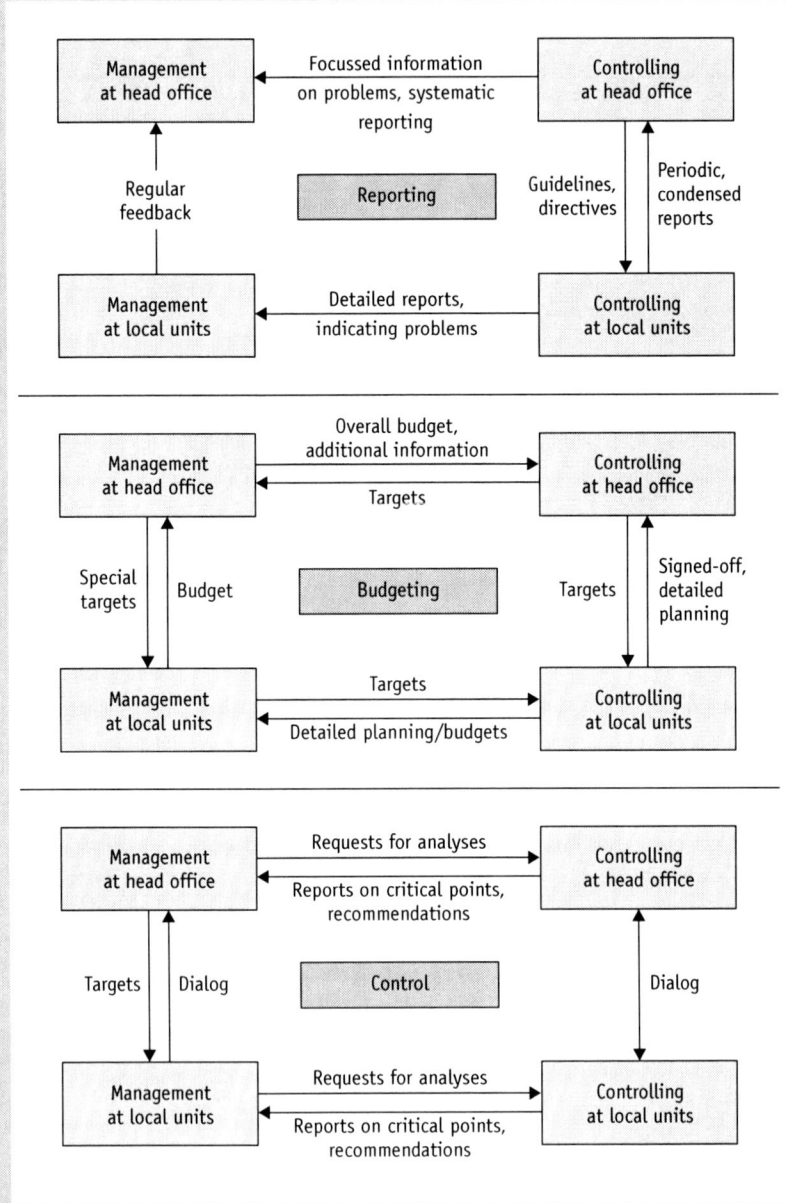

Finally, we would like to address the question of whether the division of responsibilities depends on a company's management philosophy, again using corporate groups as an example.

In integrated groups of companies, the centralized management concept would lead one to suspect that central controlling prescribes uniform standards for the entire group. It would be extraordinarily irrational to manage two comparable subsidiaries with metrics which are calculated in different ways, for instance. Therefore, local controlling should report to central controlling on functional issues in order to ensure that there is comparable, group-wide information transparency. In specific cases, for instance when reorienting a controller unit or in a crisis situation, it makes sense to create an even tighter linkage between local and central controlling. Generally, management in an integrated group of companies is still less centralized than in a sovereign company, as the units being managed are at least legally independent. In the case of a strategic holding company, central controlling is only responsible for managing and implementing strategy. There only has to be a consensus concerning the question of the degree to which targets can be prescribed and monitored. Therefore, having local controlling report to central controlling on functional issues is not necessary as a general rule, but only for special aspects (e.g. specification of results metrics etc.). As a rule, the power of central controlling over local controlling will be weaker than in the case of an integrated group of companies, and could take the form of information rights for central controlling, for instance. Finally, local controllers have maximum autonomy when they report to line management. In the case of a financial holding company, this hierarchical arrangement could be seen as a sensible option.

5.3.6 Empirical findings

The statements listed above were empirically analyzed in a study carried out in 2000 on the design of controlling in large German groups (cf. Weber/Hunold/Prenzler/Thust 2001). The key findings are listed in *Figure 5-21*, following the organizational structure. The key statements were as follows:

▸ Both in the areas of central and local controlling, a relationship was found to exist between the type of controller organizations and the management concepts of the groups. Groups with a centralized management concept reflect this preference in their controller organizations, where structures are also more centralized and give central controlling greater influence over local controllers.

Empirical findings confirm the conceptual considerations.

▸ Central controlling in integrated groups of companies typically performs more operational tasks than in management and financial holding companies. The focus of the tasks in integrated groups of companies lies on results control and information supply; in strategic holding companies, it lies on planning and consulting, and in financial holding companies, on decision making and monitoring.

▸ In integrated groups of companies, central controlling does have a strong position within controlling; however, controllers are aware that they have too little influence on management decisions because they are responsible for too many operational tasks, a state of affairs that they criticize.

▸ Its organizational status should always enable controlling to fulfill its tasks: Therefore, central controlling should always be anchored at the first or second management level. This was the case for almost all the corporate groups analyzed (22 out of 23).

▸ Central controllers with an independent board member for controlling have more influence on management decisions than central controllers who are positioned at the second management level.

▸ Controlling board members are much more common in strategic and financial holding companies than in integrated groups of companies. This confirms the assumption that the role of coordinating functions is placed higher up in the hierarchy as the degree of task decentralization increases.

▸ The trend during the past few years has increasingly been to decentralize controlling departments to individual business units. This observation holds for all types of corporate groups.

▸ In practice, the dotted line principle has been implemented in almost all companies (separation of reporting for functional vs. disciplinary aspects). Finan-

Fig. 5-21

Types of controller organization in German corporate groups – an overview
(source: Weber/Hunold/Prenzler/Thust 2001, p. 37)

	Integrated group of companies	Strategic holding	Financial holding
Tasks of group holding	▸ Business framework setting ▸ Supervision of group companies ▸ Group planning ▸ Consolidation of results ▸ Information supply	▸ Creating transparency ▸ Special analyses (share-holdings etc.) ▸ Coordination of planning ▸ Supervision/introduction of new methods	▸ Subsidiary controlling ▸ Strategic planning ▸ Valuation methods
Internal structure of central controlling	Multi-dimensional; product areas as well as selected methods	Multi-dimensional	Functional
Hierarchical positioning of central controlling	Reports to CFO	Reports to CFO	Board member for controlling
Reporting path of local controlling	Dotted line principle	Dotted line principle	Reports to line management (functional reporting only in the case of standard metrics)
Structure of local controlling	Divisional (by product area)	Divisional (units are responsible for their internal structure)	Varies by area/unit
Tasks of local controlling	▸ Supervision of product areas/production plants ▸ Implementation of plans	▸ Planning for the local unit ▸ Information supply ▸ Controlling of investments ▸ Methods of the subsidiaries	▸ Business framework setting ▸ Supervision of companies ▸ Group planning ▸ Consolidation of results ▸ Information supply

cial holding companies are the only type where local controllers tend to report directly to local management.

▸ The share of purely operational tasks of local controlling decreases as the degree of management decentralization increases.

Summary
(see guiding question 4)

▸ The organization of controller units is a complex field in large companies in particular; it is essential for the efficiency and effectiveness of controllers' activities.

▸ The basic questions deal with the hierarchical positioning of controller units (usually at the second management level, but sometimes the first or third level), the division of central and local controller tasks and the internal structure (e.g. functional task areas).

▸ When defining reporting structures for controllers and managers, it is necessary to find a balance between closeness to the actual business and a required distance and independence.

External signs of this tradeoff frequently take the shape of the dotted line principle, whereby controllers report to different superiors on functional vs. disciplinary issues.

▸ The form of the controller organization depends essentially on the form of the company's structure and its management philosophy. Controller tasks take very different forms in terms of their type, volume and distribution for each of the three types of corporate group (integrated group of companies, strategic and financial holding company).

5.4 Summary

Once more, the final chapter of the book has confirmed what we said before: Controllers are important for the companies in which they work and to whose success they contribute. They are extremely common in corporate practice; the only place they are not found is in small companies. Controllers are in high demand on the labor market. They have successful careers; many board members were controllers once or several times in the course of their careers (cf. Weber 2008, pp. 26–38). Controllers are exposed to interesting developments in their field of activity, which is expanding its scope and moving closer to the business. Their perspective on business is also broadening; they are moving away from their traditional, purely financial orientation. The same applies for the internal focus, which was at the forefront of attention to date. Today, it is part of controllers' everyday business to look at their companies »from the outside in«, or should be if it is not. All in all, the job of controller is an attractive career goal for ambitious students.

> Controllers are successful and in high demand.

However, not everything is perfect for controllers either. There are a couple of critical aspects which have the potential of darkening the positive outlook. The broad scope required of controllers nowadays places extremely high demands on them. Not every controller can live up to such demands. Generally, the breadth of requirements no longer permits controllers to specialize on technical tools and instruments; instead, controllers have to cover a range of topics so broad that it is hardly distinguishable from the topics covered by managers. One way of providing support may be to differentiate controller units internally. Consultancies use a similar concept, whereby they separate the front office from back office functions. Controllers who are intimately familiar with tools and figures would then work alongside controllers who are in direct contact with the managers.

A further potential problem is that the competitive position of accountants is improving, as has been mentioned several times in this book. This poses the question of whether the separation between these two distinct departments can be maintained. Internationally, it is the exception rather than the rule. This brings us to the next question of whether globalization will stop at controllers. As an example, there is a large German company in which controllers are responsible for risk management, a role that is uncontested. In the U.S. subsidiaries, however, this organizational arrangement was denied or prohibited by the auditors. It was obviously inconceivable that controllers could have such in-depth knowledge that they would be able to perform proper risk management.

Controllers should therefore under no circumstances take comfort in their very strong internal competitive position, but have to work actively on its ongoing strategic development. If controllers focus consistently on identifying new services for managers in the sense of »role making«, if they keep their managers' satisfaction in mind, if they measure their tasks in the same way that they plan and monitor business development, then there are strong arguments why they should be able to maintain their »market dominance« in the area of management support. The bundling of unburdening, supplementary and constraining functions is the exception rather than the rule internationally. However, this arrangement has benefits on the resource side, and it also enables a balanced relationship between the task types: Controllers who support their managers on an ongoing basis earn the right to contradict them from time to time.

> Controllers should not become complacent because of their strong internal competitive position.

Conversely, if controllers rest on their traditional position, two other developments become more likely, which are characterized by a significant limitation of their spectrum of tasks. We have mentioned both developments several times in this chapter:

> Where will the journey lead?

- ▸ On the one hand, there is the option of withdrawing to financial information tasks. As a result of the increased importance of the data from financial accounting, this development option would lead to controllers and accountants being integrated in a single department. The expression »Biltroller« (*a combination of the German word for balance sheet – »Bilanz« – and controlling, reflecting the convergence of financial and cost accounting*) serves as a direct reminder.
- ▸ Whereas being a »Biltroller« is not a desirable alternative for many controllers, the migration towards becoming a »business consultant« or internal consultant is fundamentally a rewarding goal. Consultants are in close contact to managers; they work on key topics and are not captives to a daily routine. They can request figures from others. They are important and enjoy a strong reputation, and their career prospects are excellent. Still, this alternative also has its problems. The use of consultants depends very much on the favor and budgets of managers. If there

is no demand for consulting, the controllers become unemployed. They also face stiff competition from external consultants.

The development of controller units depends on many individual and context-specific factors. They include imminent rationality bottlenecks as well as the willingness of controllers to fight for new markets. Fortunately, we do not have to provide a definitive statement at the end of an introductory textbook on controlling. Things remain interesting.

Recommended reading ...

... Designing a mission statement for controllers
David 2005, pp. 107–113
Krystek/Zumbrock 1993
Weber 1996b, pp. 26–30

... Applying the Balanced Scorecard
David 2005, pp. 160–192
Weber/Schäffer 2000b, pp. 175–342

... Organization of the controller unit
Borchers 2000
Pohle 1993, cols. 661–669
Steinle/Thiem/Dunse 1998, pp. 140–149
Vellmann 1990, pp. 535–563

Bibliography

Ahn, H. (1999): Ansehen und Verständnis des Controlling in der Betriebswirtschaftslehre: Grundlegende Ergebnisse einer empirischen Studie unter deutschen Hochschullehrern, in: Controlling, Vol. 11, pp. 109–114.

Ahn, H./Dyckhoff, H. (2004): Von der Rationalitätssicherung zur Effektivitäts- und Effizienzsicherung, in: Scherm, E./Pietsch, G. (Eds.): Controlling: Theorien und Konzeptionen, Munich, pp. 501–528.

Ahrens, T. (1999): Contrasting Involvements: A Study of Management Accounting Practices in Britain and Germany, Amsterdam.

Ahrens, T./Becker, A./Burns, J./Chapman, C./Granlund, M./Habersam, M./Hansen, A./Khalifa, R./Malmi, T./Mennicken, A./Mikes, A./Panozzo, F./Piber, M./Quattrone, P./Scheytt, T. (2007): The Future of Interpretive Accounting Research – a Polyphonic Debate, in: Critical Perspectives on Accounting, doi:10.1016/j.cpa.2006.07.005.

Amshoff, B. (1993): Controlling in deutschen Unternehmungen: Realtypen, Kontext und Effizienz, Wiesbaden.

Ansari, S.L./Euske, K.J. (1987): Rational, Rationalizing, and Reifying Uses of Accounting Data in Organizations, in: Accounting, Organizations and Society, Vol. 12, pp. 549–570.

Anthony, R.N. (1965): Planning and Control Systems, Boston.

Argyris, C. (1952): The Impact of Budgets on People, New York.

Armstrong, P. (1985): Changing Management Control Strategies: The Role of Competition between Accountancy and other Organizational Professions, in: Accounting, Organizations and Society, Vol. 10, pp. 129–148.

Auffermann, J.D. (1952): Vorwort, in: Rationalisierungs-Kuratorium der Deutschen Wirtschaft (RKW) (Ed.): Rechnungswesen im Dienst der Werkleitung, RKW-Auslandsdienst, Vol. 3, p. 6.

Bannow, W. (1983): Controlling ist wichtiger denn je, in: Harvard Manager, Vol. 5, pp. 20–25.

Bauer, M. (2002): Controllership in Deutschland: Zur erfolgreichen Zusammenarbeit von Controllern und Managern, Wiesbaden.

Baxter, J./Chua, W.F. (2003): Alternative Management Accounting Research – Whence and Whither, in: Accounting, Organizations and Society, Vol. 28, pp. 97–126.

Becker, A. (2003): Controlling als reflexive Steuerung von Organisationen, Stuttgart.

Berens, W./Schmitting, W. (2003): Zum Verständnis von Controlling, Interner Revision und Früherkennung vor dem Hintergrund der Corporate Governance, in: Zeitschrift für Planung und Unternehmenssteuerung, Vol. 14, pp. 353–357.

Berthel, J. (1991): Karriereanreize für Mitarbeiter, in: Schanz, G. (Ed.): Handbuch Anreizsysteme für Wirtschaft und Verwaltung, Stuttgart, pp. 481–498.

Bhargava, M./Dubelaar, C./Ramaswami, S. (1994): Reconciling Diverse Measures of Performance: A Conceptual Framework and Test of Methodology, in: Journal of Business Research, Vol. 31, pp. 235–246.

Binder, C. (2006): Zur Entwicklung des Controllings als Teildisziplin der Betriebswirtschaftslehre, Wiesbaden.

Binder, C./Schäffer, U. (2005a): Deutschsprachige Controllinglehrstühle an der Schwelle zum Generationswechsel, in: Zeitschrift für Controlling und Management, Vol. 49, pp. 100–104.

Binder, C./Schäffer, U. (2005b): Die Entwicklung des Controllings von 1970 bis 2003 im Spiegel von Publikationen in deutschsprachigen Zeitschriften, in: Die Betriebswirtschaft, Vol. 65, pp. 603–626.

Birl, H. (2007): Innerbetriebliche Kooperation von Controllerbereich und Innenrevision: Messung, Erfolgswirkung, Determinanten, Wiesbaden.

Borchers, S. (2000): Beteiligungscontrolling in der Management-Holding, Wiesbaden.

Botta, V. (1994): Ausgewählte Probleme des Beteiligungscontrolling, in: Schulte, C. (Eds.): Beteiligungscontrolling, Wiesbaden, pp. 25–40.

Bruns, W. J./DeCoster, D. T. (1969): Preface, in: Accounting and its Behavioral Implications, New York, pp. V–VI.

Chua, W. F. (1986): Radical Developments in Accounting Thought, in: The Accounting Review, Vol. 61, pp. 601–632.

David, U. (2005): Strategisches Management von Controllerbereichen: Konzept und Fallstudien, Wiesbaden.

Dehler, M. (2001): Entwicklungsstand der Logistik: Messung – Determinanten – Erfolgswirkungen, Wiesbaden.

Dent, J. F. (1991): Accounting and Organizational Cultures: A Field Study of the Emergence of a New Organizational Reality, in: Accounting, Organizations and Society, Vol. 16, pp. 705–732.

Deyhle, A. (1980): Controller-Handbuch, Vol. A, 2nd edition, Gauting.

Deyhle, A. (1984): Management- & Controlling-Brevier, Vol. I: Manager & Controller im Team, 3rd edition, Gauting.

Drucker, P. F. (1954): The Practice of Management, New York.

Eschenbach, R. (1994): Controlling, Stuttgart.

Eschenbach, R./Niedermayr, R. (1996): Die Konzeption des Controlling, in: Eschenbach, R. (Eds.): Controlling, 2nd edition, Stuttgart, pp. 65–94.

Financial Executives Institute (Ed.) (1962): Controllership and Treasurership Functions Defined by FEI, in: The Controller, Vol. 30, p. 289.

Foucault, M. (2004): Überwachen und Strafen: Die Geburt des Gefängnisses, 16th edition, Frankfurt am Main.

Frese, E. (1996): Grundlagen der Organisationsgestaltung, in: Eversheim, W./ Schuh, G. (Eds.): Hütte: Taschenbuch für Betriebsingenieure: Produktion und Management »Betriebshütte«, Vol. 1, Berlin et al., pp. 3/1–3/15.

Friedl, B. (2003): Controlling, Stuttgart.

Goossens, F. (1959): Der »Controller«: Chef des Unternehmens ohne Gesamtverantwortung, in: Mensch und Arbeit, Vol. 11, pp. 75–76.

Großeibl, W. (1994): Konzerncontrolling, in: Eschenbach, R. (Eds.): Controlling, Stuttgart, pp. 587–599.

Gutenberg, E. (1929): Die Unternehmung als Gegenstand betriebswirtschaftlicher Theorie, Berlin et al.

Hahn, D. (1987): Controlling: Stand und Entwicklungstendenzen unter besonderer Berücksichtigung des CIM-Konzeptes, in: Scheer, A.-W. (Eds.): Rechnungswesen und EDV (8. Saarbrücker Arbeitstagung), Heidelberg, pp. 3–39.

Hahn, D./Hungenberg, H. (2001): PuK: Planung und Kontrolle, Planungs- und Kontrollsysteme, Planungs- und Kontrollrechnung, Wertorientierte Controlling-konzepte, 6th edition, Wiesbaden.

Harbert, L. (1982): Controlling-Begriffe und Controlling-Konzeptionen, Frankfurt.

Heigl, A. (1989): Controlling: Interne Revision, 2nd edition, Stuttgart et al.

Heinen, E. (1966): Das Zielsystem der Unternehmung: Grundlagen betriebswirts-chaftlicher Entscheidungen, Wiesbaden.

Henning, D.A./Moseley, R.L. (1970): Authority Role of a Functional Manager: The Controller, in: Administrative Science Quarterly, Vol. 15, pp. 482–489.

Henzler, H. (1974): Der Januskopf muß weg, in: Wirtschaftswoche, Vol. 28, pp. 60–63.

Herzberg, F. (1968): One more Time: How do you Motivate Employees?, in: Harvard Business Review, Vol. 46, pp. 53–62.

Herzog, A. (1999): Gestaltung von Controllership: Die Zuordnung von Aufgaben zu Controllern, Wiesbaden.

Hirsch, B. (2003): Zur Lehre im Fach Controlling, in: Weber, J./Hirsch, B. (Eds.): Zur Zukunft der Controllingforschung: Empirie, Schnittstellen und Umsetzung in der Lehre, Wiesbaden, pp. 249–266.

Hirsch, B. (2006): Behavioral Controlling: Skizze einer verhaltenswissenschaftlich fundierten Controllingkonzeption, Vallendar.

Hoffmann, F. (1972): Merkmale der Führungsorganisation amerikanischer Unter-nehmen: Auszüge aus den Ergebnissen einer Forschungsreise 1970, in: Zeitschrift für Organisation, Vol. 41, pp. 3–8, 85–89 and 145–148.

Höller, H. (1978): Verhaltenswirkungen betrieblicher Planungs- und Kontrollsysteme, Munich.

Holmström, B. (1979): Moral Hazard and Observability, in: Bell Journal of Economics, Vol. 10, pp. 74–91.

Hopper, T./Macintosh, N. (1998): Management Accounting Numbers: Freedom or Prison – Geneen vs. Foucault, in: McKinlay, A./Starkey, K. (Eds.): Foucault, Management and Organization Theory, London, pp. 126–150.

Horváth, P. (1978): Controlling: Entwicklung und Stand einer Konzeption zur Lösung der Adaptions- und Koordinationsprobleme der Führung, in: Zeitschrift für Betriebswirtschaft, Vol. 48, pp. 194–208.

Horváth, P. (2006): Controlling, 10th edition, Munich.

IIR (Deutsches Institut für Interne Revision)/IIA (Institut für Interne Revision Österreich)/SVIR (Schweizerischer Verband für Interne Revision) (Eds.) (2004): Die Interne Revision in Deutschland, in Österreich und in der Schweiz 2004, Frankfurt.

Jackson, J.H. (1949): The Comptroller: His Functions and Organization, 2nd edition, Cambridge, Mass.

Janis, I.L. (1982): Groupthink: Psychological studies of policy decisions and fias-coes, 2nd edition, Boston et al.

Jensen, M. C./Meckling, W. H. (1976): Theory of the Firm: Managerial Behavior, Agency Costs and Ownership Structure, in: Journal of Financial Economics, Vol. 3, pp. 305–360.

Jost, P. (2000): Organisation und Motivation: Eine ökonomisch-psychologische Einführung, Wiesbaden.

Kahneman, D./Tversky, A. (1973): On the Psychology of Prediction, in: Psychological Review, Vol. 80, pp. 237–251.

Kappler, E./Scheytt, T. (1999): Auf dem Weg nach Jenachdem: Controlling postmodern organisieren, in: Schreyögg, G. (Eds.): Organisation & Postmoderne, Wiesbaden, pp. 211–234.

Katz, D./Kahn, R. L. (1978): The Social Psychology of Organizations, 2nd edition, New York et al.

Kieser, A./Walgenbach, P. (2003): Organisation, 4th edition, Stuttgart.

Kirsch, W. (1997): Kommunikatives Handeln, Autopoiese, Rationalität: Kritische Aneignungen im Hinblick auf eine evolutionäre Organisationstheorie, 2nd edition, Herrsching.

Kronast, M. (1989): Controlling: Notwendigkeit eines unternehmensspezifischen Selbstverständnisses, Munich.

Krüger, W. (1979): Controlling: Gegenstandsbereich, Wirkungsweise und Funktionen im Rahmen der Unternehmenspolitik, in: Betriebswirtschaftliche Forschung und Praxis, Vol. 31, pp. 158–169.

Krystek, U./Zumbrock, S. (1993): Planung und Vertrauen: Die Bedeutung von Vertrauen und Misstrauen für die Qualität von Planungs- und Kontrollsystemen, Stuttgart.

Küpper, H.-U. (1987): Konzeption des Controlling aus betriebswirtschaftlicher Sicht, in: Scheer, A.-W. (Eds.): Rechnungswesen und EDV, 8. Saarbrücker Arbeitstagung, Heidelberg, pp. 82–116.

Küpper, H.-U. (1990): Controller-Anforderungsprofil in der Theorie, in: Mayer, E./ Weber, J. (Eds.): Handbuch Controlling, Stuttgart, pp. 325–342

Küpper, H.-U. (2005): Controlling: Konzeption, Aufgaben, Instrumente, 4th edition, Stuttgart.

Küpper, H.-U./Wagenhofer, A. (2002): Vorwort der Herausgeber, in: Handwörterbuch Unternehmensrechnung und Controlling, 4th edition, Stuttgart, pp. X–XI.

Küpper, H.-U./Weber, J./Zünd, A. (1990): Zum Verständnis und Selbstverständnis des Controlling, in: Zeitschrift für Betriebswirtschaft, Vol. 60, pp. 281–293.

Lambert, R. A. (2001): Contracting Theory and Accounting, in: Journal of Accounting and Economics, Vol. 32, pp. 3–87.

Lambert, R. A. (2007): Agency Theory and Management Accounting, in: Chapman, C. S./Hopwood, A. G./Shields, M. D. (Eds.): Handbook of Management Accounting Research, Amsterdam, pp. 247–268.

Landsberg, G. v./Mayer, E. (1988): Berufsbild des Controllers, Stuttgart.

Langenbach, W. (2001): Börseneinführungen von Tochtergesellschaften: Eine konzeptionelle und empirische Analyse zur Optimierung der Rationalitätssicherung durch Märkte, Wiesbaden.

Latham, G. P./Locke, E. A. (1979): Goal Setting: A Motivational Technique that Works, in: Organizational Dynamics, Vol. 8, pp. 68–80.

Latham, G. P./Locke, E. A. (1991): Self-Regulation through Goal Setting, in: Organizational Behavior and Human Decision Processes, Vol. 50, pp. 212–247.

Libby, R./Lewis, B. L. (1977): Human Information Processing Research in Accounting: The State of the Art, in: Accounting, Organizations and Society, Vol. 2, pp. 245–268.

Libby, R./Lewis, B. L. (1982): Human Information Processing Research in Accounting: The State of the Art in 1982, in: Accounting, Organizations and Society, Vol. 7, pp. 231–285.

Link, J. (1982): Die methodologischen, informationswirtschaftlichen und führungspolitischen Aspekte des Controlling, in: Zeitschrift für Betriebswirtschaft, Vol. 52, pp. 261–279.

Locke, E. A. (1968): Toward a Theory of Task Motivation and Incentives, in: Organizational Behavior and Human Performance, Vol. 3, pp. 157–189.

Locke, E. A./Latham, G. P. (1984): Goal Setting: A Motivational Technique that Works!, Englewood Cliffs, New Jersey.

Locke, E. A./Latham, G. P. (1990): A Theory of Goal Setting & Task Performance, Englewood Cliffs, New Jersey.

Locke, E. A./Latham, G. P. (2002): Building a Practically Useful Theory of Goal Setting and Task Motivation: A 35 Year Odyssey, in: American Psychologist, Vol. 57, pp. 705–717.

Loft, A. (1991): The History of Management Accounting: Relevance Found, in: Ashton, D./Hopper, T./Scapens, R. (Eds.): Issues in Management Accounting, Englewood Cliffs, pp. 17–38.

Luhmann, N. (1989): Vertrauen: Ein Mechanismus der Reduktion sozialer Komplexität, 3rd edition, Stuttgart.

Macintosh, N. B. (2003): Participative Budgeting: For and Against, in: Zeitschrift für Controlling und Management, Vol. 47, special issue 1, pp. 13–21.

Mann, R. (1973): Praxis des Controlling, Munich.

Mayer, E. (1990): Arbeitsgemeinschaft Wirtschaftswissenschaft und Wirtschaftspraxis (AWW) in Controlling und Rechnungswesen: Beispiel der Verbindung von praktischem Management Know-how und theoretischen Controllingkonzepten, in: Siegwart, H./Mahari, J. I./Caytas, I. G./Sander, S. (Eds.): Meilensteine im Management, Stuttgart/Basel, pp. 307–323.

Messner, M./Becker, A./Schäffer, U./Binder, C. (2008): Legitimacy and Identity in Germanic Management Accounting Research, in: The European Accounting Review, Vol. 16, doi: 10.1080/09638180701819808.

Meyer, J. W./Rowan, B. (1977): Institutionalized Organizations: Formal Structures as Myth and Ceremony, in: American Journal of Sociology, Vol. 83, pp. 340–363.

Meyer, M./Schäffer, U./Gmür, M. (2008): Transfer und Austausch von Wissen in der Accounting-Forschung: eine Zitations- und Kozitationsanalyse englischsprachiger Accounting-Journals 1990–2004, in: Zeitschrift für betriebswirtschaftliche Forschung, Vol. 60, pp. 153–181.

Miller, G. A. (1956): The Magical Number Seven, Plus or Minus Two: Some Limits on our Capacity for Processing Information, in: The Psychological Review, Vol. 63, pp. 81–97.

Miller, P./O'Leary, T. (1987): Accounting and the Construction of the Governable Person, in: Accounting, Organizations and Society, Vol. 12, pp. 235–265.

Mintzberg, H. (1996): The Structuring of Organizations, in: Mintzberg, H./Quinn, J.B. (Eds.): The Strategy Process: Concepts, Contexts, Cases, 3rd edition, Upper Saddle River, New Jersey, pp. 331–349.

Mosiek, T. (2002): Interne Kundenorientierung des Controlling, Frankfurt a.M.

Müller, W. (1974): Die Koordination von Informationsbedarf und Informationsbeschaffung als zentrale Aufgabe des Controlling, in: Zeitschrift für betriebswirtschaftliche Forschung, Vol. 26, pp. 683–693.

Napier, C. (2006): Accounts of Change: 30 Years of Historical Accounting Research, in: Accounting, Organizations and Society, Vol. 31, pp. 445–507.

Niedermayr, R. (1994): Entwicklungsstand des Controlling: System, Kontext und Effizienz, Wiesbaden.

Paefgen, A. (2008): Rationalitätsdefizite im Handeln von Controllern: Ausprägungsformen sowie Notwendigkeit, Möglichkeiten und Grenzen eines Entgegenwirkens, Vallendar.

Peemöller, V.H./Richter, M. (2000): Entwicklungstendenzen in der Internen Revision, Berlin.

Pfohl, H.-C./Zettelmeyer, B. (1987): Strategisches Controlling?, in: Zeitschrift für Betriebswirtschaft, Vol. 57, pp. 145–175.

Pietsch, G./Scherm, E. (2000): Die Präzisierung des Controlling als Führungs- und Führungsunterstützungsfunktion, in: Die Unternehmung, Vol. 54, pp. 395–412.

Pohle, K. (1993): Controlling und Organisation, in: Handwörterbuch der Betriebswirtschaft, 5th edition, Stuttgart, cols. 661–669.

Porter, M.E. (1980): Competitive Strategy: Techniques for Analyzing Industries and Competition, New York.

Prahalad, C.K./Hamel, G. (1990): The Core Competence of the Corporation, in: Harvard Business Review, Vol. 68, pp. 79–91.

Preißler, P.R. (2007): Controlling: Lehrbuch und Intensivkurs, 13th edition, Munich.

Reiß, M./Höge, R. (1994): Schlankes Controlling in segmentierten Unternehmen, in: Betriebswirtschaftliche Forschung und Praxis, Vol. 46, pp. 210–224.

Richter, H.J. (1987): Theoretische Grundlagen des Controlling: Strukturkriterien für die Entwicklung von Controlling-Konzeptionen, Frankfurt a.M. et al.

Roslender, R./Dillard, J. (2003): Reflections on the Interdisciplinary Perspectives on Accounting Project, in: Critical Perspectives on Accounting, Vol. 14, pp. 325–351.

Sandig, C. (1933): Gewinn und Sicherheit in der Betriebspolitik: Das Treiben und Bremsen im Betriebe, in: Zeitschrift für Betriebswirtschaft, Vol. 10, pp. 349–360.

Sathe, V. (1982): Controller Involvement in Management, Englewood Cliffs, New Jersey.

Schäffer, U. (1996): Controlling für selbstabstimmende Gruppen?, Wiesbaden.

Schäffer, U. (2001): Kontrolle als Lernprozess, Wiesbaden.

Schäffer, U. (2004): Rationalitätssicherung durch Kontrolle, in: Scherm, E./Pietsch, G. (Eds.): Controlling: Theorien und Konzeptionen, Munich, pp. 487–500.

Schäffer, U./Binder, C./Gmür, M. (2006): Struktur und Entwicklung der Controllingforschung: Eine Zitations- und Kozitationsanalyse deutschsprachiger Controllingbeiträge 1970–2003, in: Zeitschrift für Betriebswirtschaft, Vol. 76, pp. 395–440.

Schäffer, U./Weber, J. (2004): Thesen zum Controlling, in: Scherm, E./Pietsch, G. (Eds.): Controlling: Theorien und Konzeptionen, Munich, pp. 459–466.

Scheffler, E. (1992): Konzernmanagement, Munich.

Schein, E. H. (1977): Career Anchors and Career Paths: A Panel Study of Management School Graduates, in: J. van Maanen (Eds.): Organizational Careers: Some New Perspectives, New York et al., pp. 49–64.

Scherm, E./Pietsch, G. (Eds.) (2004a): Controlling: Theorien und Konzeptionen, Munich.

Scherm, E./Pietsch, G. (2004b): Theorie und Konzeption in der Controllingforschung, in: Scherm, E./Pietsch, G. (Eds.): Controlling: Theorien und Konzeptionen, Munich, pp. 3–22.

Schmidt, A. (1986): Das Controlling als Instrument zur Koordination der Unternehmensführung, Frankfurt et al.

Schneider, D. (1992a): Theorien zur Entwicklung des Rechnungswesens, in: Zeitschrift für betriebswirtschaftliche Forschung, Vol. 44, pp. 3–31.

Schneider, D. (1992b): Controlling im Zwiespalt zwischen Koordination und interner Misserfolgsverschleierung, in: Horváth, P. (Eds.): Effektives und schlankes Controlling, Stuttgart, pp. 11–35.

Schnettler, A. (1951): Der Betriebsvergleich: Grundlagen, Technik und Anwendung zwischenbetrieblicher Vergleiche, 2nd edition, Stuttgart.

Schüller, S. (1984): Organisation von Controllingsystemen in der Kreditwirtschaft, Münster.

Schweitzer, M./Küpper, H.-U. (2003): Systeme der Kosten- und Erlösrechnung, 8th edition, Munich.

Siegel, G./Kulesza, C. S. (1996): The Practice Analysis of Management Accounting, in: Management Accounting, Vol. 77, pp. 20–28.

Siegwart, H. (1986): Controlling-Konzepte und Controller-Funktionen in der Schweiz, in: Mayer, E./Landsberg, G. v./Thiede, W. (Eds.): Controlling-Konzepte im internationalen Vergleich, Freiburg i. Br., pp. 105–131.

Simon, H. A. (1957): Models of Man, New York.

Simon, H. A./Guetzkow, H./Kozmetsky, G./Tyndall, G. (1954): Centralization vs. Decentralization in Organizing the Controller's Department, Houston.

Skousen, K. F./Zimmer, R. K. (1970): Controllership Obsolescence: Fact or Fiction, in: Management Accounting, Vol. 51, pp. 20–23.

Smith, A. (1776/1952): An Inquiry into the Nature and Causes of the Wealth of Nations, in: Hutchins, R. M. (Ed.): Great Books of the Western World: An Inquiry into the Nature and Causes of the Wealth of Nations by Adam Smith, Chicago et al.

Spillecke, D. (2006): Interne Kundenorientierung des Controllerbereichs: Messung – Erfolgsauswirkungen – Determinanten, Wiesbaden.

Steinle, C./Thiem, H./Dunse, A. (1998): Beteiligungscontrolling, in: Controlling, Vol. 10, pp. 140–149.

Stoffel, K. (1995): Controllership im internationalen Vergleich, Wiesbaden.

Vellmann, K.-H. (1990): Organisation des Controlling in einem Konzern, in: Mayer, E./Weber, J. (Eds.): Handbuch Controlling, Stuttgart, pp. 535–563.

Vroom, V. H. (1964): Work and Motivation, New York.

Wagenhofer, A. (2006): Management Accounting Research in German-Speaking Countries, in: Journal of Management Accounting Research, Vol. 18, pp. 1–19.

Walker, O. C./Ruekert, R. (1987): Marketing's Role in the Implementation of Business Strategies: A Critical Review and Conceptual Framework, in: Journal of Marketing, Vol. 51, pp. 15–33.

Wall, F. (2000): Koordinationsfunktion des Controlling und Organisation, in: Kosten-rechnungspraxis, Vol. 44, pp. 295–304.

Watts, R. L./Zimmermann, J. (1986): Positive Accounting Theory, Englewood Cliffs.

Weber, H. K. (1996a): Verbundwirtschaft, in: Handwörterbuch der Produktionswirt-schaft, 2nd edition, Stuttgart, cols. 2142–2150.

Weber, J. (1992): Die Koordinationssicht des Controlling, in: Spremann, K./Zur, E. (Eds.): Controlling: Grundlagen – Informationssysteme – Anwendungen, Wies-baden, pp. 169–183.

Weber, J. (1996b): Aufgabenspektrum und Controllingbilder: Vom Bremser zum Inno-vator, in: Gablers Magazin, Vol. 10, pp. 26–30.

Weber, J. (1997): Zur Abgrenzung von Führung und Controlling, WHU working paper No. 45, Vallendar.

Weber, J. (2003): Controlling in unterschiedlichen Führungskontexten: Ein Über-blick, in: Zeitschrift für Controlling und Management, Vol. 47, pp. 183–192.

Weber, J. (2004): Möglichkeiten und Grenzen der Operationalisierung des Konstrukts »Rationalitätssicherung«, in: Scherm, E./Pietsch, G. (Eds.): Controlling: Theorien und Konzeptionen, Munich, pp. 467–486.

Weber, J. (2005): Gestaltung der Kostenrechnung: Notwendigkeit, Optionen und Konsequenzen, Wiesbaden.

Weber, J. (2007): Aktuelle Controllingpraxis in Deutschland, Series Advanced Controlling, Vol. 59, Vallendar.

Weber, J. (2008): Von Top-Controllern lernen: Controlling in den DAX 30-Unter-nehmen, Weinheim. (»DAX 30 study«)

Weber, J./Brettel, M./Schäffer, U. (1996): Gedanken zur Unternehmensführung, WHU working paper No. 35, Vallendar.

Weber, J./Bültel, D. (1992): Controlling: Ein eigenständiges Aufgabenfeld in den Unternehmen der Bundesrepublik Deutschland – Ergebnisse einer Auswertung von Stellenanzeigen aus den Jahren 1949–1989, in: Die Betriebswirtschaft, Vol. 52, pp. 535–546.

Weber, J./David, U./Prenzler, C. (2001): Controller Excellence: Strategische Neuaus-richtung der Controller, Series Advanced Controlling, Vol. 23/24, Vallendar.

Weber, J./Hirsch, B./Rambusch, R./Schlüter, H./Sill, F./Spatz, A. C. (2006): Control-ling 2006: Stand und Perspektiven, Vallendar. (»ICV study«)

Weber, J./Hunold, C./Prenzler, C./Thust, S. (2001): Controllerorganisation in deut-schen Unternehmen, Series Advanced Controlling, Vol. 18, Vallendar.

Weber, J./Kosmider, A. (1991): Controlling-Entwicklung in der Bundesrepublik Deutschland im Spiegel von Stellenanzeigen, in: Zeitschrift für Betriebswirt-schaft, Vol. 61, special issue 3, Controlling: Selbstverständnis – Instrumente – Perspektiven, pp. 17–35.

Weber, J./Linder, S./Hirsch, B. (2004): Neugestaltung der Budgetierung: Relative, benchmarkorientierte oder absolute, intern orientierte Ziele?, in: Zeitschrift für Planung und Unternehmenssteuerung, Vol. 15, pp. 57–75.

Weber, J./Linder, S./Spillecke, D. (2003): Beyond Budgeting bei Verbundeffekten?, in: Zeitschrift für Controlling und Management, Vol. 47, special issue 1, pp. 111–120.

Weber, J./Sandt, J. (2001): Erfolg durch Kennzahlen: Neue empirische Erkenntnisse, Series Advanced Controlling, Vol. 21, Vallendar.

Weber, J./Schäffer, U. (1998): Controlling-Entwicklung im Spiegel von Stellenanzeigen 1990–1994, in: Kostenrechnungspraxis, Vol. 42, pp. 227–233.

Weber, J./Schäffer, U. (1999): Sicherstellung der Rationalität von Führung als Aufgabe des Controlling?, in: Die Betriebswirtschaft, Vol. 59, pp. 731–747.

Weber, J./Schäffer, U. (2000a): Controlling als Koordinationsfunktion?, in: Kostenrechnungspraxis, Vol. 44, pp. 109–118.

Weber, J./Schäffer, U. (2000b): Balanced Scorecard & Controlling: Implementierung – Nutzen für Manager und Controller – Erfahrungen in deutschen Unternehmen, 3rd edition, Wiesbaden.

Weber, J./Schäffer, U. (2001): Sicherstellung der Rationalität von Führung als Funktion des Controlling, in: Weber, J./Schäffer, U. (Eds.): Rationalitätssicherung der Führung: Beiträge zu einer Theorie des Controlling, Wiesbaden, pp. 25–45.

Weber, J./Schäffer, U./Bauer, M. (2000): Controller und Manager im Team, Series Advanced Controlling, Vol. 14, Vallendar.

Weber, J./Schäffer, U./Langenbach, W. (2001): Gedanken zur Rationalitätskonzeption des Controlling, in: Weber, J./Schäffer, U. (Eds.): Rationalitätssicherung der Führung: Beiträge zu einer Theorie des Controlling, Wiesbaden, pp. 46–76.

Weber, J./Schäffer, U./Prenzler, C. (2001): Zur Charakterisierung und Entwicklung von Controlleraufgaben, in: Zeitschrift für Planung, Vol. 12, pp. 25–46.

Weber, J./Weißenberger, B. E./Aust, R. (1998): Benchmarking des Controllerbereichs: Ein Erfahrungsbericht, in: Betriebswirtschaftliche Forschung und Praxis, Vol. 50, pp. 381–401.

Weber, J./Weißenberger, B. E./Guth, S./Spieker, M. (2000): Accounting Excellence: Die Kostenrechnung auf dem Prüfstand, Series Advanced Controlling, Vol. 16, Vallendar.

Weber, M. (1978): Economy and Society: An outline of Interpretive Sociology, translation based on the 4th German edition, Berkeley and Los Angeles.

Weißenberger, B. E. (1997): Die Informationsbeziehung zwischen Management und Rechnungswesen: Analyse institutionaler Koordination, Wiesbaden.

Welge, M. K. (1988): Unternehmensführung, Vol. 3: Controlling, Stuttgart.

Welge, M. K./Al-Laham, A. (2003): Strategisches Management: Grundlagen – Prozess – Implementierung, 4th edition, Wiesbaden.

Williamson, O. E. (1985): The Economic Institutions of Capitalism: Firms, Markets, Relational Contracting, New York.

Wiswede, G. (2007): Einführung in die Wirtschaftspsychologie, 4th edition, Munich.

Zenz, A. (1999): Strategisches Qualitätscontrolling: Konzeption als Metaführungslehre, Wiesbaden.

Zünd, A. (1979): Zum Begriff des Controlling: Ein umweltbezogener Erklärungsversuch, in: Goetzke, W./Sieben, G. (Eds.): Controlling: Integration von Planung und Kontrolle, Köln, pp. 15–26.

Zünd, A. (1985): Der Controller-Bereich (Controllership): Randbemerkungen zur Institutionalisierung der Controller-Funktion, in: Gilbert, J./Probst, B./Schmitz-Dräger, R. (Eds.): Controlling und Unternehmensführung, Bern, pp. 28–40.

Index

About the authors

Jürgen Weber was born on November 4th, 1953 in Holzminden, Germany. He studied business administration at the University of Göttingen, obtained his doctorate at the University of Dortmund in 1981 and qualified as a university professor at the University of Erlangen-Nuremberg in 1986. In the same year, he accepted the Chair for Business Administration, in particular Accounting/Controlling, at WHU Otto Beisheim School of Management. Since 1986, the elective courses he has been responsible for include Controlling as well as Financial Accounting and Production Management (the latter two intermittently). Further academic posts held by Jürgen Weber include a deanship and several associate deanships. He currently heads the Center for Controlling & Management (CCM) and the Kühne Center for Logistics Management at the business school. In 2006, the European Business School awarded him the title of Doctor rerum politicarum honoris causa.

Jürgen Weber also taught as visiting professor at the University of Vienna (summer semester 1990) and the Vienna University of Economics and Business Administration (winter semester 1999/2000). He is a member of several scientific commissions of the German Academic Association for Business Research and is a co-editor of the journal Logistikmanagement as well as executive co-editor of the journal Zeitschrift für Controlling und Management (ZfCM). He was offered chairs at the University of Mainz (Logistics), the Vienna University of Economics and Business Administration (Controlling and Management) and the Technische Universität Darmstadt (Controlling and Accounting), all of which he declined.

Outside of academia, Jürgen Weber follows a demanding schedule as a speaker and is a member of the supervisory boards of Lufthansa Cargo AG, Frankfurt/Main and the health provider StiftungsKlinikum Mittelrhein, Koblenz. His strong interest in business practice led him to accept numerous consulting and training mandates at an early stage. In his role as one of the 1992 co-founders of CTcon GmbH (www.ctcon.de), a rapidly growing service provider in the areas of management consulting and training, he underlined the vision of supporting business practice in an integrated fashion, particularly in the area of managing change. He continues to maintain close ties with CTcon, which has offices in Vallendar, Bonn, Düsseldorf and Frankfurt, via his roles as co-partner and chairperson of the company's scientific advisory board.

Utz Schäffer was born on November 6th, 1966 in Stuttgart, Germany. After completing his military service and a traineeship at Dresdner Bank AG in Stuttgart, he studied business administration at WHU – Otto Beisheim School of Management – in Vallendar, as well as at the EM Lyon and the Kellogg Graduate School of Management in Chicago. In 1996, he received his doctorate at the Chair for Controlling and Telecommunications of Prof. Dr. Dr. h. c. Jürgen Weber (»Controlling für selbstabstimmende Gruppen?«). During his graduate and post-graduate studies, he held a scholarship from the German National Academic Merit Foundation. In 2001, he qualified as a university professor at WHU and was the first executive director of the Center for Controlling & Management (CCM). In 2002, he accepted the Chair for Business Administration, particularly Management Accounting and Control, at the European Business School in Oestrich-Winkel. In addition to his professorship, Utz Schäffer also held the academic position of associate dean for research as well as the chairmanship of the doctoral committee from 2003 to 2007. In the same year, he accepted the offer of a Chair for Business Administration, particularly Management Accounting and Control at WHU (www.whu.edu/controlling). He declined a chair at the Technische Universität Braunschweig (Controlling and Financial Accounting).

Utz Schäffer is the author of numerous contributions to scientific and practice-oriented journals and acts as reviewer for many of these journals. His research focus lies on the development, implementation and use of management accounting tools, planning and monitoring processes, and comparative management accounting. He taught as visiting professor at the University of Innsbruck (winter semester 2003/2004) und is a member of the German Academic Association for Business Research and of several of the association's scientific commissions. Utz Schäffer is also a co-editor of the Zeitschrift für Controlling und Management (ZfCM). In addition to his academic career, Utz Schäffer gained practical experience while working with CTcon GmbH, Vallendar and Düsseldorf, as well as with McKinsey & Company, Munich. He continues to maintain close ties to CTcon in his capacity as scientific adviser to the company.